Gita was born a brahmin—never to remain one. She is a rebel at home, a rebel in the Naxalite revolutionary movement, and a rebel against the landlords of Ibrahimpatnam. For all this, she suffers expulsion from family, caste and party, and faces attacks from enemies. Yet Gita keeps herself and her ideals intact. No other story of an Indian woman has ever been told like this. After a lifetime of combativeness, still there is dil.

Kancha Ilaiah Shepherd, author of *Why I am Not a Hindu*

In recent times, a life of reading was made possible for me by the Hyderabad Book Trust... Gita Ramaswamy, though her mother tongue is Tamil, runs HBT because of her love and respect for the Telugu language. She is someone who has dedicated her whole life to a movement that serves people.

N.V. Ramana, Chief Justice of India

Gitamma coming to Ibrahimpatnam did us a world of good: she got us bullock carts, buffaloes, sheep, she had our wages increased, our debts repudiated, she got land distributed in all the villages. The reddys planned to kill Gitamma. They killed two men and Gitamma suffered a lot for about two years. But all of us benefited in the end. Now the government is wresting back all the land, and people will become landless again. Gitamma keeps saying, don't sell the land, how will you survive without land? But people have this madness—cash, cash, cash. Nothing will be left.

Gattu Basha, labourer from Eliminedu village

Gita Ramaswamy's memoir takes us straight into the trenches where a war is being waged for the soul of India. This book should be marked 'Dangerous to your complacency'. Read it before voices from across the spectrum begin to protest its honesty and its clear-eyed view of the operations of caste.

Jerry Pinto, writer and translator

For years, we have all been looking at the issues raised in *Land, Guns, Caste, Woman* in isolation. In Gita's memoir, they come together for the first time. We learn that in India, the revolution is not a one-time event. It is an everyday process. The book exposes the systemic exploitation that benefits the dominant, and the state's complicity in being against the very laws it passes. Gita takes us on a three-decade journey through the Deccan, speaking not of leaders but of the struggle for self-respect by the marginalized, the untouchables, the labouring masses. This is the story of a restless soul in search of the path towards change. As readers, we discover that the path itself is the goal. Gita's search is on even today. There is a troublesome incident in the book, when Gita garlands some village leaders with chappals: this needs to be seen as a slap on society.

Bezwada Wilson, activist

Gita Ramaswamy's brutally honest memoir recalls a life filled with fight and torment, with heady victories and deep solidarities. Every thought, action and feeling is uncompromisingly investigated, and the unconditional disclosure of her own vulnerabilities is disarmingly moving. *Land, Guns, Caste, Woman* blossoms in the entwinement of Telangana's landless labourers and Gita's lives. As the story unfolds, she unpicks her own position as a savarna involved in Dalit activism.

T.M. Krishna, musician

Whenever I ask my elders about the history of my village, they tell me one thing. The history of Eliminedu has two periods: 'Before Gita Ramaswamy', and 'After Gita Ramaswamy'. As far as they can remember, the reddys and other dominant castes of the village did not see my people as human beings. We were kept as slaves. Gita Ramaswamy is the visionary who changed our lives. To me and others, she will remain an inspiration.

Gattu Vijayendar, Eliminedu village, postgraduate student

Written with honesty, warmth, love and humility, *Land, Guns, Caste, Woman* narrates the struggles of labourers against the landlords, the state and their agents, to seize control of over 14,000 acres of land. It tells us how a young woman swept up in the idealism of the left movement of the 1970s, was disillusioned by its failure, and

then discovers the resilience and fierce determination of the poor to live a life of dignity. Disregarding the platitudes of correct and incorrect, of right and wrong, we learn how the rural people work towards solutions that are 'doable'. A must read for every idealistic person in the country.
Suhasini Mulay, actress

This is the life story of a remarkable woman in whom courage is coupled with conviction, idealism with ideology and grit matches intellect in equal measure. Though Gita refers to herself as a defeated idealist, her victories against a powerful combination of entrenched caste and class interests will be an inspiration to all.
Srinath Reddy, public health activist

I have been part of the Indian state for over four decades. The author fought it in different ways for years. I was captivated reading her remarkable life story. Over time her methods changed but her commitment to social justice never wavered. Hers has been a long saga of relentless struggle against searing oppression and discrimination that are still widespread in our society. A book written movingly with passion and candour.
Jairam Ramesh, Member of Parliament and writer

A deeply felt personal story of the struggles for justice waged by landless dalit labourers in Telangana in the 1980s. Gita Ramaswamy honestly reflects on the paths of constitutionalism and violence, and on the unity and divisions in the leftwing movement. An account that is as much about the memoirist as it is about her dalit comrades.
C. Rammanohar Reddy, Editor, *The India Forum*

I was eighteen or twenty when Gitamma came to our village, talking of minimum wages and releasing bonded labourers using constitutional methods. Over three decades, I have been in and out of many political parties. I am well-known here, but I am still recognised in every village as 'Gitamma's Sangam man'. Even today when I go to a village in the five mandals where I work, people ask, 'How's Gitamma? How're you?' I can't read English, but that our eventful struggles now find place in a book imbues them with value.

Bhadramoni Shankaraiah, Cheeded village, farmer and activist

At once personal and intense, interwoven with the mood of the times, Gita Ramaswamy shares her journey in Telangana with characteristic courage and candidness. Written with an unpretentious edge, *Land, Guns, Caste, Woman* sparkles with insight. As a young woman, Gita defies brahminical patriarchy, incurring parental tyranny. Her work has had an enduring impact on the lives of the poor in Telangana. Despite it being a chronicle of tensions and conflicts, it is a warm and endearing book. A classic for ages to come.

Shantha Sinha, activist

My family had no bonded labourers but I got involved in the Sangam's struggle. With the help of Gitamma, we freed the bonded labourers in our village, repudiated their debts, and got them cattle and land. We fought for three years to get entitlements to the forest land in adjoining Madapur. We won rights over the produce, worked on the land, and earned Rs 400 a month to feed our families. We also built houses making our own bricks, and got a concrete road constructed. We sent our children to the hostels to study. I also took active part in politics, contesting local-body elections with Gitamma's support. The Sangam transformed our lives.

Nagati Bacchaama, Pethula village, labourer

Unsparingly critical and deeply self-reflexive, Gita Ramaswamy's memoir surprises with its humility, sometimes even a kind of innocence. Here is an account of what it means to engage with the harsh realities of poverty and discrimination, to battle with your own privilege, to extend solidarity and understand your historical complicity in caste oppression. Gita does this not only with passion, but with a lack of bitterness, a lurking humour and enduring hope.

Urvashi Butalia, publisher and writer

The fading echoes of the Telangana armed struggle resonated across Hyderabad in the 1970s. Young men and women were drawn into a movement that took unexpected turns. Finding herself in the midst of this ferment, Gita Ramaswamy recounts the moment and the movement in a heart-wrenching and soul-searching account of her own life and of those people whose lives mattered to her.
Sanjaya Baru, journalist and former media advisor to the PMO

We fought the police, we trekked to courts, we were beaten and even jailed. But we did not give up in our fight for land. I won some land in Nazdik Singaram village. I was called Chinna (Little) Gitamma because I was very active in the Sangam. I visited all the villages in Ibrahimpatnam taluka and saw how the poor people profited from the Sangam, but the land struggle in my own village failed because some leaders from among us sided with the reddy landlords.
Doonimetla Satyamma, Tatiparthi village, peasant

When Gita Ramaswamy's lifelong involvement in social activism was beginning to find a practical application, I was finding my feet as a theatre worker. I'd hear about people like her and, in my naivete, would wonder what they got out of their selfless work. Reading Gita's book, with a mix of awe, admiration and envy, gave me several answers. Her prose, shorn of all embellishment, is eager to communicate rather than impress. Her unsentimental narration, undeterred forthrightness and lack of trepidation, is so startling that despite not being terribly partial to autobiographies, I found myself mesmerized by her story and a feeling of uncontained optimism filled me as I read on. Her unabashed admission of her failures and misjudgements in no way detracts from the most important lesson this book has to offer: to stick to your chosen path come what may and rely on no one else to generate your 'power of one'. After all, no other seagull crashed into the mountainside or hit a rock-hard sea except Jonathan, who realized that there was more to flying than just eating. May Gita's tribe increase. '*Main akela hi chala tha jaanib-e-manzil magar, log saath aate gaye kaarvaan banta gaya.*'
Naseeruddin Shah, actor

Land, Guns, Caste, Woman: The Memoir of a Lapsed Revolutionary

© Gita Ramaswamy

ISBN 9788194865414

First published 14 April 2022

10 9 8 7 6 5 4 3 2

Maps on pages 10 to 13 by Anurag Jadhav

Navayana Publishing Pvt Ltd
155 2nd Floor
Shahpur Jat, New Delhi 110049
Phone: +91-11-26494795
navayana.org

Typeset at Navayana

Production: Sanjiv Palliwal

Printed at Thomson Press, New Delhi

Distributed in South Asia by HarperCollins India

Subscribe to updates at navayana.org/subscribe

navayana

LAND

GUNS

The Memoir of a Lapsed Revolutionary

CASTE

WOMAN

Gita Ramaswamy

For Cyril
who inspired it, but did not live to read it

INDIAN SUBCONTINENT

INDUS RIVER

THE HIMALAYAS

CHANDIGARH
MEERUT
HAPUR
GHAZIABAD
NEW DELHI

VARANASI

NAGPUR

TELANGANA

HYDERABAD
SOLAPUR
IBRAHIMPATNAM

MUMBAI

ANDHRA PRADESH

BENGALURU
CHENNAI

HARIPAD
RAMANATHAPURAM
THIRUVANANTHAPURAM

MAP NOT TO SCALE

TELANGANA
ADILABAD
JAGTIAL
NIZAMABAD
WARANGAL
HYDERABAD
RANGA REDDY DISTRICT
KHAMMAM
VIKARABAD
PARGI
IBRAHIMPATNAM
KULKACHERLA
KALWAKURTHY
MAHABUB NAGAR
VIJAYAWADA
NAGARJUNA SAGAR DAM
KRISHNA RIVER
KARAMCHEDU
CHIRALA
SRIKAKULAM
GURTHEDU
ANANTAPUR
NELLORE
CHALLAVARIPALLE
CHITTOOR
ANDHRA PRADESH
MAP NOT TO SCALE

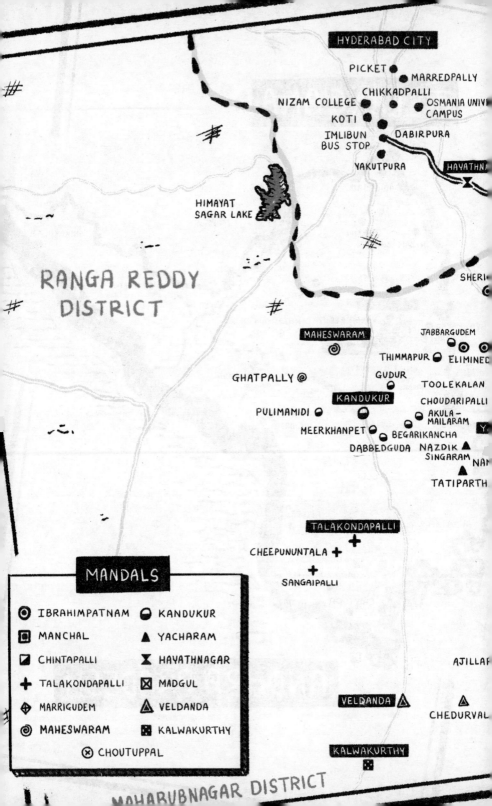

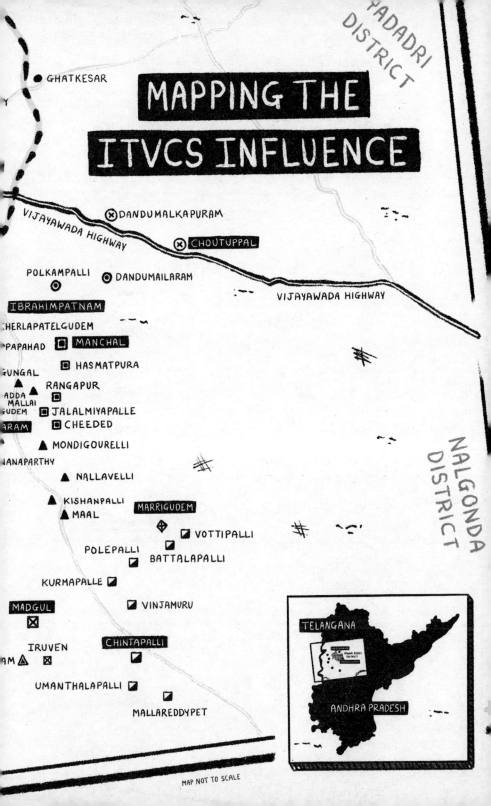

Contents

Why I had to write this book

This is the story of my reckoning with myself and the world around me. I was born into a Tamil brahmin family with roots in Kerala. For over five decades, the rugged Deccan landscape of Hyderabad and its surrounding districts has been my home. While burning the bra was considered radical in the West, in my family, wearing one when I was fourteen made me a slut. My younger days were marked by small insurrections and a passion for mathematics. I gravitated towards the Naxalite movement in the 1970s and went underground during the Emergency. My parents thought I had been brainwashed. They bundled me away to Madras, and sought to 'rebrainwash' me by subjecting me to shock treatment (electroconvulsive therapy). My memory got scrambled. Rescued and returned to Hyderabad, I could not recognize the man I wanted to marry. I was disoriented. To evade arrest during the Emergency, my husband Cyril Reddy and I moved to the north of India where we lived amongst the balmikis of Ghaziabad, teaching them English among other things. I often contemplated suicide. When we returned to Hyderabad in 1980, there was no family or party waiting for us. Yet this city was home. With the help of friends, we founded the Hyderabad Book Trust, a publishing house that specializes in low-cost books, working mostly with leftists and Ambedkarites. It worked like a drug against my depression. I soon became the face of HBT and I still am. Yet I could not settle into this role. The revolution I lived for and dreamt of was still not at hand. I was restless. I was thirty.

This is when I first came to Ibrahimpatnam. It was 1984. Ibrahimpatnam, an hour's drive south-west of Hyderabad in

Ranga Reddy district, was ruled by the reddys. In this rock-strewn landscape, people are often caught between a reddy and a hard place. The dalits, mostly madigas, were their bonded labourers and serfs. It was here that for close to a decade I was involved in land struggles, which were most often led by dalits. I was an outsider in every sense, poking my nose into affairs of which I had no experience. Working with the Marxist–Leninist movement and fantasizing about the revolution was one thing; it was quite another thing for a woman like me to ally with people who had little in terms of material holdings. Yet, they gave me a special place in their hearts and homes.

The reddys were cruel landlords. They pressed huge stones on the backs of people for hours as 'punishment'; in some villages, newly-wed madiga brides were first brought to the dora's gadi (the fortress or mansion of the landlord) for their 'breaking in'; the breasts of lactating women labourers were pressed to check if they really needed to feed their infants ... such stories abound in each village among the poor and the dalits.

I came here as a defeated idealist, in the hope that after the heady yet fruitless days of my youth I could still be of some use to someone. I lived largely among the madigas. They let me into their lives. They sang me their songs. They told me how to dress so I may look like Indiramma. They had a clear idea of their might and of the struggle they wanted to pursue. With them, I became part of an agricultural labourers' union—Ibrahimpatnam Taluka Vyavasaya Coolie Sangam, ITVCS, or the Sangam as we called it.

How did a university-educated brahmin woman with close friends among the reddys and raos land up in Ibrahimpatnam to live and work among the madigas? How and why and when did I leave this struggle? This is what you will read about.

While working in the villages, I had the unstinted support
of my husband Cyril Reddy who, at that time, was a part of
Salaha, a legal resource centre for the poor, in Hyderabad.
We worked our strategies out together, and even when he
fell seriously ill with hepatitis and was bedridden for over
a year and a half, he encouraged me to continue my work,
and sought caregiving elsewhere. I was also lucky because
Cyril constantly critiqued my brahminness. Food was an area
where I had to learn to drop much of my unease. Cyril laid
every hesitation on my part to try some new kind of meat
at the door of brahminism. The hesitation to spend money,
the tendency to bargain with small vendors, bonding with
friends (who were brahmin), compassionately understanding
the failings of brahmins while not doing the same with people
from other castes ... any wrong move, and he was on my case,
pointing out the origins of my habits and prejudices. Growing
up in a family that had suffered due to their parents marrying
across caste, religion and region, he was more intimately
aware of the malicious oppressiveness of caste than me. He
and his siblings had correctly identified Hindu brahminism as
the cause of much sorrow in India. He had no problem with
my being the more public figure and supported me in more
ways than I can tell. If it were not for him, the story I recount
here would never have happened.

Many others were selfless with the help they offered us.
Foremost among them were the lawyers Bojja Tharakam,
G. Manohar, C.V. Mohan Reddy, C. Padmanabha Reddy,
civil society activists who came forward to help at every
stage, journalists who highlighted our stories, and friends
who supported us in myriad ways. In those days, whenever
I returned home to Hyderabad, there was the risk of being
attacked by contract killers hired by landlords. Ours was a lower

middle class neighbourhood with a mix of pucca houses and tin-roofed rooms where small traders, pushcart vendors and domestic helps lived. The residents of our lane saw hundreds of people, sometimes in lorries, visiting us every day, often waiting outside when rooms were full. No doubt, the waiting villagers told their stories to curious neighbours over and over again, who then began helping us by sending food and watching out for strangers entering the lane.

I was of the generation that came of age in the early 1970s. We were extremely lucky in some ways. The women's liberation movement inspired us to be fearless. The men who were our peers did not see us as rivals or ball-breakers, and instead helped us. I was even luckier in that from 1980 onwards I was mentored by five older men, each extraordinary in his own way—C.K. Narayan Reddy, S.R. Sankaran, N.V. Raja Reddy, C. Padmanabha Reddy and Bojja Tharakam. C.K. Narayan Reddy was a lifelong communist, and the gentlest person I have met. He was my confidant in Hyderabad Book Trust, the not-for-profit Telugu publishing collective where we both worked. S.R. Sankaran, a watchful mentor, was a civil servant instrumental in several legislations and government programmes that directly helped dalits. N.V. Raja Reddy was a socialist, a zamindar, a great lover of books, curious about everything, and deeply knowledgeable about Telangana and its communities. He helped ease me into the culture of the region. C. Padmanabha Reddy was a senior lawyer who handled many of my cases. Bojja Tharakam, also a senior lawyer and a great dalit activist, was someone I worked with closely. All five gave me time and energy.

As for family, when the emotional stakes are high, a taboo against remembrance is enforced. I may now become a radioactive relative and friend. My sisters and their families and many of my brahmin friends may dislike my characterization of our families as cesspools of inequality, hidebound tradition and intolerance. Worse, in writing this I will be reopening old wounds. They believe that one does not air one's dirty laundry in public. But I am not writing about any hidden, shameful family secrets. In fact, for the most part, my family was not unusually cruel. My parents never raised a hand against us or anyone else. But the simple fact is that patriarchy and caste diktats are normalized everywhere, made to appear as natural and permanent as sunrise. Exploring this became inevitable when I started writing.

I returned to work in HBT in 1998, after about a decade spent in wage and land struggles with the Sangam. This time, whenever we needed new hands, I would call upon my friends in Ibrahimpatnam to send their wards who could work and also study in the city for a better career. Eighteen-year-olds came to apprentice at all kinds of jobs in HBT—going to the post office for mail order, bank work, maintaining accounts and debtor ledgers, hawking books at meetings, proofreading and delivering proofs and scripts between HBT and the writer/translator. When we had free time on our hands, the young ones often asked me questions about what happened in a particular village, details about stories they had heard from their elders. I was hesitant about opening up. Sometimes I saw my Ibrahimpatnam work as a personal hidden treasure. I also thought it inappropriate to talk about what I had done. In 2014, when I wrote a biography of the Osmania University student leader George Reddy, who had been murdered by rightwing goons, my young colleagues at HBT began to insist that I also write the story of the Ibrahimpatnam movement. 'Such inspiring things happened then. We need to know the whole story,' they said. Finally, in 2018, when I had time on my hands after Cyril's long illness and death, I began writing. My daughter Leila had left for the US for a PhD. The days after Cyril was gone were lonely and difficult. I had to focus on remaining afloat and active. It occurred to me that if I wrote about this joyful period of my life, it might help me tide over the despondency and also serve to give back some of our common history to my young colleagues.

The writing was cathartic and I am happy simply for having written the story. Two young readers, Abhishek Bhattacharya and Chaitra Sreeshaila, read an early draft and had many more questions for me, forcing me to rework and expand. The first draft was only about the Ibrahimpatnam work. They asked me why I had gone to Ibrahimpatnam at all. This then led me to expand on my past association with the Naxalite movement. When they asked why I joined the Naxalites, I wrote about my early childhood years and my family. The Covid-19 lockdown in 2020 gave me time to work on my first draft and consider it seriously for publication. I discussed the script with my close friends G. Manohar and Jhumur Lahiri who had been either part of or had followed the movement since its inception. They gave me useful feedback about deficiencies I needed to redress. It was only after the script came back from the Navayana team with caustic comments, pointing to several gaps in the narrative, that I engaged with it again. The book expanded in size and scope beyond my dreams.

After a gap of some twenty-six years, I slowly began contacting my erstwhile colleagues in ITVCS, the Sangam—not just to refresh my memory but also to more thoroughly reconstruct the framework of the movement that had changed us all. Accompanied by Jhumur Lahiri and Sashi Kumar, I conducted an exhaustive interview with Shankaraiah, a

23

former activist with the Sangam. It could well be the draft for a separate book. Writing this memoir also gently pushed me to reconnect with my sisters and this gives me great joy.

In remembering certain people, names, places, dates and incidents, I may well have erred. I have tried redressing all possible errors while working on the proofs; I could blame the electroconvulsive therapy, but we all remember poorly with age. Those who read the advance copies corrected some errors. Those that remain will be corrected in the next edition.

Four sets of materials helped me to reconstruct much of the work in Ibrahimpatnam. The first: I was a regular writer of articles in a periodical called *Mainstream* from 1985 onwards. These were mostly pen portraits of the people I met while working in Ibrahimpatnam. When the dalit little magazine *Nalupu* began in 1989, I wrote for it too. The second: in 2002, the Anveshi Research Centre for Women's Studies encouraged me to write a paper titled "Judicial Processes and Women: Notes on Revenue Courts". I interviewed Yacharam Buddajangaiah and Tatiparthi Satyamma for this. The third: the artist Naru, who had worked for *Nalupu*, had pasted the press write-ups about the work in Ibrahimpatnam on to big sheets so that they did not get lost. The last: I had some of the legal files used during the movement. I had retained these so that if people faced trouble in the future, I could help them with paperwork. All of these together served as foundational archives to reconstruct the timeline, content and methods of our movement.

It was a long journey, from the thrill and dismay of being a Naxalite, to becoming a publisher, to then end up becoming an instrument in the independent struggles of the largely dalit working class in Ibrahimpatnam. I made a lot of mistakes along the way and was often clueless about the path ahead. This book, though a memoir of an individual, is, more importantly, the story of the Sangam's struggles and achievements.

All memoirs are written in hindsight; all memoirs are selective. I know that I belong to the savarna side of the fence. But for those few years, I interacted deeply with those on the other side and now have an inkling of the almost instinctive and accurate critique of caste privilege that comes from being oppressed. In writing this story I am also trying to understand myself. I know that the privileged continue to be the dominant storytellers of our times. I know that I retain the power of framing, of editing, of deleting parts that don't suit me. This is a book about these very deficiencies.

I place this fearfully in your hands and ask you to read it with some sympathy for the immature thirty-year-old that I was. Ibrahimpatnam did not come to me with explanatory notes. My work was a result of the things I saw and experienced; I was trying my hardest to let go of all the pre-existing frameworks to which I had been conditioned. Dalits may critique me for taking up their space, for patronizing them (as I must have done in various situations), for glorifying my brahminical (and other) entitlements. Brahmins will take offence at what they perceive as essentializing them, for publicly parading my family and others of my community. Others will critique from other positions. And yet I think writing this story is necessary, warts and all. It is wrong to think that our mistakes are irreparable. There is always space for realization, for change. If annihilation of caste is the aim, I must hope that savarnas can be changed. This self-critique, self-exposure, stems from that hope.

1 Brahmin at home, Catholic in school

I was born and raised in an orthodox brahmin household. Our family was always on the move, and we lived in cities across the country. My parents had five daughters. I was the fourth one. The eldest was born in Thiruvananthapuram at our maternal grandmother's place, the second in Bangalore, the third in Rajkot, I was born in Solapur in 1953 and my younger sister in Bombay. Both my parents were Tamil-speaking but my mother's family had moved to Thiruvananthapuram from Ramanathapuram district in Tamil Nadu some three hundred years ago. In Thiruvananthapuram, they lived in the Karamana agraharam in row houses. The area was a brahmin settlement of yore and we visited there often. My maternal grandmother was a widow by then and I remember her as a gentle person. The brother who headed Mother's family was a sub-inspector of police. Another brother was somewhat mentally challenged, but everybody's favourite since he was always ready to help. There was a large extended family too but I lost touch with them after I entered college.

My father's family had been living in Haripad, Alleppey district, Kerala, for over a hundred years, and they were landed folk. Their house was big compared to the urban ones that we were used to. The hall was large enough to seat thirty people sitting cross-legged, and the verandahs around the house were equally large. My paternal grandfather was a sub-registrar in Haripad. He had passed away before I was born, but my grandmother, whom we called Ammami, was a strong presence in my early life. I remember her as someone who did not wear a blouse, had a shaved head, with vibhuti (sacred ash) smeared on her forehead. She cooked and served food for her many grandchildren who sat in rows in the hall to eat. She sometimes offered us theretippal—a mixture of milk, sugar and spices cooked slowy until it congeals. My mother Lakshmi, or Etchmi as her relatives called her, believed that her mother-in-law had cast black magic on her and told us not to eat it. I didn't pay much heed to this. Adults were crazy. I was different, I believed. Little did I realize that we carry our childhood experiences and internalizations into our own adulthood. The mother-in-law–daughter-in-law relationship was not good and I recall many quarrels between my parents over this.

My father K.H. Ramaswamy (Kizhakemadam Harihara Ramaswamy) was an engineer with the Posts and Telegraphs Department. When he was young, he and his brothers studied in the colleges of Thiruvananthapuram. The king of Travancore was partial to brahmins and gave them free food and shelter. Growing up, Father never stopped reminding us how they ate and lived in the maharaja's choultries and studied under the street lights. My four sisters and I were enrolled in convent schools run by nuns, and we became used to talking in English, though we talked to our parents in Tamil. My parents could only write in Malayalam. After 1980, especially during my Ibrahimpatnam years, when Mother wrote to me, she wrote Tamil in the Malayalam script. No Tamil person could read it and the bemused Malayali who read it out to me couldn't understand it. As I grew older, I came to treasure the peculiar Tamil my parents spoke and the food we ate in our early years. I once gatecrashed a wedding in Hyderabad simply to eat the food of the Trivandrum Iyers. Sometimes when I hear their intonated accent somewhere unexpected, I pause and listen to the voices with affection. Such is the allure of the fragrances, flavours and sounds of early childhood,

Aged 10

particularly to one who is cut off from them.

My parents were mild of nature. They never raised their hand to us, they did not use abusive language and they were not knowingly unkind to people—to hired help, acquaintances from other castes and neighbours. However, they felt that as brahmins, they were superior people. We had rigid pollution rules at home, and were strongly discouraged from eating outside. We never touched food with the left hand, even while serving. Specific items couldn't be touched immediately after some others—one couldn't touch ghee or curd after touching any vessel of cooked food. For a long time, we did not have onions at home, and garlic was something I had not even seen till late into college life. For a long time till after I left home, no servants were allowed into the house. The maid washed the vessels and clothes at a tap outdoors, and all the indoor work was done by our mother and us. Still, we escaped the worst kinds of rigidity because my father's job was transferable and we spent most of our lives outside Tamil Nadu. We did not stay in agraharams (brahmin-only settlements in the south) but in secular housing, where we had neighbours from other castes. My earliest memories are of Bombay where we stayed in the huge P&T building (now demolished) opposite Flora Fountain. My father's office was on the second floor and we stayed on the fourth. The staircases were made of wood, and we loved the sound they made as we ran up and down. I began my schooling in Bombay in the Convent of Jesus and Mary School, before we moved to Madras where we were all put in the Rosary Matriculation School in Santhome. I was in class four by then. My best friends there were Jessie D'Souza, Mary Anne, Shalini Kurup, Hashmi and Sheela Rani. We remained in Madras from the time I was nine till I was fifteen years old.

My earliest memories of resentment for the cross that

brahmin women carried go as far back as when I was ten. Mother often told me the story of how she was prevented from going to school in Thiruvananthapuram by her brother, who tore up her only set of good clothes. She did this possibly to instil in us the idea that we were getting the chance to do what she was denied, and that we needed to be self-sufficient and stand on our own two feet. She dinned it into us that being a woman meant a life of suffering, and that education was the only way to escape the worst of it. She never knew what a deep impression all that she said made on me as a little girl. I was eager to listen to this story over and over again. I agonized about the little girl that my mother once was and vowed that I would never be caught in a similar situation. In a way, she was probably the first feminist I knew.

Our upbringing was contradictory in many regards. While there were traditional strictures in the confines of the home around food, pollution, dress, behaviour codes and culture, there was an equal push towards English-language education and a discreet encouragement of Western-oriented leisure activities such as seeing English-language films, reading English books or listening to English songs. These were probably seen as helpful to education and career. Our Christian friends were welcomed home and we went to their homes too. All five of us sisters were trained in Carnatic music. We were woken up at five in the morning to the strains of M.S. Subbulakshmi's 'Venkatesa Suprabhatam' and were taken to all the kutcheris (as Carnatic music concerts are called) during the winter month of Margazhi (December–January) in Madras.

I began reading storybooks when I was four years old. When I had nothing to read, the telephone directory, the atlas and the railway timetable gave me hours of pleasure. They took me away from my reality, as I weaved stories around unknown people with interesting names, distant lands, rivers and mountain chains, and fascinating train journeys around India. I was a steady reader of fiction, anxious if I did not have a book at hand. From Enid Blyton through the delightful William books by Richmal Crompton, A.A. Milne, C.S. Lewis, I graduated to the likes of Tolstoy, Daphne du Maurier, Charles Dickens, Jane Austen, Somerset Maugham and Thomas Hardy in my early teens. Many of these writers had extracts in our school textbooks. Reading expanded my horizons and revealed possibilities that my family could not provide. A more eclectic reading list, say, Hemingway, Steinbeck and nonfiction, like those by E.H. Carr and Gordon Childe, developed only in college. Books introduced me to a rational, liberal world where there were explanations for everything.

In my early teens I was taken over by brand new ways of thinking: science! Biology and physics were liberating at a time when I began questioning rituals and superstitions. Science gave me a firm ground to steady myself in this quiet rebellion. I do not recall any inspiring science teacher at school but the textbooks were revolutionary. The biology lessons were about the human body and how menstruation worked, among other things. I learnt that menstruation was a natural process that was linked with childbirth. I realized that food rotted because of organisms inside it, not because a menstruating woman had touched it. Conception and childbirth occurred because of sexual intercourse, not because you talked to someone of the other sex. The earth moved, the sun shone and floods happened due to natural causes and not thanks to the machinations of a stone idol. I discovered that knowledge of nature was relevant to my social life. The physics textbook put paid to the concept of miracles and explained the laws by which the physical world operated. The history textbooks also spoke of the Enlightenment in Europe and the battles fought there. So, people had fought these battles earlier and won.

I was amazed to find that most things could be explained logically and there was no need to fear the unknown. Science was also seriously introduced to me in school when my body was changing and I was forced to confront brahmin taboos. My rational and emotional selves coalesced in a unified rebellion against the superstitions practised at home. I began menstruating at a time when I had no idea of menstrual periods. My family observed menstrual taboos. My sisters sat separately, had food served out to them separately, slept away from us, didn't go into the other rooms, and at the end of the three days, there was a great fuss about washing everything they had touched. During those three days, even bathing did not remove the pollution. I dismissed it as another of those silly customs that made no sense. One day, when I was thirteen, friends at school giggled and told me that there was a bloody stain on the back of my uniform. 'Where did I sit?' I wondered, and blithely continued to play in the school grounds. Someone rushed to get my elder sister, and she came up to me, whispering frantically that I had to go home. She was visibly upset. 'Whatever for?' I asked. 'We have to go home,' she whispered, almost weeping. When we finally reached home, she was in tears. 'She walked about in front of everybody with the stain showing on her uniform,' she cried. 'Everybody knows now.' 'So what?' my mother asked. 'It is a girls' school, and surely everybody has periods.' 'But no one is supposed to know of them,' my sister continued to sob. 'I can't go to school any more,' she announced tragically. The periods themselves did not upset me. What irritated me were the new restrictions. I had read up on 'monthly periods', and had the scientific explanation for them. Talking it over with my classmates, I found that in nonbrahmin houses, it was actually celebrated! Their parents were proud that their daughter had come of age. Here, my sister was upset that everyone 'knew' about my periods and my mother agonized over one more daughter added to the 'to-be-married' list.

We were six women at home and menstrual periods were three days of seclusion each. Of course, there was no dingy outhouse in Bombay or Madras to where we could be shunted, like in our ancestral homes in Thiruvananthapuram and Haripad. But nothing, absolutely nothing, was touched while menstruating. If we touched anything edible, be it pickle or curry, it was considered spoilt. We were told that if we went into the puja room, we would go blind. In the dreadful innocence of youth, I tried everything. I touched pickle jars and curries, and waited till lunch or dinner—had it gone bad? No. I went into the puja room, and touched the little idols—I constantly checked over the next few days if I was going blind. I wasn't.

The clothes and bed sheets were washed and we bathed from head to toe to mark our ritual return to a state of non-pollution. The period of pollution was for three days from the start of menstruation, but we often menstruated for five days. This was really what set me up against orthodoxy. 'I am still bleeding, how can I be non-polluting?' I asked my mother. 'Shush,' she replied, 'the ritual three-day period is over.' 'Does this mean that the ritual has no truth?' 'This is the tradition,' she said with finality—a most unsatisfactory reply to my mind.

My head-on collision with the weight of brahmin tradition really began here. If god had not blinded me, surely there was

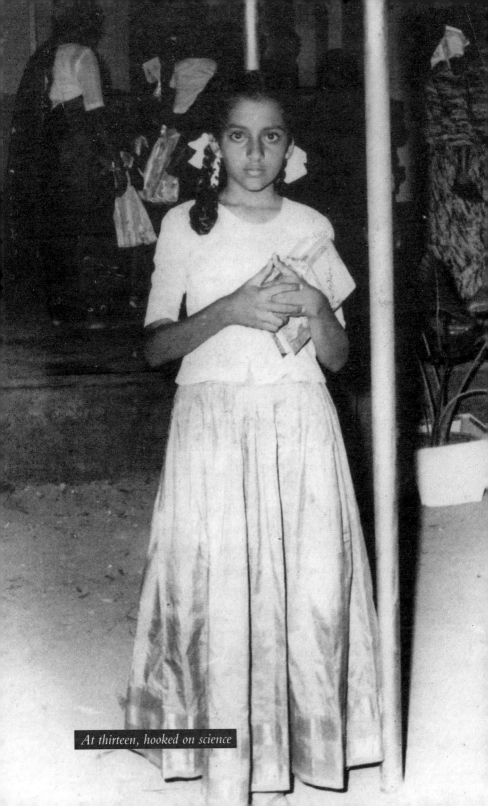

At thirteen, hooked on science

no god, or at least in the image my society had created. I learnt to question everything and anything. Often, my mother got fed up with my inquisitions, and said 'I don't know why—the elders have said so.' I countered this with what my books had to say.

We sat on the floor to eat our meals. In many brahmin households, spilling food around your plate is not frowned upon. Often, items like chewed drumstick, curry leaves, mango skins, chillies were discarded along the rim of the plate or leafplate, on the floor. These leavings were always cleaned with the bare hand, before the ground was wiped with a cloth. I was nauseated by this—why couldn't we clean up with a broom? Since I began picking up the broom every time it was my turn to clean up, the job was quickly taken up by my other sisters who did not complain.

I never really argued with my father: it was my mother who bore the brunt of my endless questioning. My father was not overbearing, but he was a patriarch nevertheless. His word was law, and he always had the last word. While my mother tried to convince me or quote the scriptures or give me horrific examples from other families, my father would just smile and lay down the law. I had regular tussles with my mother. Several times a day, she would beat her head and declare me a changeling. 'Whose child are you really?' she asked. I was also the dark-skinned one at home. My mother loudly and constantly worried about who would marry a dark-skinned girl. This constant chafing led me to silently conclude that I shall never marry. Instead of wanting to conform, I decided I would earn my own living, a good one at that, and stay away from those who coveted fair skin and traditional good looks.

Among my many skirmishes with my mother, one was

about underwear. All of us wore stitched undergarments: bodice, underpants and vest. We stitched them ourselves. The bodice was the kind that was common among rural women before the modern blouse came into fashion. It was a single piece of cloth knotted tightly under the breasts. It flattened the breasts, really bound them, and the hard knot underneath chafed constantly. Most of the girls in my school wore brassieres and I wanted one too. It was easy to know who wore what. The outline showed clearly through the uniforms. My mother flatly refused. 'This is what whores wear to accentuate their bosoms. Girls from good families do not flaunt themselves like that.' I began earning pocket money to buy my own bras. I gave tuitions, I walked instead of taking the bus, I stitched clothes for others. And I did wear brassieres. Almost immediately after my revolt succeeded, my mother let go, and all my sisters had bras. They hadn't supported me in my bitter battle, and were yet all reaping the rewards. In the years to come—after she began visiting the US for my sisters' deliveries in the late 1970s—my mother too discarded her bodices and wore brassieres.

The constant shifting of schools crystallized my thinking as an adolescent. I went from the sedate girls-only, nun-run Rosary Matriculation School to the bustling Adarsh Kendriya Vidyalaya in Royapettah, Madras. My father was finding it increasingly difficult to get admissions for five daughters in convents after his frequent transfers, and the low fees in Kendriya Vidyalayas or Central Schools were attractive. KVs were set up for central government employees and army personnel who were frequently transferred across states and found it difficult to get admission for their children. The KV system was outside the universe of private schools. There was never any interaction between the two, and KVs were looked down upon as 'government schools'. I was enrolled into one when I was fourteen. I was resentful of the shift, because KVs, in those days (and even now), were seen as inferior to convent schools where the English education was supposed to be superior. But my life blossomed.

I studied only for a year in the KV at Madras before my father was transferred again, this time to Hyderabad, in 1968. Here both my younger sister and I joined the KV at Picket. We stayed in East Marredpally, a modern agraharam of sorts, and walked to school every day. Compared to crowded Madras, Hyderabad had a pleasant climate, leafy avenues, wide roads and a more heterogeneous population. My experience at KV, Picket, was even better than at Royapettah.

Here I met the creatures I had not known before— boys, in all shapes, sizes and mental quotients. With a pan-Indian representation, unlike the Tamil-dominated convent schools, KV at Picket promised to be subversive from day one. Teachers were freer and more affectionate, a sharp contrast to the cloistered and watchful nuns. Academic accomplishments were relatively unimportant; sports and popularity among students were more valued. There was a comparatively open administration, girls were treated better than boys (honestly), we were encouraged to take part in sports, and most of all, the teaching of science set us free.

The sense of being cloistered, of being brahmin at home and Catholic at school, was gone. For the first time, there were no asides of 'Is she brahmin or not?', no peeping into tiffin boxes to guess one's caste identity from the food one brought. Many of the children came from army backgrounds and from all over India. There was a whole range of what is loosely termed extra-curricular activities: participation in inter-school meets, vigorous music training, active sports and even some amount of democratic functioning. I particularly remember a strike we had in the tenth class. It being a new school, there was insufficient furniture and there were several students in each class who had to sit on the floor. Classes often swiped each other's chairs and tables. Vexed by this, we decided to strike and absented ourselves from classes. We held meetings, took out small processions inside the school, and submitted a memorandum to the principal. In the end, we succeeded in getting some new furniture.

I was head girl during my last year at school, and proud of it because I was the first one; before there had been only head boys. Now, I led the morning prayers in the assembly and gave the commands: Savdhan (attention)! Vishram (at ease)! The KVs organized frequent competitions and fetes, both among the five KVs in the Hyderabad–Secunderabad area and with other schools. I represented the school in debating and quiz competitions. I was also introduced to the Secunderabad Hi–Y Club run by the local Young Men's Christian Association for high school students. This was a forum helmed by young people with little interference from the YMCA elders. The club was promoted by a parent of two daughters from Marredpally who, no doubt, wanted them to be engaged fruitfully in more meaningful activities than was possible in the local brahmin circle. He had studied in Rishi Valley School in Madannapalle, a boarding school founded by Jiddu Krishnamurti, and had opened his mind to contemporary liberal thinking. He met our parents and convinced them to send their daughters to the Hi–Y Club. He probably told them that he would ensure that nothing untoward happened. There were discussions and debates, quizzes, outings and picnics and get-togethers. It was a boon for young people in a city that did not encourage boys and girls to meet. More than a few partnerships were made here.

By the time I passed out of school after completing class twelve, I was a confident teenager, able to hold my own in public spaces and more than sure that I was the equal of any boy. What added to my confidence was my participation in activities outside the school.

In 1971, when I left school, I was sure that I was opting out of the traditional brahmin world—it was too burdensome for a woman to carry that cross. I thought that the way out was to carve an independent career for myself. But there were fresh complications. I had shown promise in maths during my last years at school and wanted to join an IIT. Admission at that time was relatively uncomplicated for the ten top rankers of the CBSE. I was one among them. My father however refused because he said he couldn't afford the expensive fees and that he didn't want to have a daughter staying away from home. My elder sister who was studying medicine in Madras had been admitted to a hostel when we moved to Hyderabad. He felt that he could not afford it all over again. I did know that my family was finding it difficult. Another sister had her education discontinued after her degree and had to work. I had also won a national science talent scholarship through what is known as NTSE, which gave a scholarship for five years. It was a princely sum in those days—Rs 250 per month during graduation, and Rs 450 per month for postgraduation. The scholarship was awarded only to students pursuing a bachelor's in science and my father wanted the money to be used for the family. Since IITs did not offer bachelor's or master's courses in science at the time, joining there was out of the question.

Apart from being barred from joining IIT, another event from 1971 impacted me tremendously. It was when one of my sisters—she was twenty-four years old—was beaten with a stick by her husband. I had always admired my sister. She looked after the rest of us without complaint, she was good at her studies, had completed her postgraduation in mathematics with distinction, was tactful in speech and efficient in her work, both at home and outside. Before her marriage in 1971, she had joined as an officer in a bank, something to be proud of fifty years ago when not too many women from middle class families worked in supervisory positions. The incident took place soon after her marriage (an arranged one). Her husband abused her and hit her for wanting to keep her earnings in a separate account (my mother's influence, no doubt), instead of handing them over to him. They lived in the next street to ours in Marredpally, and she came weeping with her baby in her arms, something I had rarely seen her do before—she was the unflappable one.

This was my first brush with numbing grief, with the unbelievable horror, that someone could make my sister weep in this fashion. We youngsters were only spectators; we were not allowed to speak a word, but the incident shook me to my core. What was the point of attempting anything within the system when it had the power to turn around and reduce you to nothing? To compound it, the brahmin elders in Marredpally got together and actually took my sister back to her husband, doubtless, after counselling both sides. A separation was not in the interests of the community, and it could give other young women ideas of being independent. My parents had told my sister that she didn't have to return, that she could stay with us forever, but they said nothing when she returned to her husband.

I resolved that day, silently to myself, because this was not something we could talk about even in our own home, never to marry, never to subject myself to the hateful things that men were capable of. Till my sister reads this, she will not know that her suffering affected me so.

By the time I left school, I had made two promises to myself. One, that I wouldn't kowtow to any man, and the second, that I would do my best to fulfil my potential. I would aim for the sky.

2 Ideas at a university

In 1971, I enrolled into the BSc (maths; physics; chemistry) course in the University College of Women, Koti. It was a beautiful campus that had been built by the British resident in Hyderabad in 1798, Colonel James Achilles Kirkpatrick. In my time, the building was falling apart and the classrooms in the main block had chunks of plaster hanging off the walls. There were pigeons in the rafters and the roof leaked. In fact, with some part of the collapsing building out of bounds for us, most of the classes took place in the former elephant stables at the back of the campus. Initially spread over sixty acres, its grounds were reduced to forty-two by the time I had joined. The building apart, the college was a great disappointment. Coming from a co-educational school, I found the atmosphere stifling. The girls were divided into two camps. They were not opposing ones— it was simply that everyone kept to their groups. The Muslim girls came in purdah, took off their burkhas at the college gates, left them there, and went to the morning show in the theatres nearby or sat in the Koti Taj Mahal hotel. This irked me in my ignorance; I thought that if women wanted to hide from men's gazes, they should stay at home. The Taj Mahal hotels, run by Udupi brahmins, were iconic. The Taj in Secunderabad was a favourite among youths. The one in Narayanguda was the haunt of young progressives. The Taj in Koti was frequented by more women, and the one in Abids had a heterogeneous crowd.

I was a judgemental Hindu girl back then. It took me a long while to understand that there are different ways to resist power—from direct confrontation with authority to negotiation and subversion. In time, I was myself to use negotiation and subversion with my father when I joined the Naxalites. The Hindu girls had their noses in their textbooks and did not read anything else. It was a miserable year with nothing to look forward to. All I remember from the time is my bitterness at being denied the opportunity to join IIT.

The one saving grace was the group of non-brahmin friends I made here, who were most untraditional. Sumeet Sidhu was a Sikh girl, tremendously practical and down to earth; she cured my menstrual cramps by forcing me to go on long walks. Geeta Patel and Kiran Mirchandani were also part of our group. I only kept in touch with Sumeet over the years. We usually met in her family's spacious quarters at Hyderabad's Regional Research Laboratory, where Sumeet had a room all to herself. The families of my friends were more well off than mine and quite different. The time spent with them was truly instructive. There was a near-complete absence of rituals and religious functions in their lives. Perhaps their class backgrounds had something to do with this. Their relations with their parents were easier; they didn't carry the weight of tradition on their shoulders and seemed to live a rational life. They didn't even wash their clothes every day, they hung them out to air. If they hadn't bathed that day, the skies didn't fall. They ate exciting food, it was chole bhature one day, anda bhurji the next, aalu parathe another day. Dessert was never just payasam but included custard with watermelon, shrikhand or chocolate cake. They were even close to their male cousins. In most brahmin homes, everything is segregated. My mother's daily injunction to all five of us was: 'Don't trust any man, don't even trust your own father. If you sit next to a boy, you'll get pregnant. You need to get a job and stand on your own two feet.'

Despite such different and interesting friends, the women's

college remained uninteresting. By the end of the first year, I made up my mind. I was not going to remain here any longer. Scouting around for other opportunities, I found a BSc Special course in the University College of Science of Osmania University. This was something like an honours course, with a heavier burden in all the three electives, but this did not worry me. Though I had to change one of my electives from chemistry to statistics, I took the plunge and moved to the Osmania campus. Sumeet Sidhu came along. My father did not object—if he had even an inkling of what was to come, he would have stopped my studies for good.

By June 1972, I joined the BSc second year course at Osmania, with maths, physics and statistics as my electives. The OU campus was imposing. The rooms were spacious, there were corridors to loiter in, the bathrooms were clean, and there were vast open spaces. It was a pleasure to come to campus every day. The diversity of students here was impressive—men and women from rural areas, from the city, girls in burkhas, in half saris and in trousers. The buildings of the science college were somewhat dreary but the arts college building and library were built in the classical style and were stunningly beautiful. The science college was quite boring. Here too the students had their noses buried in textbooks, but the arts college was exciting. Beautiful women, handsome young men, intelligent lecturers, students who read widely and indiscriminately .... By this time, I was reading Kate Millett, Germaine Greer, Gloria Steinem and several other feminist writers and was always on the lookout for friends who were similarly disposed.

Before I joined OU in June that year, something had happened there that was to entirely change the course of my life. On 14 April, I was part of an inter-college team

participating in a quiz at the University of Technology in
the OU campus. At about four in the afternoon there was
some agitation outside the building and the organizers told us
that the quiz had been suspended. A student had been killed
and there could be trouble. 'Who was the student?' we asked
among ourselves. 'It was a student tough called George Reddy,'
I was told. Another case of student dadagiri, I assumed, and
put it out of my mind. It was only when I joined campus that
I learnt who George Reddy was and why he had been killed.
In the late 1960s, the campus's atmosphere was pervaded by
feudal attitudes, sectarianism and petty politics. By the time
I arrived, the Akhil Bharatiya Vidyarthi Parishad was at the
forefront of such activity. The ABVP was the student wing of
the Jana Sangh, the precursor of the Bharatiya Janata Party.
It was guided by the militant Hindu organization Rashtriya
Swayamsevak Sangh, and a pracharak called Narayan Das was
active on the campus. While the Jana Sangh was not much of
a force in the rest of Andhra Pradesh, it had captured the OU
campus.

This mafia controlled the university administration, the
conduct of examinations, and also the student hostels and
bastis scattered across the campus. George Reddy ended their
stranglehold. In a short period of time, he and his small group
of friends had created an atmosphere of dissent that set the stage
for the emergence of a left–revolutionary student movement
in OU. George Reddy had been influenced by the spate of
revolutionary and student movements that were sweeping
the world—in Vietnam, Cuba, South America, Europe, and of
course, Naxalbari. His group formed the fledgling Progressive
Democratic Students which then gave rise to the Progressive
Democratic Students' Union.

Vexed at losing its citadel, the RSS had George Reddy

stabbed to death in the engineering college hostel on 14 April, in the presence of policemen. A case of murder was filed against nine people. All nine were acquitted. The state's complicity in the murder led George's friends and his brother Cyril to fight for retribution and justice.

Around this time, I befriended a small group of like-minded young men. This included my classmate, Pradeep Burgula, a staunch supporter of George's. Pradeep's brother Burgula Narsing Rao had been an active student communist during the Telangana armed struggle. His sister Rama Melkote was also a left-leaning liberal. There were Gopal and Sashi, two of my friends from my schooldays at Hi–Y. Though the two were not in the OU campus, we had remained in touch through the Uni–Y initiative of the YMCA, which was a continuation of the Hi–Y format, but for the university crowd. It turned out that Pradeep too was friends with them. We came to form a loose group of leftists and made links with others on the campus. We often sat together, discussing politics and local events in Irani cafes, watching cricket matches; we went on long walks together and attended meetings of all kinds. It was a warm group that took me quickly into its embrace. Gopal was affectionate and brash, Pradeep was quiet and circumspect, and Sashi was intellectual and somewhat unpredictable. I benefited immensely from this initiation into an outward-facing life. The world had burst into full colour. I was introduced to books that sparked in me the hope of changing the world, I attended meetings where these matters were discussed concretely—all this with a group of attractive teenage boys. This was also when I fell in love for the first time in my life. We never got physical though. I do wonder why our generation was restrained in these matters. Did the idea of revolution sublimate the sex drive? Or was it just the prudery of the society around us? I got close with others too and often wondered who would end up as my partner for life. It was an exciting time to learn to be sexual; I even propositioned an older man I admired for an affair since the men of my group were so circumspect. Sadly, he turned me down, though gently.

We attended a Youth Congress meeting in Nagpur in 1971. Being broadly on the left did not preclude us from exploring all options. We were joined by Vimala Ramachandran and Sanjaya Baru in the Nagpur meeting where we even met Indira Gandhi in a smaller group session. Vimala was my classmate in school, and an active participant in the Hi–Y and Uni–Y clubs. She went on to work in the education sector, focusing on the education of girls in government schools. Sanjaya studied economics, worked in journalism and went on to serve as media adviser to Prime Minister Manmohan Singh, even writing a memoir about his time at the Prime Minister's Office. The same year, we attended another Youth Congress meeting in Bombay but I was nauseated by the lavish expenditure and offended by the arm-candy women hanging around 'young' Congress leaders. I realized quickly that I did not want to be a part of such politics. All this activity was hidden from my parents. I bunked classes; fake cyclostyled letters of invitation from institutes elsewhere helped in convincing my parents to let me travel to distant places.

At that time, I was known to be a bold debator. I wore trousers, and was loud and spirited. When I was asked to conduct the first George Reddy memorial lecture in 1972, I agreed happily. This marked my formal initiation into politics. I identified openly and strongly with the left group. This was, as yet, a loose group of George Reddy followers—students who had loved him and identified with his politics. Here were young men who were intelligent, respectful and wanted to do something meaningful with their lives. They read about and discussed politics extensively. Among the authors I was introduced to at this time were Che Guevara, Régis Debray, Daniel Cohn-Bendit, Jean-Paul Sartre and Noam Chomsky. I tried to read Marx and Lenin but did not make much headway with them. Easier to read were Engels, Trotsky, Paul Sweezy, Leo Huberman, Clara Zetkin, Rosa Luxemburg, Erich Fromm and E.H. Carr. Mao was the clearest and most stimulating writer I read at that time. I read and reread R.P. Dutt's *India Today* which was recommended reading for Indian politics. I continued reading my 'bourgeois' books too. I was not going to give up on Somerset Maugham, Jane Austen and James Herriot. I loved fiction.

The time between 1972 and 1973 was truly one of ferment. I fell in love with the ambience on the campus. The politics of the left made great sense to me, from what I read and also in my interaction with the PDSU youth. At this time, had I been offered admission into an IIT again, I would not have moved. I had found my calling. I was part of a generation that was in step with the tide of the new, radical and subversive events that was sweeping the world, led by the young and the marginalized. It was one of those moments in history when it suddenly seemed that the coming together of many different acts of revolt could completely overturn our exploitative and oppressive society in its totality. There was the anti–Vietnam War movement in the US, the several anti-imperialist struggles in Africa and Asia, the Black Panther movement, the students' movement in Europe, the incipient women's liberation movement, and the Cultural Revolution in China. In India, there was the frustration of a large section of people over the failure of the independence project, and the subsequent Naxalbari movement. We were sure that revolution was around the corner, and that we would be its protagonists.

I became more assertive at home. I was no longer simply questioning or being a little curious, but asserting how I wanted to live my life. When my family went on summer pilgrimages, as they usually did, I refused to enter the temples. I said that I had my monthly periods. Now the arguments were no longer with my mother, they were with my father. He terrified me. If I came home late from a meeting, he stood at the gate, not allowing me in. He scolded me loudly for everyone in the neighbourhood to hear. I hated public confrontation, and his harangue, literally on the road, unnerved me. Whenever I thought of giving up my dreams and giving in to my family, the alternative loomed so large—the mindless rounds of clothes, jewellery, pujas, temple visits, gossip sessions with other mindless people, marriage to a tyrant—and my resolve strengthened again. My sister's fate made me realize that any life was better than that one.

In the summer of 1973, a year after I had joined OU, three young women joined the campus to pursue a postgraduate degree. They were a year senior to me, having already completed their graduation elsewhere. Lalitha, popularly known as Nandu, was Vimala Ramachandran's sister, hence already known to me. She joined me in the mathematics department. The other two were arts students—Rukmini Menon and Lalita. Rukmini, more popularly known as Minnie and formally as Meena Menon, was my sister's college-mate and already an acquaintance. She was in love with Srikrishna of the PDSU and therefore readily joined us. Lalita was her classmate in MA political science. The four of us had a wonderful time. Minnie was a beauty, a great mimic and a vivacious character. One saw her only in multicolour. She was to become a trade union organizer in Bombay in the 1980s with the Girni Kamgar Sangharsh Samiti

(Mill Workers Action Committee) and a consultant at NGOs in the early 2000s. Lalita is a founder member of the feminist organization Anveshi, and also works in an NGO, Yugantar. Nandu, quiet and cheerful, joined a bank but died of a heart attack within ten years, her baby barely a year old. When we got together as a group and began reading and organizing, we metamorphosed from helpless angry young women to being persons with entitlements. We were a small group of students who were consciously making our entry as citizens of India, but our rights seemed expendable.

I had seen girl after girl pulled out of the Koti Women's College because their parents felt that schooling after a point was unnecessary. We only had a tenuous right to education. We could be married off to strange men and that could mean lifelong unhappiness; our parents needed to pay substantial amounts as dowry to placate our in-laws to accept us as household slaves; we had no public spaces where we were comfortable, we were sexually harassed on the roads, in classrooms, and in hotels; there were ugly hoardings everywhere that made commerce of our bodies.

This consciousness of being a citizen with rights rested firmly on my readings and political associations in the past year. Now, as a part of this loosely knit group of like-minded friends, this shift in thinking led us to some small organized activities. We ran an anti–sexual harassment campaign on campus, an anti-obscenity campaign in the city (where we blackened posters and advertisements that demeaned women), and were active on any forum that would have us. We met frequently with B. Lakshmi Bai, a progressive feminist who taught linguistics on the OU campus and had known George. She encouraged us to think, read and discuss. But then, the sectarianism of the left predictably raised its ugly head. After

Lakshmi married someone from another political faction of the Marxist–Leninist parties, we sadly distanced ourselves from her because of the group politics of the time.

It might surprise young women to know what excited us in those days. For instance, we fawned over a teacher, Vanaja Iyengar, who taught mathematics at OU. Hailing from an orthodox Tamil brahmin family, she had studied at Cambridge, joined left students' forums, married Mohit Sen, who later became a full-timer in the Communist Party of India, and returned to Hyderabad to teach here. A beautiful and gracious woman, she smoked cigarettes in the teachers' lounge and I often peeped in and tried to catch a glimpse of her smoking. It made my day when I did. Satyamma Srinath, who taught at Reddy College, zoomed past the OU campus on her scooter—how exciting it was to watch a woman do that. Veena Shatrughna, a feminist doctor, also drove a scooter, and what was more, she wore sleeveless blouses!

Then there was the episode of M. Shantha's (later to become Shantha Sinha) elopement. Shantha is one of the warmest persons I know, and one of my closest friends. She taught political science at the University of Hyderabad, set up the Mamidipudi Venkatrangaiah Foundation, spearheading the movement for the eradication of child labour, and went on to chair the first National Commission for Protection of Child Rights. In college, however, romance was in the air. Shantha fell in love with her classmate Ajay Sinha, but her orthodox Pudur Dravida family had an arranged marriage lined up for her, and she was confined to her home. Our friends in the PDSU plotted to get her out. Mahipal Reddy dressed as a postman and went on a cycle to her Marredpally home. A car followed him close by. 'Telegram for Shantha,' he called out and when asked to give it to a family member, he refused. 'She has to sign it,' he said. When Shantha came out, she was quickly escorted to the waiting car.

There was another exciting elopement, this time involving Vijay Kulkarni—a close friend of George's and one of the founders of the PDSU who distanced himself from the group after George's death. He eloped with an MA student in the arts department who was already married, and the couple fled to Delhi.

These happenings were frowned upon by all elders, whether of left or right persuasion, but we saw them as challenges to conservatism and women's oppression.

3 Sharp left: Life as a Naxalite

In early 1973, three primary groups of Naxalites were active in Andhra Pradesh. In addition, there were several smaller formations that did not call themselves parties. For outsiders, it was difficult to distinguish all these different groups from each other because they all had similar names, with 'CPI–ML' tagged on. Worse, these names changed frequently and, in time, the split groups splintered into more, leading to further confusion. For example, there are three different PDSUs and POWs (Progressive Organization of Women) on the OU campus as I write and at least fifteen prominent ML groups in the two Telugu states of Telangana and Andhra Pradesh now. To avoid the confusion of an alphabet soup, in local parlance each group is called after its leader. Since ML groups are hierarchical, with a clearly delineated leadership structure, this is easy. The three main groups in Andhra Pradesh in 1973 were the Chandra Pulla Reddy (CP) group, the Tarimela Nagi Reddy (TN) group and the KS (Kondapalli Seetharamaiah) group.

By early 1973, many of the young men I knew had formally, though secretly, joined the CPI–ML Chandra Pulla Reddy group—the Andhra Pradesh Revolutionary Communist Party (hereafter referred to as 'the party'). I followed them. A change in clothes marked this. I no longer wore trousers and changed to saris. I took off my earrings and never wore any jewellery after that. After me, many of my friends from our women's group were quick to join the party. It was a seamless process— my group of friends inside and outside the party was the same. We continued to do what we were doing, except that it was planned and strategized now.

The years from 1973 till mid-1975, when the Emergency was declared, were filled with fervent activity. The movement was expanding. We rapidly grew from fifteen to five hundred, spreading from the Hyderabad OU campus to the entire state. In August 1973, we conducted massive agitations protesting against the rise of prices of essentials. The agitations included small and big meetings in colleges across the city and in other districts throughout the state. We took out rallies, and students from all over joined us in their thousands. Within our group on the campus, we spoke English and Deccani Hindi, commonly known just as Dakkhani. In the early 1970s, the language on the street was Deccani Hindi, not Telugu. Settlers from coastal Andhra who spoke only Telugu had not yet entered Hyderabad in a big way. Students from the rural areas who spoke Telugu quickly picked up Dakkhani once they joined colleges in the city. Studying in a central school, living in a brahmin enclave and meeting only people of my class had not equipped me to speak Telugu. I learnt to speak the language on the job, when I was sent to different districts to form auxiliary party-related groups. We met party leaders from all over and sometimes even from outside Andhra Pradesh. At the time, we also ran wall magazines in colleges. *Focus* was the wall magazine in the Arts College on the campus. We were encouraged by the party to identify young leaders, involve them in agitational work and guide them before they eventually became party members.

We often had group meetings, with both men and women present, that went on late into the night. We sat up for many nights in a row attending these, never wanting to miss out on the discussions. Since I was trained in Carnatic music, I was roped in to participate in Arunodaya, the cultural front of the party that was formed in 1974. The songs and the veedhi bhagavatham were in Telugu. The bhagavatham was a long-winded song and dance drama. Conventionally, the bhagavatham comprised stories from the epic *Mahabharata* performed in the local language. We adapted this for our own purposes as street theatre. Our bhagavathams did not tell puranic stories. I remember one we did based on the life of George Reddy and another about how the Indian capitalists were exploiting the people with the help of the government. Kanuri Venkateswara Rao, an old-timer from the Telangana armed peasant struggle, was our director. He wrote the script, improvised the tunes and played the harmonium. The plays had dances, and actors had to sing (or mime) their lines. I was one of the two narrators who stood on the side with cymbals, sang our own parts as the chorus, and provided backing vocals for the other actors who entered and exited. I wrote all my lines down in the Devanagari script as I was more familiar with Hindi. We had rehearsals every day for a few months and once we were ready, we had back-to-back programmes that lasted all night.

In April 1974, some of us women on the OU campus formed the first Progressive Organization of Women with the backing of the party. Nandu left to join the women's wing of the Radical Students' Union which was to be formed soon. At the POW's first meeting in Nizam College, we brought out a small manifesto. The organization comprised about twenty women. A lot of hard work preceded this. If memory serves me right, some four of us went to every women's college in the city—Women's College in Koti, Navajeevan in Ramkote, Andhra Mahila Sabha, St Francis College, Vanita Mahavidyalaya. We went to co-education colleges like the Nizam College, the Osmania and Gandhi Medical Colleges, Jawaharlal Nehru Technological University, Sardar Patel College and others.

It was not easy for us to 'mobilize' girls as we called it then. I remember walking into colleges, stopping by areas where there was a large group of girls and haranguing them on topics such as sexual harassment (we used to, regrettably, call it eve-teasing back then), the burden of dowry, price rise and other such issues. If we had a contact like the sister of a PDSU guy, we located and hectored her, asking her to gather some of her friends. On the OU campus, when a BJP activist Picchi Narasimha Reddy tried to inappropriately touch Minnie in the Arts College, we were really angry and organized a fairly big rally of women students from the Arts College to the Vice Chancellor's Lodge. This was the POW's first major demonstration on campus. In January 1975, we organized an anti-obscenity campaign, where we had great fun tarring obscene posters on the roads and outside theatres— we engaged with the interested spectators as we went about our work. Some posters of soft porn had women's oversized breasts and thighs highlighted. We also tarred posters that showed beautiful women in advertisements selling cars and blades. Why were women's bodies used in these, we asked.

Back in 1972 and 1973, monsoon had failed for consecutive years and most parts of the country faced droughts. Massive shortages of foodgrains were reported from all regions, pushing prices up. India was still importing foodgrains for sustenance. The Bangladesh war had eaten up a large chunk of the foreign exchange reserve, which depleted further with the rising cost of foodgrain import. The failed monsoon and fall in agricultural production led to a drop in power generation and there was low demand for manufactured goods. Industrial production went down. This led to a sharp spike in unemployment. The 1973 oil shock drained the foreign exchange reserves of India as crude oil prices quadrupled within days. The prices of petroleum products and fertilizers increased sharply. Inflation was 22 per cent in 1972–73, over 20 per cent in 1974 and over 25 per cent in 1975. There was unrest not just in Andhra Pradesh but all over India. We joined the PDSU in an anti–price-rise campaign early in 1975.

In the same period, we organized anti-dowry campaigns, not just in Hyderabad, but in all the districts where PDSU activists invited us. The POW helped in coordinating with party work that had been organized in the slums of Hyderabad by students.

The reaction from the young women students to our activities was mixed. I think we often frightened them. I cringe now when I think of how we hounded strangers. The lawyer and writer K. Balagopal's sister Madhavi studied at Andhra Mahila Sabha. The poor girl once expressed an interest in our work when I went to her college. She was then buttonholed by me several times, until finally she began running away whenever she knew that I was around. Most girls avoided us, a few gathered around to hear us curiously and only a few continued to keep contact with us.

We were only four young women in the party, but we were strong, resourceful and vocal. At meetings, we were served food first, our sleeping arrangements always took priority and generally, we were well looked after. This boosted our self-esteem and self-confidence. None of us had eaten beef earlier. During the party meetings, we learnt to do so. We had to chew and chew and chew, because the meat was stringy and prepared by men who were not great cooks. We drank very many 'single' cups of tea (which meant a half-cup), smoked cigarettes and beedis, fell in love and separated; we wore clothes given to us by our better-off friends. We learnt to walk miles, since we often didn't have money for bus fare.

We were part of a mass movement and a mass movement is liberating for everyone. Attitudes change, opinions are formed, relationships are forged, unity is discovered and courage and bravery miraculously become acquaintances. One discovers, almost suddenly, the potential in oneself. This must have been an equally game-changing experience for the young men involved. It was a unique time. The men from the PDSU must have been like other patriarchal, entitled people in society, but something of the patriarchy crumbled in them permanently. I sense this when I meet them now. The men in our group were respectful of us. I don't recall any of us having a single bad experience though we moved about closely with them. Some of us formed attachments that lasted for life. Yes, we were different, but that difference did not make us unequal to them.

I met Cyril for the first time in 1973. When we joined the party, we were given aliases to protect our real identities. It was a way of protecting those who went underground (staying away from the public gaze and having secret housing and meeting places). People in the party were usually called by their aliases. Cyril had been underground since he joined the party and was called Vijay. He was the head of the students' cell in the party which meant that we reported to him. That's when I learnt that he was George Reddy's younger brother. At that time, I was swept along by the idea of revolution. As I had never met George, he was a kind of idealistic notion in my head. Cyril was so far away from the lofty image of George I had in my head. He didn't talk much and was rather reticent with us women. It took several meetings for me to understand that this was a serious person who thought things over meticulously, and came to a fair and unbiased judgement. He had another trait which I did not know of at that time.

When he disliked a person or was uncomfortable in a situation, he reacted rudely and escalated the incipient conflict to the point of a physical stand-off.

After I married Cyril, I experienced both the good and bad parts of his personality. His volatile temper caused me much misery in the short term, but it was he who suffered in the long run, because he (and sometimes I, by extension) was excluded socially by a few people. In the beginning, neither of us had even considered each other as a partner. That only happened well into 1975. I do not think either of us were in love with each other when we decided to marry. It was based on what we thought of each other as a suitable companion in a revolutionary life.

Even today, when I look at the marriages that happened in those days, I find them so different from others. The couples have a strong bond; the wives continue to be independent. The women in the movement have all gone on to make independent careers, some left the party ahead of or behind their partners, some divorced their partners. Our male cohorts have respected all these decisions. They also cook and clean and help raise children, something unheard of in their age group in India.

The PDSU men, however, weren't so feminist when it came to their own sisters. It was as if we were privileged to exact an equal relationship, but not all women merited this. Madhusudan's sister was parcelled off to Cyril's sister Gypsy in Odisha after she fell in love with an 'unsuitable' man, someone who supposedly frittered away his time and was not husband material. In our case, the men not only let us be, they encouraged us. I think when they went back to their bourgeois lives, some parts of them ossified, though I can only speak of Cyril with certainty. At that time, I personally did not see a contradiction between feminism and communism; the two were seamless to me, though I often felt they had differing insights. Communism had a broader scope across classes and geographies, while the feminism we knew had greater insight into culture, the problems around family and relationships and attitudes. When I was in the party, communism seemed to have the answers to society's political problems and feminism had the answers to social and personal issues. One of the reasons for this twinning could be that we were really not part of the larger integrated party, the CPI–ML. We remained a kind of caucus inside the party, and within two to three years of joining the party, a large part of this caucus had left. To that extent, we did not carry the burden of the communist movement and did not feel the need to justify its blindness in various areas, including feminism.

In the left group, brahmins were teased, sometimes mercilessly—for our food habits, for our sedentary lifestyle, and of course, for all the sins of our forefathers. For the first time, I found other people critical of my family's and community's stances, but the critique was angled differently from mine. Besides the gentle ribbing, the more practical and structural influences of caste in everyday life were not yet interrogated in the left circles. You could join the left with all your brahmin-ness intact and still be comfortable. You could, for example, refuse to eat beef, like some did; you could also marry a fellow brahmin without too many questions being raised. It was as if by ignoring caste it could be wished away. Caste for me, and for many like me, did not become a serious question until 1985, when the Karamchedu massacre took place. Class was what occupied our minds. Till then, caste, unlike class, was relegated to the quirks of one's private life; a set of idiosyncracies. Caste, even in radical left circles, was not an ideological issue. It was everywhere, yet rarely discussed.

What happened in Karamchedu changed everything. Karamchedu is a village in Andhra Pradesh's Prakasam district where six dalits were massacred and dalit women raped by the dominant kamma community. This was done in retaliation to the growing resistance of the dalits against the exploiting classes. This horrific incident spawned the influential Dalit Mahasabha movement. It was really the Ambedkarites who made caste and brahminism unavoidable concerns for people like me who had happily ignored it until then. The Mandal Commission report of 1989–90 and its fallout accentuated the centrality of caste.

However, in the Naxalite years of the early 1970s, it was easy and convenient for us to gloss over caste; those who belonged to the Scheduled Castes and Backward Classes and participated in that movement would have certainly experienced an avoidance and reluctance to confront questions related to caste. To compound this, in the party it was not often easy to figure out a person's caste since people operated under aliases—a Muslim could have a Hindu name, a Christian could have a Muslim name, and so on. In the Hyderabad group, beef—not chicken—was the favoured meat of choice. This was a cultural trait unique to Telangana where most people, including the brahmins in progressive circles, had no qualms eating beef. One never bought clothes for oneself, instead relying on hand-me-downs from friends outside the movement. Sure, there were dalits and lower-order shudras among us, but only a small number—and they didn't articulate their opinions on caste matters. The Mandal Commission report of 1990—that recommended extending the idea of reservations for the Backward Classes in education and jobs—gave them the needed impetus. The little work

I saw of the party in the villages was certainly among the agricultural poor, but not slanted towards the dalits like in the Ambedkarite movements. The Hyderabad-based student group was almost entirely composed of dominant-caste activists—brahmins, reddys, privileged Muslims, velamas; among the young women, entirely so, without exception.

I remember an incident when caste was brought to the forefront in the party. In one of the city committee meetings (the party functions through committees at various levels), we were discussing what monthly stipend the full-timers among us needed. I think we agreed on Rs 150, when Rajari, a dalit full-timer, said he needed more. 'My father is dead, and my mother has retired as a Class 4 staff from Osmania University. I need to give some money at home to make up for my absence as a working member.' The comrades were shamefaced and he took his pay increase.

The times were so heady, so charged with revolutionary fervour that without a critical mass of dalit students to raise their own concerns, the subject of caste had simply no chance of being brought forward. This was not from a lack of trying though. While I was writing this book, Sashi, a close comrade of mine in the party, told me how a demand for a separate dalit students' organization was indeed raised by Dr G. Chander but this was not accepted by the party. Chander was an early activist in the PDSU; he was the elder brother of the poet Guda Anjaiah who composed the iconic song 'Ooru manadira, vaada manadira' (This village is ours, the ghetto ours too). Either Cyril operated out of their room in the old city of Hyderabad or he stayed with them, I'm not sure. We always reported to Cyril about our work in this room. Chander and Anjaiah were malas from Adilabad, and articulate and bold. Sashi also told me that students in the dalit hostels resented this refusal of the party, since it had earlier given the nod for a separate women's organization.

By 1974, my relationship with my parents was really strained. My father was quite perturbed by my increased participation in public activities, though he did not know that they were linked to the Naxalite ideology. Their bigger concern was the amount of time I spent outdoors. Every time I came home late, my father was at the gate, yelling. He did not call me names, but scolded me for doing things girls shouldn't be doing. Despite all my radicalization, I felt a whole lot of shame, often framed by the question 'what will people think'. By this time, I was barred from using the telephone. If someone wanted to contact me about a meeting, they had to get to me through my Marredpally friend, Shantha Sinha. Since she was the only person I was allowed to take a call from, first Shantha had to call me up, and then the other person could come on the line after the receiver had been handed to me. Shantha had by then married Ajay Sinha who was part of the George Reddy group but my father did not know this. He only knew that she was the daughter of Mamidipudi Anandam, a brahmin chartered accountant in Marredpally.

In 1974, I completed my BSc and applied for an MSc in statistics. I actually preferred maths, which was elegant and challenging. But I had no time for the rigorous coursework, now that I was fully involved in the student and women's movements. In April that year, my father drew me aside and asked me, 'I will ask for a transfer to Madras. Will you come with us?' I said yes. I am now more than a little ashamed at this outright lie. Of course, I knew that I would not leave Hyderabad. I was happy to stay here on my own. But I did not have the courage to tell him this. I wanted them to leave so that my troubles at home would end. He asked for the transfer to Madras and when he got it, I dropped the bombshell: 'I am not coming.'

There was a huge fight which spilt over into campus, involving my lecturers, friends and even their parents. When I wrote my BSc exams that summer, I left home and stayed in my former classmate and comrade Burgula Pradeep's home. His generous family supported me to the hilt. They were a sizeable party—Pradeep's mother, five brothers and their families, his sister Rama and her family, all in one house. All were warm to me during that trying time when I was confused, terrified, angry and irresolute. His sister-in-law Dr Mangutha Narsing Rao drove me down to campus and brought me back every day, even as my father stood about and shouted near the physics department where the exams were held. My father met the lecturers, parents of my friends and others to get them to intervene and get me back home. Sumeet Sidhu's father, an intelligent man whom he also spoke to, told him, 'Let your daughter go, Mr Ramaswamy, and she will return. Hold tight to her and she will flee.' At this point, Pradeep's family gave me the space and opportunity to think for myself. If they had not given me such an unqualified refuge, I don't know what I would have done.

This was the second turning point in my life. Now I would not back down. I had my scholarship. I could easily live on that and continue my postgraduation in Hyderabad. Finally, my family realized that there was nothing more they could do. They worked out a compromise: I was to stay with my elder sister and her husband. When they left in the summer of 1974, I moved to my sister's house in the next lane in Marredpally. Discipline here was lax. They couldn't question me like my parents. So I continued with my party

activities without much of a problem. I had completed my
graduation and enrolled for postgraduation in statistics at
Osmania University. I believed I could live on my own, away
from the control of my family. I was in every way a confident
young woman of twenty-one years. I felt I had already crossed
the Rubicon and was relieved when the Emergency in 1975
allowed me to leave home for good.

In 1974, after my parents had left for Madras, the party
sent me to Benares with a cash belt around my waist and a
heavy trunk. I was given an address where I had to report. I
got off the train and engaged a cycle rickshaw driver. Neither
of us could find the address for a long time. The rickshaw
driver threatened to put me down with the trunk. It made
me really tense because I couldn't simply walk away. When
I finally located the house, deep inside a maze of winding
streets, I found Satyanarayan Singh, Jayashree Rana and two
others there. They were ML leaders we had heard about. I was
awestruck at being in the same room with them. Satyanarayan
Singh—who had led a struggle of workers in Jamshedpur
against the Tatas in 1952 and was jailed for eight years—was
in fact the general secretary of our party. Jayashree Rana was
the petite leader from Bengal who had formed a Bolshevik
party within the CPI–ML and was an icon. The cash belt
had a huge amount of money and the trunk was full of guns
or pistols. I was horror-struck. I did not stay long and left the
next day with hardly any luggage, much relieved and happy at
having met my leaders.

I returned to quarrel with my party contact who was
Cyril at that time. 'How could a novice be sent with guns and
such a huge amount of money?' I asked angrily. Anything
could have happened—the police could have asked what was
in this huge trunk, the railway porter could have asked me

why it was so heavy. And if I did not find the place, I would have been stuck in Benares. 'Precisely why,' he replied. 'You were totally safe, no one would suspect you and you have the grit to carry it off.' I was not impressed with the reasoning. Although work like this proved to be a valuable experience.

We also read a lot. There was an immense thirst for knowledge, to know what was happening elsewhere, to know how and why movements shaped up as they did. Books that talked about this were not as easily available those days. They were certainly not available in public libraries. This made us hungrier for them. We raided the houses of older friends like Saral Sarkar, Veena Shatrughna and Rama Melkote for both books and food. Saral Sarkar taught German at the Max Müller Bhavan in Hyderabad. We often landed up in his rooms in Himayatnagar to chip away at the condensed milk tin that he hid from us and discuss politics. In time, he married a German ex-nun, Maria Mies, famous in her own right as a feminist and writer. Veena Shatrughna was a doctor who was to become one of the founder members of Anveshi. Her husband M. Shatrughna was a cheery and welcoming sort who taught in a college in Hyderabad and reported for the *Economic & Political Weekly*. He often cooked for us. Not that Veena didn't, but we remember the men who cooked with greater appreciation than the women who did the same.

We prepared ourselves for torture by speaking to each other and reading accounts of how people held up under such conditions elsewhere. Of course, we were to subsequently learn how nothing could really prepare a person for torture and how our dear friends caved in at different times.

I joined Arunodaya, the party's cultural front formed in 1974. No one pressured me. I was more than willing at first. But my interest waned when in 1975, before the Emergency,

I heard Gaddar and Bhoopal Reddy performing at a cultural conference in Anantapur. Lalita and I had gone to perform our own veedhi bhagavatham. Gaddar and Bhoopal Reddy were associated with the cultural wing of the Communist Party of India (Marxist–Leninist), the group that became the People's War Group in 1980. Gaddar's fame preceded him even at that time. Their performance was staggering. It was immersed in the working class tradition. Gaddar's songs, that adapted the popular burrakatha folk form traditionally used to narrate Hindu mythological stories, were in the regional Telangana dialect. They came across as spirited, spontaneous, evocative and creative, although I am sure a lot of planning, practice and thought went into their work. We sang in standard textbook Telugu and our songs stuck to the more brahminical classical groove. Besides, we were only singers, we could not emote like Gaddar did. He was a powerhouse made for the stage. We were paltry pretenders.

I decided that I would not perform for Arunodaya any longer. It felt pointless. I was tired of the never-ending touring and public display of myself. It must have been a blow to the party because two young women up on the stage was an attraction. Others objected but Neelam Ramachandraiah (or NR as we called him) supported me and told the others to let me be. NR was from Kurnool district and had been a member of the Legislative Council of Andhra Pradesh (when it had a bicameral legislature). He was someone I liked and respected. He listened with attention and care, and only spoke when he had to respond to a query. He made comments only when absolutely necessary. When NR was liaising with us in the early days, he pretty much let us do what we wanted. He sometimes gave us suggestions that were based on the practices of communist parties in the past, which often made for valuable advice. For instance, when we discussed setting up the POW for the first time with him, he only listened, never telling us what to do. He spoke more when PDSU functioning was being discussed.

The other organization I was involved in, POW, both lost and gained from its association with the party. It gained in terms of learning strategies, planning events, and having a broader reach, but lost because of the party's image as a feared group; after all, we were the dreaded Naxalites. Publicly we denied all contact with the party, but whom did we fool really? Even today, I am known as a 'Naxalite' in some circles in Hyderabad, though it has been over four decades since I ceased to be one.

POW was quite close to the PDSU, and being students, we were in close contact with our counterparts in the other organization. Two problems disturbed the fledgling organizations. One was the urgent need to recruit cadres for the party and the other was the sudden onset of the Emergency. Every leftwing party has an ever-present need to recruit cadres: this is common across all shades of the left even today. Left party leaders give great importance to this matter. They often deliberately split mass movements and force people to join one group or the other. Their reluctance to join forces with other like-minded groups stems from their fear of 'losing' cadre. Free and frank discussion and open-ended reading were discouraged for the same reason. Students are quickly pushed into full-time work and made professional revolutionaries. This really means that there is little preparation in the kind of mass work that involves meeting and working with people from all walks of life. There is little discussion on how their relationships with their families can continue. No thought is given to children born to women who are party cadres and the tragedies that unfold from the situation are disregarded. There is barely any discussion on the process of transformation or what the immediate future may hold. The young cadres are not prepared for the inevitable burnout that sets in after a period of idealistic party work. They are not trained or supported to confront a psychological or existential crisis that can develop in the course of such precarious work. They aren't taught to build a support structure around themselves. It could be due to this that the cadres leave as quickly as they join the party. The attrition rate in the left parties is extremely high.

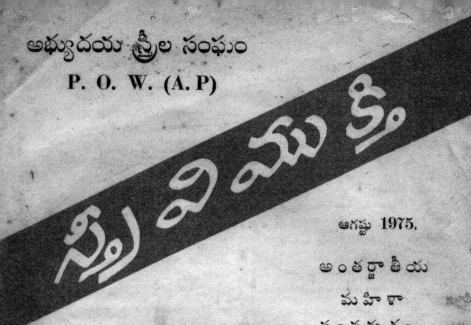

అభ్యుదయ స్త్రీల సంఘం
P. O. W. (A. P)

స్త్రీ విముక్తి

ఆగష్టు 1975,

అంతర్జాతీయ
మహిళా
సంవత్సరం
ప్రత్యేక సంచిక

ఇందులో......

సంపాదకీయం
రిపోర్టు P. O. W.
స్త్రీ జాతి కథ
భారత స్త్రీలు
పోరాటు మెందుకు ?
విప్లవపథంలో స్త్రీ
నవసమాజంలో స్త్రీ

వెల : 1.00

The August 1975 issue of Stri Vimukti, the Telugu magazine of the
Progressive Organization for Women, Andhra Pradesh, priced at Re 1

4 The revolutionary road breaks off into shadows

I was twenty-one when the Emergency was declared on 25 June 1975. It was a landmark for me and many of my friends who were politically active. Forty-five years later, as I write, we still use it as a marker of many events in our lives. Soon after the Emergency was proclaimed, the party asked most of us to go underground. I do not think we would have done so on our own. Around that time, I was heading the city committee of the party, which oversaw the student, women's, trade union and basti movements (where the poor, living in cramped settlements, were mobilized). The Emergency was a new situation, a near fascist rule, something we had only read about in books, and so we obeyed the party's directives without question. Cyril had been underground since 1973 even though he had no cases against him. We were told that since he was high profile, being George's brother, his movements would be watched and noted, and this would prove disastrous for the party and expose its operations among students. Over time, we were given to understand by the party that mass work and the identity that went along with it were precarious, to say the least. We could not expect to stay overground for long.

At the time, being told to go underground merely came across as a precautionary measure. In hindsight, it does make sense, since a number of us were arrested quickly. Immediately after the Emergency was proclaimed, M. Shatrughna, Dr Veena Shatrughna and C.N. Chari were picked up. All three were lecturers and professionals. Elsewhere in Hyderabad, radical intellectuals like Bojja Tharakam, Varavara Rao, Nikhileswar, Jwalamukhi, and even former CPI–ML activists like C.K. Narayan Reddy were arrested.

Jampala Prasad was a dynamic leader of the PDSU. He was bold, uncompromising and active, someone whose life completely changed after George was murdered. The party sent him to the coastal Andhra region to organize the workers there. Caught along with party leader Neelam Ramachandraiah (known as NR) in Vijayawada, he was arrested, tortured and killed in November 1975. The euphemism used was the usual: they were 'encountered'. We knew that if he had not been arrested in Neelam Ramachandraiah's company, he would not have been killed. While NR was dear to us, his murder was expected as he was a top leader of the party, but Jampala's murder shook us up. It meant any one of us could be the next. All across the state, people of our group and of other ones were arrested and tortured.

The Emergency created the first major schism among us. Not everyone was willing to continue participating in the movement, some wanted to write their examinations (the Emergency was proclaimed in June, which was right at the time when semesters were ending), others didn't want to upset their families. We had entered the campus as students, as potential scholars. Were we to study and prepare for careers as our teachers and parents wanted? Or did we, as students, have a responsibility to both educate ourselves and the people around us and work for change, for revolution? We were often torn between the two choices. I was ambitious. I had earlier resolved that I would never marry, I would get a great job and support myself. I was anyway quite successful academically. Was I to throw all these away? Some of my friends were careful in hedging their bets—they wrote their exams and kept close to their families who would be their safety net some day. Why should I be foolhardy then? But the idea of revolution swept all my doubts away.

Not that this was an easy decision for the men, but leaving home and disappearing was something they did frequently anyway: they went on trips, they stayed out, they stayed with friends. For us young women, it was a do-or-die situation. Once you left home, you could not return easily. In my own case, the days before the Emergency were already hellish and tension-ridden. I felt I had already pushed my family to its limit and was relieved when the Emergency allowed me to separate entirely.

The sheer number of activists going underground had immense ramifications for mass movements. The continuity of our work was broken, especially since a lot of us were still relative novices. We were immature and hadn't had sufficient time to learn from our own experiences. Our bond as a group was not strong enough to keep us united and focused. Overnight, several friends had been arrested and the party relayed to us that we were to stay out of the police's reach. Initially, it was fun and why not: it was a new experience for a curious and enthusiastic bunch of youths. While the men took up rooms, we women stayed with other families. Given that parents usually kept tabs on girls, going underground changed family equations forever. The party farmed us out to stay with unknown families, most of whom were poor. They were usually relatives of party cadre who had agreed to host one student. Our lives changed like never before. From a middle-class environment, we were thrust into a lower middle class or poor one.

My stay was rotated between a fixed set of families. I stayed with a family, for instance, that lived in one room. Lunch and dinner were rice with a watery tamarind soup. There was no tea or coffee. Sometimes, a mirchi bajji was bought to spice up the meal. The bathroom was shared with several other families. Water was scarce. Besides, there was not much to do, with all of us cooped up in a single room. Housework was minimal since the cooking was simple. I talked with the family but the experience was so new that I was not comfortable with them—I was only used to being around my peers. I had been in Hyderabad since 1968, but I still couldn't speak Telugu too well. Added to this was my lack of contact with students from rural areas. Our friends spoke either English or the Dakkhani Urdu. Except for women whose exposure to the outside world was minimal and students who had freshly come from villages, most people spoke Urdu. With my limited knowledge of Telugu, I tried hard to make friends with the families but found it difficult. Life here was so much more different and difficult than what I had known so far. Romantic ideals of emancipating the poor now looked far more difficult if this was how the poor lived. I was chafing to get out and take up a room of my own. I often retreated to a corner and read all day, until it became safe to move around in the city by nightfall.

Party meetings invariably happened late in the evening, and they went on into all hours of the night. The meetings were held in the houses of friends who were not already sheltering underground comrades. One such room was that of Patlolla Indra Reddy who was a PDSU activist in the Social Welfare hostels. He was renting out a room along with his friends, and was the elected president of the Law College Students Union. Indra was arrested during the Emergency and was in prison for eighteen months. He joined the Telugu Desam Party in 1985 and served as a minister in the N.T. Rama Rao cabinet.

The rooms we selected for our meetings were always small, and the doors and windows closed. They were usually filled with a pall of cigarette smoke, mostly thanks to the men. The smoking was so irritating to us women that we constantly quarrelled with them to stop it. In return, they cleverly got some of us to smoke with the jibe, 'Girls can't smoke.' After the meetings, we went back to our 'shelters', by rickshaws. Travelling by bus was out of the question. In those days, rickshaw drivers insisted on waiting by the gate when they were dropping women, to make sure that we made it safely into the house. I wonder now why we were never mistaken for sex workers. Of course, back then I had no idea how sex workers operated.

Naturally, we had to drop out of college and could no longer meet our non-party friends. Our world became circumscribed and that's when the fun began waning. Prior to the Emergency, one could still meet people in the day. Parental control could be sidestepped on the pretext of going to college, seeing a film, going for a picnic or simply staying over at my friend Sumeet's house. In one instance, when I had to go for the Nagpur meeting of the Congress where we met Indira Gandhi, I typed and cyclostyled invitation letters from an institute announcing a seminar. I signed and posted these letters to mine and my friends' houses. But staying underground had definite rules. Now, we could move about only before dawn and after dusk, we could not go to any public places, or to the houses of people known either for their leftwing sympathies or for their connections with us. Since we lived in small rooms, we had to be careful to dress and behave appropriately. I remember that I could not sing in the room. When I hummed, the host told me that I could be mistaken for a sex worker. In effect, it meant the end of the world as we knew it.

Even meeting our own party colleagues happened at specific times. It took a while to get used to such rules. There were other difficulties too. Whenever someone was arrested, the rooms they frequented were immediately vacated because it was presumed that they would give away these locations when tortured during interrogation. This left us suddenly homeless. I went to friends' houses only to be turned away—they were too frightened to give shelter. In one instance, I had malaria and was burning with a 105-degree fever. My friend took me to a known doctor's house for treatment, but we were told to leave.

Despite the Emergency, romantic relationships continued to flourish. We met at friends' homes, often we had the whole night to ourselves (to talk, of course). Sometimes, we walked around the city late in the evening, but only in the areas where we were not known. It was difficult for police and intelligence officials to make out faces at dawn or later in the evening, and acquaintances whom we knew otherwise were not normally out at such hours. We worried over whether marriage or even a sustained partnership would come in the way of our political work. We pored over the works of Alexandra Kollontai—her books: *The Autobiography of a Sexually Emancipated Communist Woman* and *Sexual Relations and the Class Struggle: Love and the New Morality* were of biblical significance to me. She was the only Marxist party leader I had read who was also a feminist. Of course, there were others like Sheila Rowbotham, who was a Marxist and a feminist, but Kollontai worked in the party and I felt more of a connection with her. She advocated for the rights of women and wrote that sexuality is a human instinct as natural as hunger or thirst. She was especially important because we did not discuss sexuality with our party elders. If it were not for Kollontai, I would not have married at all. It was also reassuring that most communist leaders outside India were married to active women. There were the four wives of Mao, not to mention those of Lenin, Fidel Castro and Che himself.

We didn't use any of the Indian communist leaders as points of reference since so few of the ones we had heard of had wives who were their partners in the revolutionary movement. All the leaders in our party had left their families behind. Some were even known to have extramarital affairs.

In July 1975, Cyril and I decided to get married and informed the party elders and our friends. Shortly after this, I was summoned home with a lie. It was like a Bollywood film script. My family called up one of my friends in Hyderabad to say that my mother had suffered a heart attack. The message went to the party. I was sceptical, but the comrades insisted that I go home. I took the train to Madras, only to end up trapped. My mother was hale and hearty, my elder sister had had a second baby, one sister was to be married, and they had all decided to rein me in. They locked me up in a room, and fearing what they would do to me, I locked myself in too. There was a small garden outside my window and right past it was the main road of the CIT Colony, behind the Madras Music Academy. This was an upscale area where Tamil brahmins lived in large independent houses.

I was locked in for three days. All through I called out to passers-by for help. I told them that I was twenty-one years old, locked in by my parents, and needed to be freed. My elder sister stood by the window and informed them that I was a Naxalite. Horrified, they'd move on. Some even told me that I should be shot and was lucky that my parents had only confined me. I was rudely brought down to earth by the absolute lack of response from the public in those three days. There were people gathered outside my window, hardly twenty feet away, but no one was moved by my plight. The city had let me down, abandoned me. Ashamed and agonized, I yelled and shouted loud enough for the whole street to hear, but no one responded. I had no food inside the room though I had access to a bathroom and could drink water from the tap. The room also had some cans of a baby food product called Enfamil, which were brought from the US for my newborn niece. I opened one up and tried the powder but couldn't keep it down.

After three long days, I let my family in. I don't know why. Perhaps I was hungry. Immediately, they took me to the polyclinic of a psychiatrist, Rama Rao, on Poonamalle High Road. I recall pleading with him, telling him how old I was, that I was a free adult citizen, and that my parents had detained me against my will. I told him that I was of sound mind, I had no disconnect with reality, I was fully aware of it, and was conscious of wanting to change it. He completely ignored me and assured my father that he could 'cure' me. He had cured a young man from Bangalore brought to him with a similar complaint. He would 'rebrainwash' me to counter the brainwashing the Naxalites had done, he said. I was sedated and given electric shock treatment at his clinic. Tears still fill my eyes when I recall that feeling of total helplessness. Why weren't they simply killing me? Why were they torturing me, treating me like an animal? I watched the others who were being given similar treatment, wheeled out like zombies, their eyes unfocused, saliva drooling out of their mouths, their limbs flopping. I hated Rama Rao desperately for a long time. Could I file a case? Could I expose him to the media? Sometimes, I fantasized at night about killing him. If I had seen him on the streets, I would have surely attacked him.

I disliked going to Madras for a long time after this episode. For years, I did not discuss my electroconvulsive therapy with anyone. It hurt too deeply and I dissociated myself from the young woman who had suffered so much. It hurt to even think about the memories and I wept silently whenever they came back to me. It took me a full twenty-three years to open up about it. In 1998, while working on the mental health chapter of the book *Taking Charge of Our Bodies*, which I co-authored with Veena Shatrughna and Srividya Natarajan, I told Veena and mental health activist Bhargavi Davar (co-author of a chapter) about the incident and wept for a long time. I wept as I wrote this in the book. Every time I read and reread the drafts, I wept and had to pause for a long time. I can never understand why I grieve so much. It cannot simply owe to the suffering at that time, or the loss of memory and certain brain functions, or even the loss of the vitality and exuberance I had prior to the ECT. I think that when our own family turns against us, we are left with no means of reckoning with the betrayal. There is no enemy, there is no justice or revenge when those we think of as our own are out to get us. I can understand my parents who were horrified that their daughter had joined the Naxalites and wanted desperately to 'save' me, but surely my sisters, all of whom were educated adults, should have supported me.

In 2019, forty-four years after the incident, news broke out about a Hindu woman in Kerala who had married and converted to Islam. Hadiya was confined to her house by her parents and this was supported by the courts and civil society. This news troubled me greatly; this is the fate of so many of us even today.

After a twenty-day 'psychiatric treatment' I was taken to the doctor's clinic several times for check-ups. Here, I pretended to agree with whatever plans my parents had laid out for me. I applied for IAS and IIM courses and agreed to take up classical music classes. As the new routine began to set in, I tried making an initial attempt to escape, but this ended in disaster. My father had taken us to a wedding, and there I asked to go to the bathroom. Slipping away, I ran out of the function hall, hailed a taxi and asked him to take me to IIT Madras where I had friends. I had no money and must have been close to hysterical when I spoke to the driver. He did take me there, but after dropping me, he perhaps informed the police. Meanwhile, my father had lodged a police complaint of kidnapping. By the time I located my friends, the police, my father and some family friends had gathered at the institute.

The dean of IIT also came down. We were in some sort of an open square, and I vividly recall all the actors playing their parts in the predictable tragicomedy that unfolded. The dean said that there was no way he was allowing an outsider on the campus and asked me to leave. My friends were quiet. The police said that I had to tell them where I was staying for three days because there was a pending complaint of kidnapping and that I had to report to them every day. My dear school friend Jayashree Srinivasan's father was also there, though I don't know why. I appealed to him and to my other family friends to allow me to stay in their house till the mandatory three days were over. Then I could leave for Hyderabad. No one responded. I left with my father that day. But I didn't lose hope.

Meanwhile, my friends in Hyderabad sent Sashi to rescue me once they realized that I was trapped. Through our IIT friends, Sashi contacted Jayashree Srinivasan whom my family trusted. He gave her a note to be handed over to me in a book and I responded likewise. In a short time, we worked out a plan. My elder sister was to marry in a week's time. (She has never forgiven me for what she terms 'spoiling' her wedding.) At the decided time, I left home, accompanied by my niece for the music class. Once out of the house, I ran towards the street corner where another friend was waiting on a motorbike. My niece started yelling, 'Chitthi is running away, Chitthi is running away!' I jumped on to the motorbike and was taken to yet another friend's house where I changed clothes and had something done to my hair. I was driven, on a bike again, to Arakkonam, some seventy kilometres from Madras, on the Bangalore route. I had to get out of Tamil Nadu state limits because my father was sure to lodge yet another police complaint. At Arakkonam, I met Sashi and we went to Bangalore from where we took a bus to Hyderabad. I was not to meet my parents for some years after that. While I was writing the book and cross-checking facts with my friends, Sashi told me that he had found me oddly disoriented. During the journey, he told me that our close associate Jampala had been shot dead and he was surprised that this shocking news did not register with me.

I realized that all was not right with me when I returned in November 1975 to a completely different landscape. Police watch, arrests and torture had frightened several of our people. Jampala Prasad had been 'encountered' along with our mentor Neelam Ramachandraiah. This great loss had shaken up many of my comrades. They were glad to see me but didn't really notice how confused I was. I realized this when I met Cyril and couldn't recall who he was. He had grown a beard during the months I was away. When I told someone present at the meeting that I didn't know who this man was, I was told that he was the man I was to marry. I was upset. 'I don't even know him,' I said. Over the next few days, I reacquainted myself with all my old friends and comrades. Madhusudan Raj was a dear comrade, also to be 'encountered' soon. His house was open to us all and his family warm towards us. Madhu's father was the superintendent of the Erragadda Mental Hospital. I told him about the shock treatment in Madras and my present disorientation. He asked me to hold up my fingers, then my hands, to move them around in different positions, walk in different positions and asked me several questions. Finally, he told me that some part of my memory was lost but I could get on with life. That was all, he didn't elaborate. I was relieved because I was free and alive and physically whole. I found out that I could not recall any of the phone numbers I had known. Prior to this, I had a photographic recall for numbers and pages. I could scan them at lightning speed and remember them perfectly. I never needed to note down telephone numbers. I lost this ability. I also lost my love for mathematics. None of my comrades noticed this. They were too caught up in the events of the time. I could not speak of my ECT or my subsequent difficulties with anyone, not even Cyril.

Many young party members surrendered, some were arrested, and some disappeared to stay with relatives outside the state, away from both the party and the police. Dens were raided, people lost contact with their immediate cell members, the hierarchy was broken and everything was in chaos. I married Cyril soon after my return, late in November or early December, in a 'party wedding'. We had decided to marry before I went to Madras, but I was unsure and disoriented now. The party leaders wanted us to marry soon; they said it would lift the morale of our cadre. Usually, party weddings are conducted in the open and are like public meetings. The couple is seated on the dais, people in chairs or on the floor before them, a picture of Marx and the red flag on the dais. A leader makes an appropriate speech about loyalty, love and revolution. The couple exchanges vows, something along the lines of 'We will care for each other and remain true to the revolution', and the whole thing usually ends with them garlanding each other. Voila, wedding over! Chandra Pulla Reddy, the leader of our party, presided over the wedding.

He came from a landed family of Rayalaseema and had been active in the freedom movement as a student. The event took place in the cellar of Ramachandra Reddy's farm by the Himayatsagar lake—an underground wedding in every sense. Bananas were distributed to the few people present after the short ceremony where we read out our vows. CP gave a small speech and pronounced us married.

In Hyderabad, Cyril and I stayed in places like Dabirpura and Yakutpura, in tiny eight-by-eight-foot rented rooms where we shared bathrooms with several families. Here, I learned to cook on a kerosene stove. I had never cooked before, only helped around in the kitchen. Cyril and I (and I suspect most of our comrades too) had just one vessel with a lid. Rice was cooked in the vessel, omelettes on the lid; one of us used the lid as a plate and the other ate directly from the vessel. When we first moved to a room, I bought a mangalasutram for five rupees, worried that the families staying nearby would judge and question me for the lack of one and suspect that we were not married. Unlike men, women are expected to display this visible sign of marriage, parading their enslavement and unavailability to other men. But its cheap wire broke within ten days. I never found the time to replace it and have lived happily ever after in several types of accommodation without any symbol of a married Hindu woman. Since then I have felt that anxieties with society's symbols are more inside our heads than anything else. People can be stopped from judging us sometimes if we possess a degree of confidence.

As the repression deepened and our rooms were raided often, I was forced to move in and out of Hyderabad several times between 1975 and 1976. Cyril was able to find a place to stay, but it was becoming increasingly difficult for us to do so as a couple. I went on my own to Delhi where I stayed with the IAS officer B.N. Yugandhar for a month in his flat opposite Vigyan Bhavan. As secretary to the Andhra Pradesh government, Yugandhar would be the man behind several welfare measures including the popular two-rupees-a-kilo-rice scheme introduced by N.T. Rama Rao in 1983. Yugandhar was living on his own as his wife Prabhavathi taught in Tirupati. He was a great conversationalist, but we quarrelled over food because we had differing tastes and wanted to cook different things. He used onions in his rasam which horrified me. It was here that I learnt that Cyril had an older brother, Karl, who was also an IAS officer. Yugandhar and Karl knew each other. When Karl and his wife Satwant Kaur, also in the IAS, learnt that I was in Delhi, they wanted to meet me. I was mortified that I knew nothing of Cyril's folks, but it goes to show how little connection we had with our families.

The experience of the Emergency and going underground for so long led to the destruction of our faith in the party. For the first time, we met other comrades in Hyderabad whose hideouts in the city and in towns like Warangal and Khammam had been raided. They were forced to ignore party protocol and go to friends in Hyderabad in search of shelter. They told us uncensored stories about life in the party and the lies spun to keep members loyal. We had earlier been told that the forest was a liberated area and that revolutionary laws prevailed there. Our friends, particularly Sarangapani, Mohan Raj Yadav and Papla Venkateswara Rao who were sent to the forest, and had fled to the city after being hounded out by the police, told us that the propaganda was a lie. We heard how women were treated, seduced, raped even; how brother betrayed brother, how weeping mothers had to abandon their newborns—all terrible stories. No doubt, a revolution is no dinner party, but it is leavened by the love of the people and the comradeship among revolutionaries. Being underground meant that we were separated from people, could not lean on them, and were left to face our tribulations in isolation. Similar stories cascaded out of one young comrade after another.

The party's approach to us young members was initially one of caution. I think there is something to be said about Neelam Ramachandraiah's grace and tact in handling us before he was 'encountered'. We, as an English-speaking group, several of us non-Telugu, and somewhat charismatic on the campus, were quite different from the party. The party was used to younger replicas of themselves—students who were children of comrades or had been inspired by the party's activities. We were different, an entire batch that came in, inspired by George Reddy and his fight on campus. We were largely from the privileged, middle-class, urban background; most of us were brahmin and quite outspoken. This was not the profile of the party cadre from districts other than Hyderabad, but even they were savarnas with many of them coming from the landed gentry.

It was only in 1976, maybe in March, when Chandra Pulla Reddy and his partner Radhakka came to live with Cyril and me, that I understood this. After NR was killed in November 1975, Chandra Pulla Reddy became our 'handler' and that is when the problems began to crop up. The difference in Chandra Pulla Reddy's and NR's functioning was staggering. CP was autocratic, he never listened, only lectured. In hindsight, the Emergency itself was huge in turning us away from the party, but CP exacerbated the problem. We had joined the party because we thought that a revolution was for the good of the people. In March 1976, CP's cover was blown and his den was raided. Probably, the cover of a joint family was attractive and functional, and it was decided that the four of us would take up a larger house with three rooms in the Amberpet area. CP and his partner Radhakka's behaviour put me off completely. She took over the running of the house. She cooked chicken, whereas we had entered the party eating beef. We did not eat expensive meat. We thought we should eat the food of ordinary people. Radhakka frequently bought fabrics and got them stitched by a tailor. We thought that we should wear used clothes given to us by our sympathizers. She also shopped a great deal. Among us, both men and women shared the work equally. Here, Radhakka laid the bathwater out for CP, rubbed him down with soap, towelled him, laid his food out, stood behind him and served. Besides, she did the entire housework and washed his clothes. Seeing the couple at close quarters made me wonder if they could lead anyone to a new life.

I made an issue of this barely a fortnight into their stay with us. I asked CP why the party was lying to us about 'liberated areas'—regions where the party's diktats are obeyed, and the arms of the state by way of the revenue, police and panchayat raj departments were virtually non-existent. We had been told that the forests had been liberated, but then we had met so many of our cadres from the forests who had no shelter there. What was happening then? The cadres from the forests were themselves surprised on coming to the city and learning that we were in trouble too. They had been told that the campus was a liberated area. I asked CP why Radhakka performed all these tasks for him, and why they ate chicken and stitched clothes for themselves. Why the differing standards for them and for poorer cadres? CP threw a book across the room. 'Can they read this?' he asked. 'You and I can, they can't. Don't confuse us with the *people*,' he said. 'We are different. We are leaders.' He followed this up with a lecture on how we were to lead the people, how they were to be led, how we knew things they didn't, and so on. He said that there were many things we did not know and did not need to know. This was the time of armed struggle, not idle debate.

This happened at a time when intense discussions were brewing amongst younger cadres. We were becoming critical of our own movement. The bastis in Osmania University which we had organized since George's days to rally for their local problems had quickly turned into recruiting grounds for the party. There was little consideration or thought about building up the movement based around people's issues. We used questionable tactics when we worked with activists of other ML factions. If we were in a position of power, we were aggressive and tried to boot them out. If they were powerful, we tried to sabotage their programmes. Other parties behaved in a similar manner towards us. Our differences with the Democratic Students' Organization (affiliated to the CPI–ML Nagi Reddy group) and the Radical Students' Union (affiliated to the People's War Group) were hardly based on ideology. We worked in other bastis in Secunderabad and Hyderabad with G.M. Anjaiah only to attempt to take over his work and then fail to organize the people in any way. Anjaiah was a lawyer, a former socialist who worked for slum dwellers in the Secunderabad area. He organized several bastis on questions that concerned their immediate lives, like those of house patta (papers), water and electric connections. He was a fiery orator and contested on the Jana Sangh ticket for the Secunderabad Assembly seat in 1967. He was also known for some unsavoury real estate deals. Sashi and I were sent to work with him. We worked hard in many of the bastis and when we tried to undermine his leadership and take the people to our own rallies, he kicked us out, and instructed his followers not to have anything to do with us.

Our attitude towards other organizations was similar, based on increasingly narrow concerns. We criticized the Radical Students' Union for raising slogans like 'Armed struggle zindabad', 'Naxalbari zindabad', 'China's chairman is our chairman', 'Power comes from the barrel of a gun', in the processions, but not ourselves for similar provocative slogans that did not make any sense to the people, instead exposing our organizations to the police. People began openly saying that we had taken up earlier agitations against rising prices in the cities so that police pressure on our squads in the forest would decrease. Summer was a difficult time for the squads who were hiding in the jungles—water was available only in ponds which were often watched over by the police.

My own efforts were hardly ever democratically inclined, never considering what the people wanted nor showing any empathy to their needs. All I worried about was winning people over to the party line. In the second half of 1976, for all purposes, ML activity—broadly defined as party-based fora that veered left of the CPI(M)—was led from above, dictated by considerations of capturing political power rather than by issues of change and people's welfare. The possibility of democratic functioning in a party so deeply hierarchical was bleak. I recall an instance when a leader of the CP faction of the CPI–ML, Ram Narsaiah, complained bitterly about us, the young city activists. He said, 'People from rural areas get up when we tell them to get up and sit down when we tell them to sit down. These people [students from the cities] think they can conduct debates during an armed struggle.' The actual practice of democratic centralism was also problematic. One was bound not to question a decision taken by the majority or by the leadership. Theoretically, you could raise your concerns time and again in your particular cell, but you found that the others, even if they were your peers, soon tired of your concerns since the discussion never led to any change in policy. Democratic centralism was nothing but centralism, and discussion was allowed only when the leaders thought it politic. Democratic centralism was the single weapon with which the left destroyed itself by actively sabotaging debate and discussion.

The blinkered politics of that age made us realize that we could not widen the area of people's mobilization if we remained in the party. The understanding of the ML factions was stuck on three conceptual mountains that they used to explain oppressive conditions in India—semi-feudalism, semi-colonialism and comprador bourgeoisie. How I came to hate the clichéd use of these three mountains, the terms irritated me for decades together. Any discussion, ranging from dowry deaths to farmers' suicides, led back to the conclusion that these three mountains were responsible for what we were talking about and these were what we needed to fight. These terms even haunted me in my nightmares. There was no attempt to analyse a problem devoid of these empty formulations. Every document from the party and its various committees reiterated the formula of fighting the 'three mountains'. Another baffling belief was that 'the ends justified the means', something I found deeply troubling. Could we at all create a new state if we used the state's own methods to overturn it? Isn't change brought through all of society instead of just capturing power by rallying towards a specific strategic point called the revolution? I also disaffirmed the party's belief in violence. We heard shocking stories of mindless carnage and this was attested by the unwritten belief, particularly of the People's War Group, that violence was intended to create terror and thereby exercise control over the dynamics of a situation. The worst sufferers of the violence created by ML factions were the poorest people. ML violence invited worse violence from the state, and the Indian state armed with the best of technology and superior force was not about to brook any challenge to its might. The use of violence felt counterproductive. The ML movement was premised on a primary challenge to the existing communist parties, and armed struggle often boiled down to the use of petty violence against individuals.

By 1976, Cyril and I began preparing documents critical of the party and circulated them in different committees. We also worked out rebuttals to the party's literature that had been brought against us. The situation had changed from the days when NR listened attentively to us. Now, the party regarded those who differed with them as troublemakers and proclaimed that the dissidents were merely fearful of Emergency repression. The concerns that we raised also plagued other young members of the party. People who had been sent as far away as Visakhapatnam to organize there shared the same feelings about the party. There were perhaps twenty to thirty of us thinking on similar lines, but Cyril and I were the only ones to circulate documents openly stating our position. We were therefore targeted by the party as troublemakers and our stipends of Rs 150 each were stopped. Others were asked not to meet us.

I still remain a little cautious about taking a stand on violence in revolutionary movements. Maybe there are times when violence is justified. If you pin me down and ask me when, I will have to scratch my head and think hard. But in the movement that I worked, and in the case of PWG's activities, which I followed closely, I will say that violence by the party was never justified. I cannot say this about violence by the people themselves, but violence by the party in the two Telugu states was cruel, intentional, and more a statement of power than a necessity. We did not take recourse to violence in the city and none of us had firearms anyway. Still, we heard about the cruelty that was being perpetrated. Satyanarayana, one of our senior PDSU comrades, was killed by the party dalam in the Warangal area because one of the members of the local dalam mistakenly thought him to be a renegade. Sometime during the Emergency when I was secretary of the city unit, we came to know that Chalapathi Rao wanted to surrender. If he did, several shelters would be compromised. In the meeting held to discuss this, I suggested, 'Why don't we kill him?' To my great relief and fortune, no one took this up seriously. When I met Chalapathi again after many years and renewed my friendship with him, one of the first things I told him was how I had suggested in the party meeting that we kill him. I rested easy after unburdening myself.

Today, there's more clarity on this question than there was in 1975–76. The Narmada Bachao Andolan, the Chhattisgarh Mukti Morcha, the Chipko movement and several other movements that came up, clearly indicate how mass movements can be taken up, how the masses are the lifeblood of any revolutionary movement and why democracy in practice is crucial to the health of any revolutionary party.

With the party escalating its hostility towards us, things came to a head. Our small group of students had given up a lot to join the movement, and we weren't going to endure put-downs from anyone. How should we work among people? What should be our mode of activity? How should we ensure that people controlled the movement? Should the agenda of the revolution not be close to their hearts and lives? These points were never a part of the discussion in the party proper, even though it plagued us students quite a bit. To the party, all that mattered was how we took our programme to the people. They busied us with concerns about what we needed to tell the people and the techniques of mass mobilization that maximized gains for the party. There was considerable tension on this subject. At the time we joined the party, Mao's works were popular among us. At their core, Mao's writings emphasized respect for people and the importance of the ground realities of the situation. We constantly discussed these points. But party programming was not based on these principles, rather it had considerations of expanding the sphere of influence and increasing cadre strength as its main focus: all for the party project of capturing political power.

We constantly told our bosses: 'We are not prepared, this is not the kind of slogan we can take to the people, we won't get far with this kind of programming from the top.' We were not questioning the need for revolution or armed struggle but merely making arguments about strategy. When we finally left the party, it was with the strong desire to work among people without any kind of constraints, without dictating any slogans from the top. It was clear to us that we did not simply want people to affiliate themselves to our programmes. Rather we wanted to work on programmes that people wanted, and help them get going.

About twenty to thirty of us, including Cyril and I, left the party in November 1976. In turn, the party declared that they had expelled us. This was to be expected. The party could not stomach the fact that people were *leaving* it. We had to flee Hyderabad because we had neither money nor shelter. Sandwiched between the police and a now hostile party, we felt it was not wise to stay on in Hyderabad. The larger part

of the student group left the party. Many more surrendered to
the state authorities or quietly moved out.

Taking up a non-political life now was not an option
for Cyril and me. Both of us had strong reasons to continue
working with people. He had entered the movement as a full-
timer, initially to fulfil his brother's mandate, which became
his own conviction. As for me, I had burnt my bridges in a
spectacular manner. There was no way I could return to my
family.

In December 1976, we left Hyderabad for Chandigarh
where Cyril's eldest brother Karl lived. We took a tortuous
route of trains to avoid police surveillance, with our meagre
belongings in two sacks. It was a fraught trip. Cyril and I
quarrelled about the best route. At the Itarsi junction, in
Madhya Pradesh, where we had to change trains, the quarrel
resulted in both of us throwing our clothes and utensils out of
the sacks on to the platform in front of a bemused crowd. But
then we made up. As we made our way up north, I learnt more
about Cyril's family. They were five siblings. I already knew of
Karl and his wife Satwant. And George was obviously known
to me. Their oldest sibling was Dawn (also called Gypsy), who
was married to an Odiya man, and taught in Bhubaneswar.
She went on to run a school in Jeypore, Odisha. The third,
Joy (Lavanya), married to a Kannadiga, taught in Mysore;
The fourth was George, and Cyril was the youngest. Both
Gypsy and Lavanya kept open homes, not just for refugees
from the party, but also for the marginalized people who
lived near their homes. They educated them and supported
them till they were employed. They had gone through a
tough childhood, having seen first-hand how a brahminical
society could destroy relationships and abandon children, and
so they readily supported any movement or individual who

promised to change such a system. They continued to support us through our lives, and did so even after Cyril died.

In Chandigarh, Karl offered us a monthly stipend until we could find work. We did not stay with Karl though. It would have been unsafe for us. We took up a room, paying for it and our expenses with the money he gave us. We wanted to work with poor people and discover for ourselves if there was a way to do this without charity or reform work. We needed fresh identities to work safely. No one could foresee that the Emergency was about to be lifted shortly. We had heard of P.K. Murthy and Neeta working in central Madhya Pradesh under assumed identities. Murthy was a Tamil-origin Vietnamese who had returned to India to foment the revolution. He married Neeta from Bombay. Both joined the CP group and left to work in Chhindwara in central Madhya Pradesh where Murthy worked as a regular miner. (Murthy died early in 2020.) In another instance, Shankar Guha Niyogi had built up an independent workers' movement in Chhattisgarh. He had incorporated the daily needs of working-class families like education and healthcare in the work of the Chhattisgarh Mukti Morcha. These were inspiring examples for us.

Cyril and I began learning Punjabi and wrote the tenth class public examinations in the language (passing in the first class!) to create new identities for ourselves. However, these identities remained paper documents, since it turned out that we didn't need them at all. The Emergency was lifted in March 1977 and the new Janata Party government took power after it defeated Indira Gandhi. Despite this, we did not leave Chandigarh till it became clear that there was no ongoing witch-hunt.

One serious loss the Emergency caused me was that of my voice. Since the Emergency, I have never been able to speak confidently in public. When I go up on stage anywhere, I feel like a total impostor. I think this has got to do with my loss of faith in the revolutionary politics that we espoused so vigorously among other students and the basti people. I came to distrust educated men and women who speechified easily and led people into impossible situations.

5 After the Emergency: Our lives elsewhere

After the Emergency, life should have been better, but it wasn't. When it was lifted in March 1977, we left Chandigarh to come to Delhi. We remained in north India till 1980, unsure of what kind of police repression awaited us in Andhra Pradesh. We also wanted to work with people but Andhra Pradesh was not an option, given our difficulties with both the party and the police. Besides, there was no family to return to, unlike our friends who relocated to Hyderabad and rebuilt their lives, no doubt, with great difficulty.

In Delhi, we needed jobs. I worked for six months with Vijaya Mulay in the National Council of Educational Research and Training on a project for children. Vijaya Mulay, or Akka, as everyone called her, took me under her wing and became a lifelong friend. She smoothened some of the rough edges caused in me by the Emergency and our exit from the party. Cyril and I stayed with her many times and we were welcomed with much warmth. She cooked wonderful meals, listened to good music, and talked about the several people she had met over the years. She also opened up to me about her own difficult life. She insisted that Cyril and I marry legally and we heeded her advice; the deed was done at a registrar's office at the Tees Hazari court. Pratap Pothuloori, a doctor and one of George Reddy's best friends, along with his wife, Manmohini Kaur, served as witnessess. Pratap was the son of P.R. Venkatswamy, the legendary Telangana activist and chronicler of the dalit movement from 1900 to 1950.

Cyril was an engineering graduate and took up a job in that field for a few months. After my work at NCERT with Vijaya was done, we moved to Ghaziabad in Uttar Pradesh on the outskirts of Delhi. We went around the small town and identified the balmikis (manual scavengers) as the poorest people there. We honed in on a small colony near the Ghaziabad railway station and rented a room nearby. The balmiki colony itself did not have place for us. The men of the community worked in institutions like the railways as scavengers and their wives cleaned dry toilets in Ghaziabad. We went to the balmikis one evening and said that we wanted to be of some use to them. 'What can we do?' They saw this educated south Indian couple, and said, 'Teach our children English.' At the time, it was a great disappointment to me. But we did exactly what they asked; we taught the children English and I taught the women sewing. Soon, the adults came to learn to read and write Hindi. We did it well and they were pleased with the work. We also helped them with other problems, like accessing healthcare, but the possibility of working politically remained remote.

We didn't draw any attention to our activities because we had no wish to be targeted by the police. Our balmiki friends took us to weddings and family functions and proudly displayed us. Very soon more and more people came to us with the same demand from as far away as Meerut and Hapur. I prepared a basic Hindi text woven around their lives with the help of Vijaya Mulay. I also illustrated the text with drawings from real life. The protagonist of the text was Asha, a sweeper woman with a broom, and each page had text and drawings from her life. I was very proud of this little book. It proved quite useful in teaching children the Hindi script. Each page introduced five new letters, words made from these letters, and a text about Asha and her daily life.

The balmikis took great care of us. We often had dinner with them—thick well-roasted rotis and pork every night. The pork was from the pigs that ate shit in front of the colony and I worried about tapeworm. When one of the families prepared a sweet dish, we were taken to their house for a treat. My special escorts in the basti were Jogender, a balmiki boy, and Charan Singh from the chamar basti a short distance away. Both were about twelve years old and curious about us and our lives. They visited me frequently, looked around the house, picked up books and bombarded me with questions. When I went into town and they had a holiday, they accompanied me. When we finally left Ghaziabad to return to Hyderabad, I missed these boys and always wondered what they were up to. In 2021, when I visited Delhi briefly, I went to Ghaziabad and searched for the colony because the landscape had changed considerably. What had happened to my Ghaziabad people? It had been forty-one years. We had exchanged postcards for a few months. In Hyderabad, since I had changed many addresses, they had no way to get in touch with me unless I wrote, which I didn't. I have this habit of putting aside the past and getting lost in the present.

I found a balmiki basti near the Ghaziabad station and I told the people there my story of teaching the women and children more than forty years ago and wanting to see them now. The curious crowd was young, their basti was recent— about twenty years old, they said. 'You may not find your particular balmiki basti,' they said. 'Even if you do, will those you are looking for be alive? We balmikis drink ourselves to death before we are forty years old.' When I persisted, they directed me to an older balmiki basti behind theirs and we walked through sewage swamps, with pigs mucking around, to reach a block of dilapidated buildings which looked like nothing I had known before. The frontage of these buildings were all shops manned by people from elsewhere. I went from shop to shop trying to locate any balmiki elder. They asked me for names and the only name I could remember was Jogender. 'Yes,' said a woman, 'his house is nearby though he has moved out. His brother and sister-in-law are there, but can they help? She is ill and he is near-blind.'

I went there, called out 'Koi hai?' Anyone there? When a man emerged, I narrated my story. He was Gyani, Jogender's brother. He asked, 'Are you Gita Ramaswamy?' I said yes and he invited me in. It took him a while to place me after a few questions and then he was excited. Gyani said, 'You changed the lives of my brother and the others; they studied because of you and went on to get good jobs.' He said that most people had moved out of the basti, families had grown, some had sold their houses to others, there were only a few original inhabitants left. He recalled small incidents when I was there, and insisted that I stay for lunch and the night. I declined the offer, but when I was leaving the basti, Gyani pressed a Rs 500 note into my hand. I was taken aback. 'No,' I said. 'When my sister visits, I always give her some money,' he said. 'Will you deny me that?' he asked. I took it with tears in my eyes.

Pretty soon, I received telephone calls from Jogender and Charan Singh. Jogender, who must have been twelve years old in 1978, is now the manager of the Amritsar airport, and Charan Singh, who was from the chamar basti in Ghaziabad, is a lawyer in Noida. The calls came ten minutes apart, both recalling different incidents, they were really excited. 'Our lives changed because of you,' they said. I caught up with Charan Singh in Ghaziabad later in the day and he tried to touch my feet. At the end of half an hour, he said, 'Dil nahin bhara. My heart has not had its fill. Please stay, I want to talk so much more.' We now remain in touch, as do many of the youths whom Cyril and I taught. They have secured jobs in Bengaluru, Guwahati and elsewhere. We were in Ghaziabad for more than two years. Cyril commuted by train to an office in New Delhi. He worked in the Public Enterprises Centre for Continuing Education, doing surveys and training programmes. This was an institute for labour studies. Cyril got the job because Yugandhar put in a word with Nitish De, the director of the centre.

Yet, life was disappointing because I still had political dreams. Here, it looked like we were going to end up as charity workers. In the 1970s, NGO work was known and derided as 'charity work'. The Naxalbari dream had not faded and the only work that felt respectable to some of my generation was political work—work that directly led to mobilizing people on their problems against the state and the wresting of political power. We had yet to read Ivan Illich or Gramsci or any of the theorists whom you read today. I could teach English to all the balmiki children from Delhi to Meerut and we would get no closer to the revolution. We could be their darlings but this was not going to lead them to overthrow the state. Maybe I am being uncharitable to myself and to the balmikis in my bitterness. The balmikis knew the importance of an English education back in 1978. They recognized it as their door into the modern world, and a scavenging-free future for their children. In many ways, our work in Ghaziabad was preparing us for a future that we did not know. It led us away from party work and towards the realization that there was no straight path to revolution, and that possibly, revolution was not a single goal but a million achievable goals every day in every sphere of life.

❧

I did not meet my parents for a few years after the 1975 house arrest and ECT episode. In 1979, I came to know from my old friend Gopal that they wanted to see me just once. Gopal also told me that they were sorry for what had happened. I couldn't be sure if this was just another ruse to convince me to go back home. He added that they had gone on a pilgrimage to Kedarnath in penance, but this could be some yarn. I was travelling from Delhi to Hyderabad when I suddenly decided to go back home. When Warangal approached, I got off the train and took another one to Madras. When I reached my parents' home, the same old CIT Colony house, my father opened the door. The first thing he said was, 'I am sorry for what happened.' And lo, my heart melted. It was as if all was good between us once again. The heated quarrels, the bitter recriminations, all vanished in that split second for me, and I began loving them more than I had done earlier. All of us had suffered; they too. The child they thought was the brightest in the family, the child who could have been the son they never had, had been drawn into the worst possible situation to their minds.

Now, they were eager not to offend me in any way. If they wanted to buy me something (and of course, they did) they were careful to ask first if it was okay by me, if I would like it. Right up to the end, when my father died in January 1981 and my mother in 1998, there was never any heartache between us. I visited them frequently. When travelling to Vijayawada or Chittoor I often stopped over at my parents' home in Madras. I also agreed to their occasional requests to help out with my sisters' deliveries and other needs related to childbirth. I was considered the only one who was 'free', that is, free of children and a needy husband. I attended to both the deliveries my younger sister had and one of the elder. Yet my sisters and I remained somewhat distant and we never discussed the 1975 episode till I finished the second draft of this book. There is no closure. I feel let down by them for never standing up to those horrors, and they feel that I caused them and my parents much unwanted trouble. My parents came from a severely orthodox background and were not exposed to people from other communities, my mother especially so. But my sisters were well educated, had friends from all communities, and were employed in jobs where they met people from all walks of life. My father apologized to me. And when I wanted a baby in 1992, my mother said, 'You are the happiest of all my daughters. Continue what you are doing. Don't have a baby like the others. You don't know what it entails.' I had made peace with my parents but not with my sisters, one of whom thinks and says today that Cyril's long and terminal illness was a punishment to me for what I did to my parents.

Perhaps, some day I will come to terms with some of my sisters. This is what they told me when I told them about the book and raised the issue of ECT for the first time in forty-five years: 'Don't blame our parents,' they said. 'Don't blame us. You were the son they never had. They believed that you would become an important person whom others would look up to—an IAS officer, a leading scientist, maybe even a chief minister … and they saw their dreams collapsing when you threw everything away and joined a movement that only saw its members killed or living in penury. Our mother desperately wanted to save you and we had to follow her decision.'

Sometimes, when I see my friends with their natal families, I get this feeling of loss, a void within me which can never be filled. Cyril's family has always been my family and they care deeply for me. Still, I feel this profound sense that something precious has escaped me forever. Somehow, we remain children no matter how old we grow. I identify deeply with the child I was at thirteen and the girl I was at twenty, and often grieve for her. It feels like I am still that child, but have lost the old moorings, the old world, and can never recover it. Families are supposed to accept you for what you are. Some even accept murderers and rapists. Yet I feel an outsider among my people. Is it because women have to pay the price for leaving the trodden path?

▶

While in Ghaziabad, we began supporting the Telugu magazine *Viplava Sandesham* (News of the Revolution) run by Inguva Mallikarjuna Sharma who had quit the PWG and was, like us, searching for alternatives. Cyril's monthly income was Rs 600, of which we sent Rs 300 to Sharma, besides writing articles for the publication. On the days when I had some free time, I explored Ghaziabad town and its markets and sat outside tea shops, listening to the conversations, and the accents of the people …. I switched to the local cuisine almost entirely and tried hard to get assimilated into the local culture. I cooked on a coal chulha like my neighbours and learnt several dishes from them. We lived in the railway colony adjacent to the railway station in a neat one-room quarter and I quite liked our home. The evenings were fragrant with wheat rotis cooked on the coal chulhas all over the place, and the neighbours were friendly. Yet I longed to return to Hyderabad, my political and emotional home. I was dreadfully unhappy. I had wanted to do something and had failed at it. I had given up my family, thinking that the party was a substitute. Now, both were gone, and worse, I was in a place where I had few friends.

I was in an alien culture. Life seemed to have no meaning whatsoever. Prior to the Ghaziabad work, I had applied for a bank officer's job, had written the exam and was selected.

When the time came to join, I did not. I applied for a master's in the nearby Meerut University, but did not write the exams. I did not even return to collect my original certificates. What would I do with them, I reasoned. I was not going to finish my postgraduation and look for formal employment.

It was at this time that I nearly had a nervous breakdown. Everything was grey and I moped around all day. Cyril left early in the morning for office and I went in the noon to the balmiki basti, but without energy or passion. I barely read a book, hardly spoke to the neighbours. The balmikis saved me from a complete collapse with their affection and demands on my time and energy.

Once or twice, I went to the railway tracks close by, wanting to commit suicide. The only thing that stopped me was Cyril telling me, 'Go ahead.' That put my back up and I would return. I was furious with him for not stopping me, for not commiserating with me. Lump it, he seemed to say. We were made so differently. He took tough times easily, adapting to the situation whereas I agonized unendingly. It took me years to understand that this was my first brush with depression. I did not even know that it had a name, clinical or otherwise. I only knew that there was this huge weight of sadness, of tragedy even, that I was carrying. Nothing made sense, life felt worthless. I also heard that some others, mainly women, had suffered breakdowns after leaving the party. Women suffered particularly because they usually made immense sacrifices to join the movement and work in it. I had lost almost all my old friends who were apprehensive of the ML movement. So when I, and so many of my peers, realized that the revolution wasn't coming, and that the ML organization was autocratic and narrow-minded, when we discovered that the very reason for the movement's existence, annihilating the unequal system, was not as important to its leaders as the continued existence of their particular party, our world shattered.

We had to slink back to the old world, to the old society. Men transitioned more easily—they picked up from where they had left, be it academics, or getting jobs, or setting up their own businesses, getting into the liquor business, or even joining regular politics. Not that some women didn't join the mainstream, but most women stuck to a modicum of the politics that changed their lives. Do we retain our politics because we can't return to the old family norms? Or is it that we have internalized the politics of change so much that we cannot discard them as men appeared to do? Life no longer felt worthwhile on old terms; we had to find meaning in our new sense of being. And that was difficult, given that we quit the party and had to frame new systems of life, livelihood, friendship and family relations.

Sheela Reddy, a dear friend from Hyderabad, who worked as a reporter in Delhi, was a great help during this time. I often stayed, travelled around and shared my anxieties with her. But for her, I wouldn't be here now. I also became good friends with another unlikely person, years older than me, Dr Sarojini Reddy who had practised gynaecology in Hyderabad and was then in Delhi with her husband K.V. Raghunatha Reddy. He was a member of the Rajya Sabha from Andhra Pradesh and they had their quarters on Shahjahan Road in upscale Lutyens's Delhi. I used to visit Sarojini Reddy in Hyderabad when I was in the PDSU and POW for contributions. She gave me Rs 25 every month. Her son Srinath was a friend of ours. In Hyderabad, I was scared of her—a beautiful, gracious, famous gynaecologist who was superintendent of Niloufer Hospital. In Delhi, she was another lonely housewife. Talking to her and sharing an Andhra lunch was like a trip to Hyderabad. She was relatively free here. Raghunatha Reddy was almost always out on work, and we spent hours discussing all things under the sun. She never knew how important she was in restoring some degree of normalcy in my life and when she died in August 2015, I realized that we must tell people while they are still living how important they are to us.

I longed to return to Hyderabad. I was beset by several illnesses at this time: chronic bronchitis, chronic urinary tract infection and malaria—and these wore me down. My lifelong engagement with matters related to health began here. I was diagnosed with chronic urinary infection which had reached the kidneys. The doctors advised an operation to remove a part of the diseased kidney. Rajesh Tandon, who founded the civil society group Participatory Research in Asia in 1992, then husband of yet another dear friend and co-founder of Saheli, Kalpana Mehta, gifted me a copy of *Where There Is No Doctor: A Village Health Care Handbook* by David Werner. Werner explained urinary infection as an overload of virus cells and advised washing it out of the body with high water intake. I stopped all work and outings for a month, drank water by the jugfuls and of course peed by the bucketfuls. Within a month, my urine tested normal and has always tested normal since. With this, I began to understand the importance of knowing my own body well and working with it to cure ailments.

For years after the Emergency, I was looking over my shoulder wherever I went. I had great difficulty going to new places with friends and even in making new ones. I was suspicious of everything, suspecting the police to be behind anything unexpected that happened. The effects of the Emergency stayed with many of us for a long time. It was not just an apprehension of the police or shying away from making new friends. It was also in how we looked at our near and dear ones. Cyril's name when he was underground was Vijay. I called him Vijay, not Cyril, for several years after that. I continued to be called Jyothi or Nalini by several people for decades. Our names changed, our identities changed, our relationships changed, everything changed.

Yet I do not and never have regretted my few years in the ML movement. The crisis in idealism, the personal suffering—these tested our values and stiffened our spines. The radical movement, the Emergency, counterbalanced by the struggles of people for democracy and entitlements, was a watershed in our lives.

6 Hyderabad Book Trust: The world of words

We were finally able to return to Hyderabad in 1980, primarily encouraged by Ajay Sinha who felt that we could gainfully contribute to the politics there. Ajay, a close associate of George and Cyril's, was a lecturer of political science at Osmania University. He died at the young age of twenty-nine of an epileptic seizure, soon after we moved back to Hyderabad.

Before moving, we had explored several options. There were many people who were in a similar position as us with similar questions. I travelled to Pune and Bombay to meet groups there, activists who had quit various ML formations and wanted to continue to work with people. The conundrum on everyone's minds was what to do next. Cyril had decided that he wanted to study law and equip himself with tools to support the movement in legal matters. At about this time, we met his uncle and former CPI–ML Charu Majumdar group activist and twice MLA from Chittoor district, C.K. Narayan Reddy, at Hyderabad. He was called CK affectionately by nearly everyone. It was a practice among communists of the generation between the 1940s and the 1960s to call people by their initials. Chandra Pulla Reddy was called CP, Neelam Ramachandraiah was called NR and so on.

CK was jailed during the Emergency and he decided not to join the party again. He began publishing leftist literature after 1977, foremost among his books being Telugu translations of Mary Tyler's *My Years in an Indian Prison*, William Hinton's *Fanshen: A Documentary of Revolution in a Chinese Village*, Edgar Snow's *Red Star Over China* and Ted Allan and Richard Gordon's *The Scalpel, the Sword: The Story of Doctor Norman Bethune*. It was a peculiar meeting. Cyril and his siblings had kept a distance from their paternal family. Their parents' inter-caste, interfaith, inter-region marriage had not gone down well on that side. Cyril did not acknowledge them as family and did not like my doing so either. He had no problems associating with CK as a comrade though.

CK was born as the youngest son in a landlord family in Challavaripalle, a village in Chittoor district. He studied at Tirupati and became politically active with the socialists during his college education at Madanapalle. He accompanied Jayaprakash Narayan on his southern trips. In the early 1950s, he broke with the socialists and joined the Communist Party of India. When the CPI split, he went with the CPI(M), and after Naxalbari, he joined the Charu Majumdar-led CPI–ML and even participated in the first meeting of the group at Gutthikonda Bilam, a hillock in Guntur district famous for its caves. In 1971, after he was arrested, he quit the group. He was arrested several times and was also jailed during the Emergency. After his last stint in prison, he began publishing, first as Janata Prachuranalu and then as Anupama Prachuranalu.

As I came to know CK, I fell in love with his serene personality. He became, in time, the supportive father figure I never had. There was nothing I had to hide from him even if he disapproved of it; he was the gentlest of men. However, when he took umbrage at something, nothing could pacify him and he became extremely stubborn. I was secure in knowing that nothing I did could anger him. He took great care of me as he did of the several people whom he considered 'good'. He made this sharp distinction: people were either good or bad. His most valuable quality was that, unlike other communist leaders who love talking interminably, CK actually listened.

Every morning, he made his rounds calling on people he met

everyday. He called on a wide variety of people. As an MLA, he met administrators and politicians. As a communist, collecting donations for the party, he met fellow-travellers working in cinema and other businesses. As a publisher, he had extensive contacts with writers, translators and readers. He helped people in Chittoor and elsewhere with their health issues, taking them to hospital, talking with doctors and arranging money where required; he helped people settle family disputes by acting as mediator; he helped people get jobs—there was nothing at which he had not tried his hand. Most importantly, he was ethical in all that he did and lived by his principles.

We often travelled together on work all over Andhra Pradesh by bus and train, and I saw him working at close quarters. He often went around picking up discarded banana peels along the roads, because he knew that people slipped on them. He did not tolerate or meet men who mistreated their wives and hired helps. It was a joy to work with such a communist who brooked no double standards in his private and political lives. In the early 1990s, he took up the cause of stray dogs on the streets of Hyderabad as they bit poor people walking on the roads. I turned to him for my personal issues too. My quarrels with Cyril, painful disagreements with friends, difficulties with my sisters and parents—I placed them all on his shoulders for a solution, and he never failed me.

CK and I only disagreed when it came to our opinions on books. Immersed in the culture of orthodox Marxism for several years, he was uncomfortable with any criticism of the ideology. We argued endlessly about the atrocities of Stalin's regime (atrocities to me, necessary collateral damage to CK), the Khmer Rouge in Cambodia, and even Arundhati Roy's stray criticism of E.M.S. Namboodiripad in *The God of Small Things*. But we concurred on the really important issues: those raised by the women's movement, the dalit movement, and the great importance of health and education in the lives of poor people. When I began working with him in publishing, and suggested a Telugu translation of Gandhi's *Hind Swaraj*, CK threatened to resign—he was incensed by the suggestion that Gandhi could have written anything remotely useful to people.

Cyril and I also met with other activists who had left their ML factions. We keenly felt the lacuna of any eclectic reading and debate in the ML groups and discerned the need for publishing books and essays that would contribute to raising the level of debate among activists. Such knowledge was not being produced in Telugu and we planned to step in. When we finally tied up with CK, the group expanded to include the veterinarian and activist Veeraiah Chowdhury, son of another communist leader, Kolla Venkaiah, and C. Bharathudu, who taught at a college in Guntur and was a book lover and an associate of Kolla Venkaiah. Together, we set up a trust (rather than a society or a private company) on the advice of Shantha Sinha's father Mamidipudi Anandam, a chartered accountant. He argued that a trust would give us the greatest freedom, which was important in the context of a repressive government curbing publishing freedom. We selected the name Hyderabad Book Trust, a neutral name, which was meant to signify to our readers that we didn't want to necessarily polarize opinions. Names of publishing houses in those times flaunted ideological leanings—like Arunatara (Red Star), Peace Book Centre, Navodaya (New Sunrise), Prajashakti (Peoples' Might). We wanted to avoid such signals. The Hyderabad Book Trust was registered in February 1980 with CK, Bharathudu, poet and journalist M.T. Khan, Vithal Rajan and me—Rajan having recently returned from Canada and joined the Administrative Staff College of Hyderabad. He

Hyderabad Book Trust

A GROUP of us have formed the Hyderabad Book Trust to systematically bring out progressive publications in Telugu. Our main objective is to bring out low-priced works in Telugu, which while assisting the democratic movement, will reach out to the widest sections of people, educating, enthusing and developing scientific and rational values from the actual problems and contradictions within society. We are planning to translate great works in other languages, publish works by Telugu writers, bring out low-priced series depicting people and events that have changed society and man, bring out illustrated books and comics for children too. Our objective is one of starting a book movement, encompassing neo-literates and illiterates.

Our first set of books include translations of

(1) "The Scalpel and the Sword" by Ted Allan and Sydney Gordon.
(2) "Two Measures of Rice" by Thakazhi Sivasankara Pillai.
(3) "Poems of Vemana" edited by Dr N Gopi.

We appeal to those interested in this venture to send us their ideas, suggestions, etc. All contributions to the Trust are tax-deductible under Section 80G.

GITA RAMASWAMY
Hyderabad Book Trust,
10-1-17/2 First Floor,
Shyamnagar,
Hyderabad-500 004,
June 24.

An appeal from HBT published in the Economic & Political Weekly *on 2 August 1980* resigned from HBT within the month, but the others stayed on and several others joined along the way.

We planned a set of three books to start with—these were *Rakthashruvulu* (Tears of Blood), a translation of *The Scalpel, the Sword: The Life of Doctor Norman Bethune*, already published by CK's Anupama Press and quite popular, *Coolie Ginjalu* (Two Measures of Rice, a translation of *Randidangazhi* by Thakazhi Sivasankara Pillai), and *Vemana Vaadam* (Poems of Vemana), an annotated selection of Vemana's poems edited by N. Gopi. Vemana was a seventeenth-century poet and philosopher whose poems were known for their simple language and native idioms that explored caste and morality. These three books represented both our ideological leanings (to the left) and our desire to be different from the existent forms of the left.

To begin, we raised about Rs 25,000 to print the three books. The only cost involved was that of the printing, all other services, including editing, were voluntary. Our outlay was modest. I, along with another fellow employee, Krishna, drew a salary of Rs 500 every month. J. Rameshwara Rao, chairman of Orient Longman, graciously gave us two rooms behind his office free of charge, and these served as our office. His daughter Lakshmi is a good friend of mine. We began a fund-raising initiative soon after and enrolled members to the trust, who were promised a discount of 25 per cent on all our books. We used public transport wherever we went, lugging cartons of books with us. I usually carried one carton in each hand, with my personal luggage in a sling bag. In the initial years, this was not difficult, but as the book list grew, it slowly became impossible for me to carry twenty-kilogram boxes and led to chronic back pain. I wish I knew about ergonomics back then.

Forming the Hyderabad Book Trust in 1980 turned out

to be the best medicine for my depression. I plunged into the work with enthusiasm. I loved books and what better than founding a publishing house? HBT made huge strides in the first few years. CK and I trudged through every small town, city and big village, to meet writers, thinkers and activists; we set up mobile book stalls with two tables and a petromax light in the centre of town. We met activists of all kind, both to sell our books and to listen to their ideas. We ate and stayed with comrades and writers of all hues, from the CPI to the ML, and when in a town or village where we knew no one, we slept in the bus stand or railway station. Through all this, we were commissioning both translations and accepting original scripts. *Edutaralu* (Seven Generations), an abridged retelling of Alex Haley's *Roots*, came soon after the first three titles and became one of HBT's best loved and most reprinted titles of the last forty years.

HBT happened at a time when publishing in Telugu had come to a virtual standstill. Most major books were published by the two communist parties—Prajashakti of the CPI(M), and Visalaandhra of the CPI. And even they were sluggish in their output at the time, churning out old communist reprints. Not for nothing did the great communist writers, historian Kambhampati Satyanarayana and fiction writer Mahidhar Rammohan Rao, both giants in their fields, walk into our office. Kambhampati's two-volume *A Study of the History and Culture of the Andhras*, had been published in 1975 by People's Publishing House, the CPI's publishing wing. It was the first of its kind to trace the political, economic and social history of the Andhras from a materialist standpoint. Mahidhar had translated the book and it turned out that their parent organization, Visalaandhra, was unwilling to publish it because it strayed from the orthodox party line. They came to us in the hope that we would not be narrow-minded. Kambhampati recalled that he had marched in the tail end of our POW processions prior to the Emergency. 'If I can be eclectic, so can you,' he seemed to say, in an effort to convince us. For us, the manuscript was a blessing. After we published it in 1981, it received rave reviews and Mahidhar's translation was rated flawless. We ended up reprinting the two volumes several times over the years. Both men continued to be close friends till their deaths. I stayed with either of them whenever I visited Vijayawada and always had a warm welcome. They told me stories of the communist movement, stories of the famous writers of yesteryears like Kutumba Rao, Sharada and Chalam, and a vista of the Telugu literary world opened up to me like never before.

Very soon, we had other writers and translators lining up to work with us. In 1981, we published *Uppena* (Hurricane) by Saripalli Krishna Reddy, a novel about the Telangana peasant revolt in the 1940s. *Polisulu Arrest Cheste* (If the Police Arrest You) was the highly successful serial in a magazine by advocate Bojja Tharakam. We published this in 1981 and it continues to be one of our more popular titles. Generations of activists have cut their teeth on this book. The eighth book we published in 1981 was *Grahanaala Katha* (The Story of the Eclipse) by Mahidhar Nalinimohan, a space scientist of repute. For the first time, science and its methods were explained in a popular style for laypeople. Nalinimohan, who had a PhD from Moscow University and worked for the National Physical Laboratory, also wrote many science books for us.

The year 1982 was momentous. We published many milestone titles. We tried our hand at translating the ...*for Beginners* series started in the late 1970s in English. We began with *Marx for Beginners* by the great Mexican cartoonist Rius, with K. Balagopal as its translator. This was the first title that we printed in an offset press. Till then, all our books were laboriously composed in a letter press and then imposed on to plates. In the years to come, we were to translate and publish *Lenin...*, *Mao...*, *Cuba...* and *Das Kapital for Beginners*, though none of these titles was successful for a long time. B. Vijayabharathi's biography of Ambedkar, based on Dhananjay Keer's original, was also published by us in 1982, signifying the beginning of a long list of Ambedkarite literature. Another landmark was *Vaidyudu Leni Chota*, the translation of *Where There is No Doctor* by David Werner. This book translated by Dr Aluri Vijayalakshmi was a bestseller for many years.

We also began translating Mahasweta Devi the same year. Her *Sri Sri Ganesh Mahima* was translated from the Bengali by Surampudi Seetharam. It was Devi's first book in our catalogue. We went on to translate and publish *Hazaar Churashir Maa*, *Aranyer Adhikar*, *Daayin*, *Basai Tudu*, *Rudali* (a collection of four stories) and *Choli ke Peechhe* (Breast Stories). She gave us her consent in a terse letter. We were lucky to have Surampudi Seetharam with us to translate several of these works directly from Bengali to Telugu. Seetharam worked in Calcutta. His landlady regaled him every day with bits from Bibhutibhushan Bandyopadhyay's *Aranyak*. Seetharam was so fascinated by the tale that he learnt Bengali to be able to read it in the original and eventually translated it into Telugu.

We were fortunate in that authors gave us permission gratis. Alex Haley sent us a letter with just two words—Permission granted—for *Roots*. Rius, Mary Tyler and several others (especially authors staying abroad) were equally generous. Those were times when authors were swept along by the left and feminist movements and were not hemmed in by their agents. HBT does not have its books licensed or copyrighted. We allow others to use and reproduce our materials freely, recognizing the importance of accessible knowledge for everyone.

In the first five years, from 1980 to 1985, we had a good response from writers, translators and readers. Our average print run was 3,000 for the letter press and 5,000 for an offset title. This was at a time when other Telugu publishers were not attempting more than 1,000 copies for anything other than pulp fiction. Some notable titles from this period were *Ma Katha* (*Let Me Speak! Testimony of Domitila, A Woman of the Bolivian Mines*) by Domitila Barrios de Chungara with Moemma Viezzer, *Spartacus* by Howard Fast, *Charitra Ante Emiti?* (*What is History?*) by E.H. Carr, the NCERT books (which were rescinded by the Janata Party government between 1977 and 1980), *Taratarala Bharata Charitra* (*Ancient India*) by Romila Thapar and *Adhunika Bharatacharitra* (*Modern India*) by Bipan Chandra. We began our bestselling series on pedagogy with *Railu Badi* (*Totto-Chan: The Little Girl at the Window*) by Tetsuko Kuroyanagi, followed by all of Gijubhai's books available in English (Gijubhai Badheka was a pioneer of children's education and literature in Gujarati), and the influential Soviet (Ukrainian) educator Anton Makarenko and Krishna Kumar's books.

In this period, we experimented with smaller booklets of about sixteen to seventy pages, priced at Re 1 each. These were usually short essays by writers like Kodavatiganti Kutumba Rao, Dr Gurukula Mitra and Romila Thapar on topics like rationalism, exposing the Vedas and developing a scientific outlook. They became immensely popular. When we stopped selling books through our own makeshift stalls and began getting stocked in bigger stores, the production of these booklets was reduced since shops refused to stock them—booklets had no spines, they couldn't be displayed well in shops. We also attempted making children's books; but these were expensive and involved considerable artwork, the use of colour, better quality paper and a new marketing network, and we soon abandoned the idea.

Working at HBT gave me the traction I needed. In the party, I had not seen the everyday life of Telugu people. My work among students and in the bastis was brief. The Emergency had cut it short, and after that, we had moved only among people like us. The Ghaziabad work, away from friends and radicalism, did not give me the emotional grounding I needed. HBT did that. I visited all parts of the two Telugu states (though administratively one then), met a variety of people from all walks of life (the educated, predominantly though) and visualized the lives of the poor through their pro-poor lens. I learnt to read and write Telugu and was even able to speak its two major dialects with some ease. I met writers and translators, poets and activists, lecturers and professors, booksellers and publishers. I must have visited hundreds of homes all over the two Telugu states. We never stayed in hotels. Apart from saving money (of which we had little), this brought us closer to the people who could help us. Staying in people's homes and interacting with women gave me a broader idea of Telugu culture, food, music, entertainment— something I had lacked before. I sat selling our books, outside meetings of all kinds: from those of the rationalists to those of the Bharatiya Janata Party. I thought that we could find readers even in the BJP meetings. This way, I met hundreds of curious spectators who wondered why a young woman sat selling books in the centre of a town, and I learned to carry on conversations about books with them.

Through all this, I was under the watchful and affectionate eye of CK. While he accompanied me in the beginning, later he simply guided me about where I could go, where I could stay and whom I could approach. I took all my problems to him, sure of finding a solution together. There was, however, one time when his reaction left me a little nonplussed. It was when I was in Vijayawada on my own, for work, when the lawyer and former communist, Karnati Rammohan Rao, propositioned me. I was completely thrown by this and when I returned to complain to CK, castigating him for introducing me to this horrible man, CK said, 'But nothing happened!' I still don't understand his calm reaction and he, in turn, didn't get my overweening anxiety at the lawyer's insistent propositioning. I avoided Vijayawada for the next ten years. Whenever I passed through the city on a train, I kept my head down.

Apart from this incident and a similar one involving a professor in the Indian Institute of Science in Bangalore, I learnt to move with confidence in a variety of circles and was slowly able to shed the paranoia of the Emergency. I learnt to sidestep suspicious-looking, middle-aged men and developed a tough exterior. I learnt how to do the second and third proofs of our books, work with artists to design covers, push writers and translators to do their work on time, and most important, collect dues from creditors. The last was important because the kind-hearted CK was no good at that kind of work. If he had a chance, he would give away books for free. I learnt to talk forcefully to the bookshop owners and managers of chain shops, like those of Visalaandhra and Prajashakti, to recover our dues. On one occasion, I picked up stones and threatened to break the glass frontage of the shop. My reasoning was that I would only get a police case on me (and even the police would wonder why a woman was pushed to throwing stones) while the shop owner would have to spend thousands of rupees replacing the glass. I certainly earned a bad reputation. I was called a pisanari, mingy miser, to my face—though I was merely demanding what was due to us. But HBT did not lose money.

By the end of 1984, HBT was well established with a network of readers across Andhra Pradesh and a good stable of writers and translators. Our titles were selling well, money was flowing back, and we had two more employees to organize tours and sell at meetings. Some friends like Bal Reddy (who went on to found Malupu Publications) and K. Suresh (who was to found Manchi Pustakam) also gave us their time to tour the districts with HBT books. Some people employed in HBT like Visweswara Rao (Sri Sri Publications) and Subbaiah (Charitra Publications) went on to establish successful publishing organizations themselves and some others became activist leaders—like Sandhya of the POW. When we started HBT, some of the left and radical circles were unsure about us. But as the book list revealed itself, we received unstinted cooperation from all their sections. Publishing Ambedkarite literature, we came in close contact with dalit political groups and soon began working with them. Books like *Vaidyudu Leni Chota* (*Where There is No Doctor*) had proved useful to NGOs working in the health sector and helped develop connections with them. Governmental projects like the Sarva Shiksha Abhiyan and the Rajiv Gandhi Mission came into our sights when we published our first pedagogical texts. We began considering co-publishing with other organizations in this period. One of the first such books was *Bharatiya Parishramika Parinamam*, a translation of the 1924 classic *The Industrial Evolution of India* by D.R. Gadgil which we co-published with the Indian Council for Historical Research in 1988. We went on to co-publish many books with the National Translation Mission, the Bojja Tharakam Trust, the Anveshi Research

Centre for Women's Studies, and the Centre for Dalit Studies.

The low prices of our books were matched by our low salaries. We had wage parity at HBT right from the beginning. Everyone drew the same amount, Rs 500 to start with in 1980, Rs 5,000 in 2000, and Rs 12,000 in 2019. The wage parity helped because the staff involved in routine jobs like packing, delivering and errands remained loyal and honest. It worked against us because our senior staff eventually looked for more remunerative work elsewhere. Our office and our books were and are always open to the scrutiny of the staff, and the phones and computers were used by everyone. There was always someone using the office for accommodation until 2010. Even Cyril and I lived there till 1997. This practice stopped after we found misuse of the telephone and an affair conducted in the premises after office hours.

Meanwhile, Cyril completed his law degree and registered with the Bar Council of Hyderabad in 1984. He soon began working with senior lawyers like J. Parthasarathy and V. Satyanarayana. We started befriending many young and enthusiastic lawyers, as Cyril involved himself with legal and paralegal activities for the marginalized. Together with his friends, he set up Salaha, a legal aid resource centre for the poor.

▶

My father died in January 1981 of a heart attack. He was sixty-one. The same year he built a house in Madras's Anna Nagar, to settle down and spend time with his grandchildren. His death was a great shock to me. We had barely spent any time together. I wish we had understood each other better. I had visited Madras a month before he died and he insisted on accompanying me in the bus all the way to the station. It was late in the night and I was taking the train out of Madras to Vijayawada. I was furious with him, both because I could manage on my own and because he was old and did not need to travel at night. I sulked all the way to the station and continued to scold him till my train left. This troubled me a great deal for years and I was full of regret. Why had I not been kinder to him?

When he died, I stayed in Madras for a few days and Cyril joined me. There were rituals going on every day with hordes of brahmins being fed while Cyril, my younger sister and I played cards in an adjoining room. My mother was not yet sixty and would now have an unsettled life, sometimes staying on her own in the new house, sometimes shuttling between her daughters, three of whom were in the United States. When she came to visit me once, she said she would like to stay with me—I was the least complicated of her daughters, she said, and did not interfere with her. I was mostly in Ibrahimpatnam at that time and wondered how I could keep her comfortable in Hyderabad as we stayed in a room in the office. Cyril would not have minded, but would have expected me to look after her. I continued to meet her often. She had become needy now. I felt like she was the child and I the mother.

7 The perils left to conquer

By the end of my fourth year with HBT, the old longing for active political work took hold of me again. During that time, between 1980 and 1984, I mostly met middle-class people, all of them leftists and Ambedkarites. Slowly, the work began to get unsatisfying. Writers and translators are often egotists, and it was sometimes unpleasant working with them. We also had to follow the retail market closely to collect our dues. As HBT picked up momentum, I was complimented for my work on many occasions. People often attributed HBT's success in those first few years to my hard work. In truth, HBT was the right idea at the right time, and we were a great, heterogeneous group that worked well together. Radical activity in Andhra Pradesh was on the upsurge in the 1980s and our books thrived in this atmosphere.

In such a situation of post-Emergency ferment, we came in contact with many inspiring figures. We were already hearing positive things about Shankar Guha Niyogi's work in Chhattisgarh. Niyogi was influenced by Charu Majumdar's politics and had fled Bengal to escape imprisonment. He worked in the Dalli Rajhara area of Chhattisgarh with miners and set up the Chhattisgarh Mines Shramik Sangh in 1977, which paved the way for the Chhattisgarh Mukti Morcha in 1982. CMSS was a broad-based democratic movement of workers and also enveloped their everyday concerns of health, education and gender. In 1983, we met A.K. Roy, a member of parliament and a Dhanbad-based trade union organizer, whom we had invited to speak at the inauguration of the George Reddy Publication Trust. We had established it in 1983 to publish overtly political books in Telugu that would not find a place in HBT's book list, like the translation of Charles Bettelheim's *China Since Mao*. A.K. Roy had worked as a chemical engineer and left his job in support of a workers' strike. He was expelled from the CPI(M) after Naxalbari and founded the Marxist Coordination Committee in Jharkhand. This again was a wide-ranging organization and I was greatly impressed by this quiet man when he stayed with us for three days. About fifty years old, he spoke sparingly, in a measured tone, but with exceeding clarity. He had no bank account, I learnt, and had only two or three sets of clothes which he washed himself. On one of my HBT tours, I called on Katthi Padma Rao in Ponnur. He was the general secretary of the Andhra Pradesh Rationalist Association and a Sanskrit scholar. He taught at a local college, was an eloquent speaker and a prolific writer. A mala by caste, he was later to become famous for leading the Karamchedu victims' struggle along with Bojja Tharakam. He was one of the founding members of the influential Dalit Mahasabha. He told me, 'So you publish great literature. But your books lie unread in the shelves of well-to-do people. The people who desperately need change cannot read.' I had no reply. HBT's reach was limited. It was as if there was no alternative to direct work among poor people.

After marriage, Cyril and I had decided not to have children. We had dedicated ourselves to full-time activist work and we had witnessed up close how the children with activist parents often suffered. One parent—and this was always the mother—had to work and raise the children. I was not willing to do that. With the decision not to have children, we had no dependants to worry about. My father was dead and my mother was slowly developing mental health problems. I was distant from my natal family, and between

Cyril and me, there was the understanding that each would do what interested them, and the other would cooperate wholeheartedly. I was thirty years old, confident and full of energy, and the world was beckoning.

The early 1980s were conducive to activist work of many kinds. The Emergency had been soundly defeated and a plethora of leaders of novel political hues had emerged all around the country. Feminists were actively questioning much that was taken for granted. Regional parties began making inroads into Congress strongholds. There was no Hindu right worth its name yet and the central authority was weakened; what the media and state called 'fissiparous tendencies' were on the ascent. There was a resurgence of peasant movements in Sircilla and Jagtial in Telangana. On the far left, the People's War Group, under the leadership of Kondapalli Seetharamaiah, had captured the public imagination, boldly challenging authority with their unusual tactics. The state's attitude towards them oscillated between repression and conciliation, and the PWG used this flip-flopping to their advantage, expanding their influence in a vigorous fashion. They organized the peasantry and planted red flags on the territories occupied by the landlords, forcing them to flee to the cities in Telangana. Separate glasses at tea shops for dalits were smashed and PWG squads and local cadres held open and summary court in villages to punish wrongdoers, landlords and political opponents. The coal mines of Singareni were brought under the control of this group, even though their union, Sikasa, was not a recognized one. The group targeted the police (and not civilians), and kidnapped politicians and IAS officials. All this earned them the goodwill of the people and the admiration of the youth; there was an upswing in their favour.

Even NGOs were speaking a radical language at the time. Comprehensive Rural Operations Service Society that worked in the Bhongir area and the Rural Development Advisory Services, a consulting development NGO liaising with grassroots NGOs, were two such. They experimented with organizing poor people and speaking the language of revolt, shedding the earlier image of a charity organization. Left activists who had quit the party joined these NGOs in droves. These organizations worked with malas, madigas and backward communities to unite them on rights-based issues. As they did not take up arms and worked with local public functionaries and government offices, many fellow-travellers, anxious about avoiding the ML tag, worked with them.

Cyril and I sometimes met up with ML cadres, particularly those belonging to the People's War Group. We respected them and recognized their sterling qualities. The few people we met discussed matters in a frank and intimate manner—their use of violence against poor people and members of other revolutionary groups, their sidestepping of the issues of caste and gender, the abusive behaviour and sexual harassment of women by their leaders, the extortion from beedi and tendu contractors in Adilabad, Khammam and Karimnagar, compromising people's struggles in these areas, the extortion from realtors in Hyderabad and other major towns of Telangana, leaving their cadres susceptible to bribery and kickbacks, their privileging of settlers over adivasis in the forest areas (with many of the settlers being ex-communist kammas from coastal areas and relatives of ML leaders). The people we met were affectionate, respectful and committed to their work. We mourned them when we heard of their deaths in police 'encounters'. But a party that stifled discussion in the name of democratic centralism, a party that worked in a hierarchical system, that privileged attainment of power over people's actual issues, was not for us. While the radical leaders acknowledged all this in private, their party refused to acknowledge them publicly or in open fora.

Salaha was formed in early 1984 by Cyril and his friends, G. Manohar, J. Parthasarathy, Janardhan and C.V. Mohan Reddy, to explore new ways of using the law to the advantage of people's movements. Each of them went on to have a successful practice in the Andhra Pradesh High Court in Hyderabad: Manohar was a public prosecutor and Mohan Reddy served as the advocate general of Andhra Pradesh for two terms. The other lawyers who worked with them were Kondaveeti Arjun Reddy, K. Jairaj and Nallapu Prahlad. Salaha comprised lawyers who worked pro bono in cases where poor people had to face the rich. Cyril believed that law, with all its limitations, could be used to a certain extent as a tool by the poor. But this required lawyers to have the organization and mobilization of the poor as their starting point, and the active involvement of government functionaries and laws in a helpful capacity. Another requirement was a certain amount of lobbying and advocacy at the official level. Salaha met with NGOs working on people's issues and conducted workshops for them. Cyril's work in courts and outside led him to have close relations with lawyers like Bojja Tharakam, Padmanabha Reddy and B.S.A. Swamy (who became a judge in the Andhra Pradesh High Court from 1995 to 2004). Bojja Tharakam, the son of former independent MLA Bojja Appalaswamy and son-in-law of the poet Boyi Bheemanna, was a crusading dalit activist. I have mentioned Tharakam earlier in two contexts—first, during the Emergency when he was arrested, and second, for translating Ambedkar's texts that we published. Since I got to know him well in this period, I should say more about him.

Bojja Tharakam was a human rights warrior, he was an Ambedkarite, an eminent poet and writer, and a senior advocate. His work reached every village in Andhra Pradesh and Telangana, and his words went out to every dalit home in the two states. He inspired all sorts of activists, be they feminists, ecologists, human rights defenders, those working for the homeless, the factory workers, the urban poor, Muslims, adivasis, and those belonging to other marginalized sections—a reach beyond compare. When I met him for the first time at his house, I heard him ask an activist, 'You haven't gone to jail yet? You haven't been arrested? How can you call yourself an activist?' I was wonderstruck. This was in the early 1980s when erstwhile revolutionaries were scrambling to distance themselves from any movement and run after the pot of gold in the mainstream. He was not a Maoist leader, exhorting people to jump into militancy. He was, even during the Emergency, noted as a man with a broad understanding and open convictions. His reading was eclectic, his interests wide-ranging, from poetry to theatre, and our long journeys to and from Karamchedu were marked by conversations on many topics, including music. He often said that if he wasn't what he was, he would have been a musician or a thespian.

He was born in the small village of Pachchalanadukuda in the Konaseema area of East Godavari district, on the coast where the river Godavari joins the sea. His father, Bojja Appalaswamy, was a remarkable Ambedkar-inspired dalit leader, who was a two-time MLA contesting and successfully winning as an independent. He set up schools for dalit children, taught his wife Mavullamma to read and write, and was a Brahmo Samajist dedicated to social reform. In 1942, Appalaswamy established a local unit of Ambedkar's Scheduled Caste Federation. A revolutionist, he organized militant land struggles of the dalits in the area to retain control of their assigned lands. He named his son after Kambhampati Tharakam, the brahmin social reformer and district education officer of East Godavari district, who hosted him in his home all through his teacher training course.

It was in the mid-1960s that Tharakam came out of his father's towering shadow. As an advocate in Nizamabad, where his wife Vijayabharathi taught in the local college, he took up cases of the poor, organized fact-finding missions for cases of atrocities against dalits and the village poor, and helped form the Ambedkar Yuvajana Sangam that campaigned vigorously against untouchability and caste atrocities in the villages of the district. All this led to his two-year imprisonment during the Emergency. In 1978, he moved to Hyderabad after Vijayabharathi began working as an officer with the Telugu Academy in the city (where she eventually became the director). Tharakam began practising in the AP High Court, continuing his ceaseless fact-finding work in hundreds of villages and towns where dalits and poor people were tortured, harassed and jailed. He was a government pleader in 1984 when the Karamchedu massacre took place and resigned in protest. Many people had remarked that with this he had lost the chance of being appointed a judge in the high court.

After the Karamchedu massacre, he led dalits there to organize themselves and helped in the rehabilitation and the court cases of the affected families. All this work directly led to the foundation of the Dalit Mahasabha. In 1989, he helped found the Andhra Pradesh chapter of the Bahujan Samaj Party. He resigned from it in 1994, opposing its alliance with the BJP in Uttar Pradesh. He joined the Republican Party of India in 1995, but broke away from the national body after Ramdas Athawale allied with the BJP in 2011. He continued with the independent state unit of the RPI till he died in 2016. He was the warrior who fought both in the courts and outside. He fought the cases that nobody else wanted. Karamchedu (1984), Tsunduru (1991), Lakshmipeta (2012)—he carried the weight of these massacres on his shoulders. Few people know that the landmark judgment of the Supreme Court ordering compulsory registration of criminal cases in 'encounter' murders, was initiated and fought for by Tharakam. His booklet, *Police Arrest Cheste* (If the police arrest you), that HBT published, sold lakhs of copies and saved the lives and bodies of countless young men and women.

Padmanabha Reddy was a top-billed criminal lawyer in the Andhra Pradesh High Court. Often called the poor man's lawyer, the soft-spoken man devoted the same amount of energy to defend an indigent accused as he did for any other person. He was also president of the All-India Lawyers Association. B.S.A. Swamy was a gregarious and dynamic lawyer who espoused the rights of the Backward Classes. In such exciting company, there is little wonder that I wished to foray out again on my own. When I voiced my dissatisfaction with HBT work, CK and Cyril encouraged me to think of other options, even though this meant that the greater burden of running HBT fell on them.

Could a non-ML, non-violent, yet militant movement be built? Could humanism and democratic practice be made integral to a people's movement? I must admit that I had a specific programme in mind when I went to Ibrahimpatnam. I wanted to see if a self-sustaining, strong organization of the rural poor could be set up. In most peasant organizations of the left—those affiliated to the CPI and CPI(M)—we saw middle and rich peasants taking the leadership role, with their demands dictating the programme of the organization. I thought that someone who was educated, had access to various networks, legal and otherwise, government institutions and the media, could help people who had very little of this. I thought I could offer a capsule of all that I had learnt to the people and they could use it as they saw fit. That was my confused thinking. I had no idea how it would actually pan out. I assumed that class was the key concern of the rural poor.

Early in 1984, I was working on the women's health book, *Savaalaksha Sandehaalu: Sthreelu-Aarogyam, Samskruti, Rajakeeyalu* (A million questions: Women's health, culture, politics) with the feminist group Stree Shakti Sanghatana. This group, formed in the late 1970s, focused both on feminist activism and scholarship. The pioneering book *We Were Making History* emerged from this group. *Savaalaksha Sandehaalu* was the Telugu version of *Our Bodies, Ourselves*, the book written by an American feminist group that had so inspired a generation of women in the early 1980s. We wanted to reimagine our approach to health and illness in the Indian context from a feminist standpoint when we began work on this book. I was part of a core group that worked on several chapters: it was decided that I should research the health problems and other concerns of poor women and interview them. In doing this, I was hoping to slowly acclimatize myself to staying and working in villages.

By this time Cyril and I had grown ever closer to the dalit organizations in Andhra Pradesh. HBT had already published a Telugu translation of Baburao Bagul's Marathi stories as *Dalit Kathalu*. This was closely followed by Ambedkar's biography by B. Vijayabharathi titled *Ambedkar Jeevitha Charitra*. *Dalit Kathalu* was launched by the rationalist Katthi Padma Rao in a well-attended meeting in 1982 in Hyderabad. Soon, I began attending Ambedkarite meetings. In the early 1980s, these meetings were usually organized by the Ambedkar Yuvajana Sangam and the Scheduled Caste Employees Welfare Association. Grand meetings were held every 14 April at the Ambedkar statue near the Tank Bund to celebrate Ambedkar's birthday. I sold books at these events and from the sidelines I observed and heard what was being said and how. These meetings were markedly different from those of the left. Ambedkar's photo replaced that of Marx or Lenin or Mao. Yes, there was a platform—but the crowd, what they spoke and the slogans they raised were new to me. The people here were dark-skinned (compared to the fairer-skinned savarnas predominant in left meetings) and wore white clothes (leftists wore all kinds of clothes, but rarely white). The speakers did not rail on about the ruling class, the capitalists, and the three mountains that were imperialism, feudalism and the comprador bourgeoisie. Instead, they spoke of the daily lives of a class of people whom the left should have embraced from the very beginning. They spoke of how they were denied decent housing and employment in towns because of their caste and how they were deemed untouchables and kept at the outskirts of villages. They talked about the atrocities they endured and the exploitative conditions in which their children grew up.

The Tharakam family lived at a walking distance from our house in Chikkadpalli and we were frequent visitors. At their home, I made several new friends from among the dalits, and became immersed in Ambedkarite politics. Vijayabharathi drew me close to her, and they slowly became my second family.

Cyril also knew Paul Diwakar through his paralegal work with NGOs. Paul, his wife Annie Namala, and their eldest child, Anand, who was an infant then, stayed in Jalalmiyapalle in Ibrahimpatnam taluka, some forty-five kilometres from Hyderabad. Paul, the man behind the National Campaign on Dalit Human Rights founded in 1998, worked with an NGO called Water Development Society. He offered to host me and generously shared not only his home but also his wide network in the area. He was planning to relocate to Chittoor and set up his own NGO there.

That is how I came to Ibrahimpatnam and began working on the book *Savaalaksha Sandehaalu*. Here, my life would change forever.

8 Between a reddy and a hard place

I was thirty years old when I first went to Ibrahimpatnam, about thirty kilometres to the south-east of Hyderabad in Ranga Reddy district. To reach Ibrahimpatnam, which the locals called Eerapatnam and I did too, I took a bus from the Imlibun bus stand—named after the huge tamarind (imli) grove that surrounded it, once an unassuming spot in the south of the city. The old bus stand was razed in 2018 by the Telangana government to construct a massive modern bus station across the road. My usual bus started from Imlibun on a narrow road leading to the Nagarjuna Sagar Dam and reached the outskirts of the city within five kilometres. Here, the road veered sharply away from the Vijayawada highway, and the undulating terrain began.

From June to October, one saw fields of jowar and castor, and small emerald green bits of paddy near ponds and wells. Custard apple trees dotted the landscape, and from September to November, they were heavy with fruit. They were so plentiful that passers-by were allowed to help themselves to the fruit. Occasionally, one saw thumma (acacia), neem and tamarind trees and, once in a rare while, the banyan. Shepherds accompanying their sheep and goats were common through the year. They were recognizable from far away, with their trademark blankets called gongadi, which was usually black with a red border. A stick slung across his shoulder with a bag of food and drink, a shepherd was always curious about passers-by, and if you stopped, he would stroll up to you for a quick chat.

Further down the road, one comes across a sudden and

massive outcrop of granite rock—huge boulders in all shapes and sizes that conjured imaginary scenes as one peered at them from out of the moving bus window, like a sleeping man, a mother carrying an infant, eggs in a tray, a woman carrying a pitcher, the proud head of a lion. I watched these behemoth rocks balanced precariously over one another with intrigue to check if their angles remained constant over the many journeys I made along this route. Were they the left-behind toys of a civilization of giants? I kept an eye out for my favourite rocks and, eventually, home became a landscape filled with rocks. Whenever I was in coastal Andhra Pradesh, I missed my rocks; whenever I was returning from Delhi, and the train passed by the huge outcrops near Ghatkesar on the outskirts of Hyderabad, I had butterflies in my stomach and tears in my eyes—I was returning home.

The roads that led to the villages were populated by different characters at different times of the day. Early in the morning, boys took their sheep, goats or cattle out to graze, men were seen with a pair of oxen and a plough, women and older girls carrying pitchers of water and littler girls with infants on their hips. Peasants with some money in their pockets sat on rickety benches outside solitary tea shops drinking tea; aspiring politicians sat underneath venerable trees holding forth to an audience of sidekicks. When the sun was high, the streets and the village centres emptied out and only the village drunkards stayed behind, singing to themselves. As the evening progressed, it was as if the tape played itself in reverse. The boys returned with their animals, men returned with their oxen and ploughs, women carried water for the evening meal and little girls ran around with babies on their hips. Well into the night, tipplers returned from toddy shops and dogs barked at strangers and at other dogs entering their territory.

Ibrahimpatnam is not dissimilar in its social arrangement to the rest of southern Telangana. Before Independence, the region was under the dominion of the nizams. Under them, a vast network of feudal lords, called doras, administered and controlled the lands. The doras mostly hailed from the reddy community, though there were some velama ones as well. In the brahminical scheme of things, reddys (and velamas) are considered shudra; yet, for long they have been the ruling community in the villages of Telangana. The nizam's dominion was marked by extremes in wealth—the rich in the city and the landlords, both Hindu and Muslim, in their gadis (fortresses) lived a life of incredible luxury while the poor died of hunger, ill health and hard labour.

Before 1948, the doras collected extortionate rents, for themselves, and land tax for the nizam, from the peasants. They maintained private armies, laid down the law in their villages, and extracted free services from the artisanal castes, and from the 'service castes', malas and madigas. Then came the Telangana armed struggle, which swept through most parts of the nizam's state. The Telangana peasant movement or the Telangana armed struggle (as it is called by communists) is a defining period in the modern history of the state. The nature of landownership in the region was extremely exploitative. Forty per cent of the land was either directly owned by the nizam (sarf-e-khas) or given by the nizam to elites in the form of jagirs (special tenures). The remaining sixty per cent was under the government's land revenue system, which gave no legal rights or security from eviction to the people actually cultivating the land. Exploitative practices like the vetti (forced labour) system were widely prevalent.

The First World War worsened the condition of peasantry and increased their debt burden. In the 1930s, large landowners had taken over significant tracts of land, either through forced occupation or debt sales. Some landlords owned lands in the range of 30,000 to 100,000 acres, and 550 landlords owned land amounting to about 60–70 per cent of the cultivable land. When the communists began organising in the rural areas of the Hyderabad state under the banner of the Andhra Mahasabha in the mid-1930s, they met with great success. In the early 1940s, entire swathes of villages in northern and eastern parts of the Telangana region were under their control.

The support given by the princely state and the Muslim gentry to the feudatories in the countryside was coupled with the activity of the Ittehad-ul-Muslimeen, a Muslim separatist organization that worked for the independence of Hyderabad from a fledgling India, with the tacit support of the nizam. In 1946, the peasantry began an open revolt under the leadership of the communists and when the state sent its police, which, assisted by the razakars (the private militia of the nizam) defended the landowners, the communists formed their own armed squads in retaliation. By 1948, the communists had established control over four thousand villages. The same year, the entry of the Indian Army and the accession of the nizam to the Indian state brought the communists into open conflict with the Indian state. In 1951, the struggle was formally given up.

The struggle broke the backs of the bigger jagirdars who owned tens of thousands of acres, but the power structure in the villages remained unchanged for the most part. After the nizam ceded power to the Union government, the latter took up half-hearted land reform legislations, but only after violently stifling the burgeoning peasant movement. The reddy doras continued to exert dominance over all other castes and played a major role in the region's politics. All reddys are not doras, most are called 'patel'. This derives from the posts they traditionally held—that of the mali patel (village officer) and the police patel (law enforcement officer). It is not as if every reddy is a landlord. There are thousands of them who work as agricultural labourers. Even the labouring part of the community is addressed with the 'patel' honorific though. I have seen a mala landowner approach the hut of a reddy labourer and call out, 'Patela, panikostava?'—Patel, will you come to work for me? However, as is the case wherever untouchability and the caste system prevail, a venerable dalit elder can be addressed by even a reddy child with a shortened first name: Ellamma can be Elli.

Back when I was beginning my work in Ibrahimpatnam, caste was the first thing that struck me in its ubiquity. The first question you were asked when you entered a village was not your name. It was your caste. To be more precise, it was worded like—perhaps as in other language landscapes where caste is the be all and end all of existence—'Meeru emitollu?' Literally, it is not a caste question as it is 'What exactly are you?' Only after placing you in the caste order of things was further communication and socialization possible. Castes here are tightly knit, solidly welded groups that dictate everything. They govern what work you do, who your co-workers are, who your friends are, your education level, the kind of house you live in, where in the village you live, the health levels of your family, what you eat at home, your taste in culture, what songs you sing and appreciate, how soon or not you can recover from a crisis of any kind, whom you pray to, and how and when you die.

The castes that form the labouring classes in Telangana invariably hail from Scheduled Caste communities. They include the malas (who watch and ward tanks, carry out cremations and burials, and are also agricultural labourers) and the madigas (cobblers, jeetagallu—farmhands, and militant foot soldiers for reddy landlords). There are also castes from the OBC community—mangalis (barbers and midwives), chakalis (washermen and women), kummaris (potters), kammaris (carpenters), vodla (blacksmiths), golla-kurma (shepherds), telaga (oil-pressers and keepers of orchards), besta (fisherfolk), gouds (toddy tappers), and several other minor castes. Their populations can vary from region to region, but in southern Telangana, madigas are far more predominant than the malas. There are several sub-castes among the malas and madigas, but Ibrahimpatnam saw only a sprinkling of these—baindla (a sub-caste of the madiga), begari, dommari, dakkali. Untouchability was rampant here. Dalits lived in small colonies outside the main village. They were served separately, if at all, at weddings and public functions. Other castes did not eat in their houses, and if people from other castes were invited to their weddings, their food was cooked by non-dalit cooks. In most villages, tea was served to all in common glasses, but the madigas and malas washed their glasses before placing them back on the counter. In the tea shops of the villages adjoining Mahabubnagar district, dalits were served in separate glasses altogether. Untouchability seemed less severe in schools, but with most dalit children working as animal grazers, the question was cleverly sidestepped.

Most villages had smaller hamlets attached to their peripheries. These were either exclusive to one caste, like the malas or lambadas (originally nomads, listed as a Scheduled Tribe), or simply a smaller village that did not qualify to be designated as a revenue village. Such hamlets usually did not have elected bodies and had to depend on the largesse of the main village for funds, anganwadis, schools, ration shops and other public utilities.

During my work here (and even now, I suppose), I came to suspect every reddy from Telangana of crimes in their villages, crimes of bonded labour, low wages, usurping land which was not theirs, brutalizing the poor, appropriating the bodies of their women .... This was because wherever I went, the poor only spoke ill of their landlords. The landlord could be a liberal, an activist, a radical in the city, but in the village, he was always a tyrant.

When I visited Marrigudem mandal, which is situated forty-four kilometres south of Ibrahimpatnam, I heard how the family of environmentalist and university professor Purushottam Reddy had by-passed the land reform laws. The family of Madhusudan Reddy, once head of the political science department at Osmania University and the leader of the liberals there, had also done a similar thing and his whole village knew it. When we invited Professor Thippa Reddy of the economics department of Osmania University to one of our meetings, he gently refused, saying that his wife was related to the Pulimamidi doras and he would get in trouble with his family. Mohan Rao, who was a special government advocate representing a case for us in the village of Jabbargudem, where a madiga had been murdered by reddy landlords, was himself on the wrong side of the law in a tenancy case in Tandur. The bad reddys easily outnumbered the good reddys; and there often was a bad reddy hiding inside a seemingly good one.

Land reform laws were openly flouted in Telangana. Congress MP Chokka Rao who favoured our land struggle in Ibrahimpatnam told me that in 1971 when the second land reform law was passed, velama landlords in Jagtial found themselves unable to tamper with the land records because of a lack of trained personnel. So the land records of several years were taken in lorries and buses to Hyderabad where retired

tahsildars and revenue inspectors were put to work, changing
and overwriting the documents. These were then transported
back to Jagtial. How then did one reconcile the liberalism on
campuses and in protest squares with what the reddys did in
the villages? How did the liberal reddys deny the feudalism
that was practised in Telangana?

Those of us born in the dominant castes often wonder
why people of marginalized castes are so angry with us.
We think that we are redeemed by acknowledging caste
exploitation and trying to do our bit to redress it. But people
from marginalized castes remember how our ancestors behaved
with them, they remember the laborious work at low wages,
the forced labour, the grabbing of peasant land and produce,
the rape of their women, their little children being forced
to work as cattle hands, the terrible beatings and torture,
the cruel politics played by the doras to ensure that the poor
do not unite. They know that the children of these doras
have flown to greener pastures—to the city, to the US, to
Europe—where they can claim that they have nothing to do
with caste. Indeed, where is caste around them, they say. The
poor know that the greener pastures are available precisely
because of the surplus extracted from their own forefathers. Is
it right to forget the past? With my work in Ibrahimpatnam, I
came to know that the descendants of the Kundaram reddys,
the Pulimamidi reddys and the Eliminedu reddys are now
in the US raising their children in the liberal values of that
country. Can they afford to forget what their fathers and
grandfathers did in their villages? The landlords of Telangana
have a bloody history, make no mistake. This is not to say
that there were no outliers; there were a few reddys who did
support the agricultural labourers' union I was a part of— the
Ibrahimpatnam Taluka Vyavasaya Coolie Sangam or ITVCS.

Most of these reddys were from other places; I wonder if they would have supported similar struggles in their own villages.

In popular memory, a wall of silence has long surrounded the subject of despotism and caste slavery, a wall nowhere more soundproof than among the descendants of the doras. There are two arguments or justifications that are constantly on the tongues of most of the families who at one time literally owned people. First, that their ancestors were gentle masters. They did not beat their jeetagallu (plural form of jeetagadu)— bonded labourers. And second that the men in their family did not sleep with the wives, daughters and sisters of jeetagallu. Others may have done so, but not their ancestors.

Much of the prosperity of the Telangana reddys and velamas today is linked to a past of exploitation of their serfs. Can you blame children for the sins of their forefathers? Can you blame people for being part of the ethos of that caste society? Can you blame the Manchireddy children for their forefathers killing people deemed expendable? Today, we have come around to the consensus that feudal despotism and caste slavery were crimes against humanity. The families of former doras are not responsible for the past in the way that a criminal is culpable for a crime. We cannot influence our ancestors. However, the descendants of doras are accountable for exploitative acts done in their name, because they have benefited from this system of exploitation. We can acknowledge and speak about the difficult acts in which our families took part, rather than hide or distort them. We can retell those stories and try to make sense of them.

Given the clout reddys wield, several place names in the two Telugu-speaking states bear the names of famous feudal reddy caste men. Ranga Reddy district—where Ibrahimpatnam was the political epicentre—is named after Konda Venkata Ranga Reddy, a freedom fighter of the independence movement. Rayalaseema's Kadapa district was officially renamed as YSR district in honour of the former chief minister Y.S. Rajasekhara Reddy in 2009. The reddys make up only 6.5 per cent of the population of Telangana and Andhra Pradesh, but still are the most politically and socially dominant constituency in most parts of the two states. In 2018, forty of the 119 MLAs in the Telangana Legislative Assembly were reddys. Of the sixteen chief ministers that took power in Andhra Pradesh since the state's formation in 1956, reddys accounted for twelve—and since two of them wielded power twice, the number effectively totals fourteen terms. Back in 1984, it was the kamma caste, stewarded by actor-politician N.T. Rama Rao, that held most of the power in the state. In fact, the demand for the statehood of Telangana was partly a result of the dissatisfaction that powerful reddys and velamas felt after the decrease in their share in power and the increased dominance of the kammas of the coastal regions.

The name Ibrahimpatnam can be translated as 'the town of Ibrahim'. It is named after the lake that Sultan Ibrahim Qutb Shah planned and built at the end of his thirty-year reign between 1550 and 1580 CE. It was built after the Hussainsagar lake in Hyderabad. The Ibrahimpatnam lake, spread over 1,300 acres, was one of the last in a chain of lakes planned from Dindi in Mahabubnagar, some 150 kilometres away. This was to ensure water for irrigation and household needs. When the Dindi lake overflowed, water flowed into the next lake in the chain and then into the Ibrahimpatnam lake through a sluice gate. Today, there is barely any water in the Ibrahimpatnam lake, after the chain of lakes was demolished. The names of the villages in Ibrahimpatnam taluka have a sweet Dakkhani–Telugu mix. The nizams of Hyderabad ruled the areas of Telangana, Marathwada and north Karnataka for several centuries, hence their influence on the region and its nomenclature.

The nizam ruled through his feudatories: the paigahs (the senior aristocracy who maintained their own courts, palaces and standing armies), the samsthanams (minor princely kingdoms), jagirdars and deshmukhs (both of whom held vast tracts of land). The jagirdars were granted land for their service to the nizam while the deshmukhs were revenue collectors who had to hand over revenue tax to the government. The jagirdars were largely Muslim while the Hindu deshmukhs belonged to the reddy, velama and brahmin castes, although the Dichpally samsthanam near Nizamabad once had a Backward Caste deshmukh. Besides these feudatories, the nizam had his own landholdings—the sarf-e-khas, which amounted to about 30 per cent of the total land in Telangana. The taxes levied from these regions went directly into his private treasury. The jagirdars and deshmukhs were crucial in maintaining this dynamic and constituted the nizam's support base. Extortion from the peasantry was high throughout Telangana as were the illegal eviction of peasants and the extraction of free goods and services—known as vetti across the southern states. Citizens had scarce civil or political rights.

By the 1930s, opposition to the feudal rule was brewing. The Andhra Mahasabha, which was formed in 1929, was of this disposition. It was taken over in 1940–42 by the communists who further demanded the abolition of vetti, protection of the rights of tenants, and granting of land to the tiller. The movement was intense in northern and western Telangana and slowly turned into an armed movement by the mid-1940s, when the communists deployed armed squads to fight the armies of the local deshmukhs and the razakars. In 1947, the nizam refused to accede to the Indian Union. So the Indian Army marched into Telangana in September 1948, operating under the code name Operation Polo which was a police action to annex the state. The nizam's army surrendered; and a large number of Muslim jagirdars fled the state leaving behind vast tracts of land. In western Telangana, Muslims were massacred in thousands by an incipient Hindu right (represented by the RSS, the Congress and the Arya Samaj). Thousands of Muslims lost their jobs and livelihoods across the state, particularly in Hyderabad. The conservative estimate was that between twenty-seven thousand and forty thousand people died during and after the police action. The Pandit Sunderlal Committee's report of 1948, hidden from public eyes until its declassification in 2013, sticks to this figure. Other scholars have put the toll at two hundred thousand or even higher.

The nizam was co-opted by the Central government, and he was made the first rajpramukh (governor) of the state of Hyderabad. Effective control, however, now lay with the Indian Army. Major General J.N. Chaudhuri, who led Operation Polo, stayed on as military governor until December 1949. M.K. Vellodi of the Indian Civil Service was appointed the first chief minister of Hyderabad in January 1950.

The first comprehensive land survey in the state had been conducted under the nizam's rule between 1932 and 1934. In 1954, the new administration conducted another, more intensive survey. Between 1954 and 1955, the Indian Civil Service prepared a comprehensive account of landownership in Hyderabad and drew up documents that indicated who owned what land; this document is called the khasra pahani. This was an important event. Before this, all the records of ownership were prepared under the supervision of jagirdars and zamindars. After 1954, the records were kept by petty government officials under the sway of landlords. But in that year, the documents were authentic, since they had been prepared by a somewhat impartial party.

With the nizam's fall came the time of the land grab. In village after village, reddy and velama landlords drove out the Muslim landlords and took over their property. Since they were also the patwaris (the accountant or administrative officer responsible for maintaining land records of the village) and patels, the marauding landlords simply wrote their own names in the pattas (ownership deeds) and became 'legal' occupants. In the villages in northern and eastern Telangana (specifically, the districts of Nalgonda, Warangal, Karimnagar, Khammam and parts of Nizamabad), that saw the Telangana armed peasant revolt, the rich and middle peasants acquired the lands of both the jagirdars and the Muslims. Here too, Muslim landholders fled even if they were not full-fledged landlords.

After the military took over the administration of Telangana, the Protected Tenancy Act was legislated in 1950 to quell the aspirations of peasants. This act gave some guarantees to cultivator tenants. Tenants could not be evicted by force and were given the first option for purchase of land at a reduced rate. Rent was also fixed at a reasonable rate, one-tenth to one-fourth of the market rate. Officers from coastal Andhra were brought over to survey the region, and in many places, people from marginalized communities were recorded as protected tenants in the 1955 khasra pahanis, which are integral to the Telangana revenue system. Landlords understood the import of this legislation as possession was nine-tenths of ownership. Tenants were evicted by brute force. Many of their certificates were seized or taken away under false promises and inducements (liquor, promises of gifting back a fraction of the land). Where tenants were strong (such as in Suryapet in what was Nalgonda district) or belonged to the dominant castes (usually the two went together), they virtually took ownership of the land. No rent was paid to the landowner, and in most cases, neither was the purchase price paid. Bribes to revenue officials ensured changes to the title deeds or disappearances of the original files. In Kodad, which was part of a National Institute of Rural Development survey I was to undertake along with others, we were surprised to find that all the tenants (all reddys) listed in the protected tenant register—known as PT register—were in place. The opposite was true of Vikarabad where the PTs were dalits. Caste played a crucial role in determining whether you could own land.

In 1956, the state of Hyderabad was split. What is now Telangana was merged into Andhra Pradesh; the Marathwada region went to Maharashtra; the Kannada-speaking areas to Karnataka. In Telangana, land was always owned by the reddys, velamas and, to a lesser extent, by the brahmins. The intermediate castes like the gouds, telagas and munnuru kapus held small tracts and the dalits were virtually landless. Every village had inam land ('inam' is a gift in return for services) and every caste was entitled to a small portion of this pot. The mangali (barber) had his mangali inam, the chakali (washerman) had his chakali inam, as did the madigas and malas. Each madiga and mala household got its turn at cultivating the tiny inam holding of half an acre or less on a rotation basis, once every few years.

The Telangana peasant movement brought landownership to a wide range of castes, including the reddys and velamas. The latter were already cultivators and so took the best of the land. The intermediate and artisanal castes managed to recover what they had lost to the jagirdars and deshmukhs. The common pastures and wastelands were left for the malas and madigas, and when, over time, these were encroached upon by the landlords, they became bones of contention. Many dalits had been tenant cultivators and the khasra pahani even recorded this fact, with their names entered in the PT register. As soon as this happened (after 1954), most dalits were evicted by their landlords who obviously feared such entitlements.

The communist movement of the 1940s barely touched Ibrahimpatnam. In that period, the reddys used the movement to grab the land of Muslim jagirdars. Yacharam Buddajangaiah, the leader of the madigas in the village of Jabbargudem, says: 'The reddys led us to attack the house of the jagirdar. They took the gold and the title deeds and left us the rice bags and toddy.'

Prior to June 1985 when mandals were formed, Andhra Pradesh had the taluka or tahsil as its basic revenue administration unit. The tahsildar, a gazetted officer, was responsible for the collection of land revenue and supervising the village accountants (patwaris) and revenue inspectors (girdhawaris) in his charge. Ranga Reddy district, which envelops the southern part of Hyderabad city, had eleven talukas. Ibrahimpatnam taluka consisted of sixty-three revenue villages with many more hamlets. In June 1985, the taluka was divided into three mandals—Yacharam, Ibrahimpatnam and Manchal. The mandal then became the basic revenue unit. I worked in Ibrahimpatnam for nearly a year before the mandals were formed. The region was considered backward: its main sources of irrigation were rainfed tanks, monsoon streams and open wells. The most common dry crops were jowar and castor; only about 10 per cent of the land was irrigated, and it mostly yielded paddy and vegetables like tomato and brinjal.

Most of the landless labourers were madigas, but there were also telagas, chakalis, mangalis, gollas and kurmas, kammaris, vodrangis and kummaris. Malas were few in number compared to the madigas. In this region, the malas had better access to education as compared to the madigas, and most mala families often had an employed member. The middle and rich farmers included kapus (who called themselves reddys or kapu-reddys sometimes), a few brahmins and the stray kurmas (herders). The reddy farmers monopolized the bigger businesses and government jobs. They also owned assets like tractors, tillers, mills and other such instruments of industrialized farming. They operated all the village contracts, be they related to electricity, road work, construction of buildings or the deepening of tanks.

Reddys were often the sarpanches and self-selected members to local bodies. Wherever reservations prevented them from exercising direct political control, they had their stooges to stand in for them. Many big farmers left their agricultural operations entirely to their farmhands. Farming was their secondary occupation, with most of them having day jobs or running their businesses in Hyderabad. Yet farming gave them the political clout necessary to dominate village life, maintain their grip over politics, control vote banks and contracts, and to influence policies that suited them.

During the lean season, most agricultural labourers and small peasants migrated away from the villages. Some went to the Nagarjuna Sagar Dam's left canal area (in Nalgonda) for agricultural work, the rest headed to the city for construction work, to ply rickshaws, lay roads and so on. Summer was a long season of unemployment; the women called this a time of desperate waiting, a time spent 'scratching the mud walls of their huts'. In families with two or three young sons, one was inevitably sent to the city and put to work in a bakery or a hotel or a factory, which earned him Rs 150 per month in the 1980s along with food. At that time, the hamsa (coarse-grained) variety of rice cost some two or three rupees a kilo while fine rice cost about seven to eight rupees. The wages were extremely low considering the expenses, and the work demanded hard and long hours. There were two categories of agricultural labourers—the daily wagers, both men and women, and the farmhands or jeetagallu, who were bonded labourers. The jeetagallu were always male. The daily wagers, despite the name, received their payments at the end of the week. The farmhands often had to take out loans that equalled their entire annual income, sometimes even more. This usually happened during Ugadi—the start of the agricultural season. The farmhand's monthly wage was adjusted against the loan. Some landlords did not calculate interest on the principal, others did. The farmhand had irregular hours of work unlike the daily-wage labourer. He could be on duty from four-thirty at dawn till late in the evening.

In 1984, farmhands earned around Rs 600–700 a year. Daily wages for men at that time ranged from three to four rupees, and for women from eight annas to two rupees. Even this was subject to the prevailing season and the intensity of work. At the time, Andhra Pradesh was divided into four zones based on productivity and economic status. For the zone in which Ibrahimpatnam fell, the Minimum Wage Authority had prescribed the minimum wage as Rs 135 per month in 1984. This rose to Rs 150 in 1986. The reason for the lower monthly wage was the regularity of employment as also the implicit understanding that this came with a substantial loan.

As you can imagine, there was a huge gulf between what the law prescribed and how things actually worked. The jeetagallu often had specific tags based on how much they earned. Most little boys were called 'kundedu jeetagallu', one kunda being twenty seers (one seer equals 933 grams) of paddy. That is, they got twenty seers of paddy a month as payment—at the time worth twenty rupees. An adult was referred to as a 'moodu kundelu jeetagadu' (three kunda jeetagadu) since their payment was three kundas, or sixty seers, of paddy.

Madiga women had to sweep the courtyards of the landlords, coat it with a mixture of cattle dung and water, and clean the cowsheds. This was a lot of work given that some courtyards were nearly an acre in size. In return, these women were given a cheap sari and a blouse once a year—which amounted to some fifteen paise per day. If the landlord was generous, he allowed them to collect the leftovers from the threshing yard, but this happened only if they worked in his fields.

In all my visits, I often found men sitting around tea shops, smoking beedis, but never found women idling about. They were always pacing, always to or from work. On lean days, when the men had no work, they lazed about, went to the weekly shandy (the Wednesday market where vegetables, fruits, groceries and all kinds of meat as well as live cattle were sold) or watched a cinema at the only single-screen theatre in Ibrahimpatnam town. But women used those days to fetch firewood, weave rush mats and stitch quilts from old clothes. When their children were older and had set up their own families, the women had more time for leisure and the societal nod to take up other activities. But they were never a part of the caste panchayats.

In most poor families, children had minimal schooling. Anganwadi—rural childcare centres set up with government support since 1975—coverage was sporadic and available only in the bigger villages. Often, anganwadis were located in the bigger villages and dalits were discouraged from sending their children there. Even if a girl did go to school, as soon as a new child was born in the family, she was pulled out and brought back home to care for the little one, since the mother had to go out to work. Any crisis in the family forced the boys to get working, often tending cattle and sheep.

Ibrahimpatnam was on the margins of the Telangana peasant movement of the late 1940s. In the main, the villages had not been influenced by the movement though some people had joined as activists. The malas and madigas in most villages had kept away from the movement. In my time there, the CPI(M) continued to control some villages. I was told that they did this with a more vicious hand than the Congress or the BJP, for they tolerated no outside influence. They forbade their cadre from debate and brooked no dissent. Over time, I experienced this brusqueness first-hand.

9 The lay of the land

My first visit to Ibrahimpatnam was in August 1984 when I went to stay in Paul Diwakar's house in Jalalmiyapalle, a hamlet of Rangapur, eighteen kilometres from Ibrahimpatnam town. The owner of the house was a man called Jalalmiya, miya being a respectful suffix in the Deccan. Before the 1948 police action and the fall of the nizam, Jalalmiya lorded over around a thousand acres, and the area was named after him. He built himself a big house and had a small colony of servants to attend to his needs, all belonging to different castes: a potter, a blacksmith, a barber and malas. After the events of 1948, Jalalmiya found it unsafe to stick around as the only Muslim in the area. He left for Hyderabad and rented out his home to several tenants. I found this out in 2020 while writing this book. Paul was his tenant in 1984 when I was trying to find my feet there. Paul's father, N.D. Ananda Rao Samuel, was a bishop with the Church of South India and often visited him in Jalalmiyapalle. He was a widely respected man and played a key role in legitimizing priesthood for women. As bishop and moderator, he shed light on the topic through discussions and debates at synodical platforms, and in 1980, the CSI passed a resolution granting ordination for theologically trained women. I did not know this when I stayed with Paul. His father was a simple, austere and quiet man. Paul's brother Solomon was also there. About twenty-two years old, he was to leave for the US soon for his studies. For the first day or two, I wandered about the house and in the tiny village outside. I met Buggaiah (who was later to work with me), his family and his paternal aunt, who was the only woman in the entire taluka to take up the plough. I felt a great sense of dislocation—what was I doing in this strange place, this strange house? Did I ever think that I could live in a village like this and engage with villagers?

I had come with the ostensible reason of researching marginalized women's health problems for the book I was working on. I went around Jalalmiyapalle as also Cheeded, a neighbouring village at a walking distance, with a draft questionnaire but did not really engage with what I had come for. The sights, sounds, smells and language were overpoweringly different from what I had known earlier. There was too much to absorb and I was in a hurry, trying to figure everything out in a day.

I spent about one week there and then returned to Hyderabad to catch my breath. I had to take the plunge, now that I had seen the area and met some people. I also had to get some means of transport. Paul was to leave soon for Chittoor, down south in the Rayalaseema region, and I was on my own. In my thirtieth year, I learnt to ride a bicycle, because there was no public transport in Ibrahimpatnam. Distances between villages were not very large and could be covered by cycling. But the learning happened near home in Hyderabad. I was zipping down the lanes of West Marredpally on a cycle borrowed from Shantha Sinha. I fell down and grazed myself innumerable times, but Vidyarani Narasimha Rao, the gracious principal of Kasturba Gandhi College for Women and a great activist, was always there to soothe me, clean my wounds and apply thin strips of cotton soaked in iodine. By then I had given up wearing trousers and was in the sari mode. Since saris didn't aid cycling, I had to borrow a few salwar kameez sets from friends.

Returning to Jalalmiyapalle, I found that Solomon had time on his hands till he left for the US. I do not recall who suggested this, but we decided to tour the villages of Ibrahimpatnam on our own. Solomon spoke Telugu well enough though he was not conversant in the Telangana dialect. The two of us took off on cycles with sleeping bags. We ate whatever food people gave us. It mainly consisted of rice or jowar roti with pickle, and we paid the hosts two rupees for each meal. We slept wherever someone offered us a place. This was in September or October 1984. It was a lovely time. The weather was pleasant, Solomon and I did not have to report to anyone, we had no work to take up, we cycled where we wanted, stopped where we wanted, sometimes for hours, to look at amazing rock formations and talk. By night, we stopped at the nearest village.

We had three routes to cycle out of Jalalmiyapalle. To the north-west, we rode past Rangapur, Gaddamallaigudem and Gungal to reach National Highway 565 which connected Hyderabad to Nagarjuna Sagar that is home to a large dam across the River Krishna, dividing the two regions of Telangana and Andhra. When we crossed the highway to head west, we hit Pethula, then southwards to Chintula, Nandiwanaparthy and turned west to Yacharam to hit the national highway again. Northwards from Jalalmiyapalle, we crossed Rangapur again to ride along Japala, Arutla and Manchal. Southwards, we cycled past Cheeded and Dadpally to skirt the rocky terrain of Rachakonda, then turned towards southeast—the Rachakonda rocks obstructed us to the west— to go past Mondigourelli, Chintapatla, Nallavelli and again hit NH 565 at Maal.

Cycling in Ibrahimpatnam was no joke. When I started out, I often lost balance and fell whenever I spotted children or cattle at a distance. Gradually I began to improve. Solomon was a wonderful companion, easy to talk to and cheerful. The villagers were companionable too. The two of us had no regard for caste, so we stopped wherever we wanted food. We told them openly about ourselves when they asked questions. We must have cycled like this for about two weeks. After he left, I stayed a while in Jalalmiyapalle and soon rented a room for myself in Gungal. Paul and Annie were also to leave for Chittoor.

Gungal—the villagers called it Guniganti—was some four kilometres from Jalalmiyapalle, and about half a kilometre off the Nagarjuna Sagar highway. Gungal was better connected to other villages. My room also had an outdoor pit latrine which was a big relief, since I was tired of doing my business out in the open. I learnt to sprinkle bleaching powder over the toilet after using it, and every day I fetched water from a handpump some distance away. I bought fresh milk and used clay pots to cook my food over a kerosene stove. The food was simple— rice and a vegetable or dal, sometimes accompanied by the most delicious curd made from fresh milk. Sometimes I made chicken. Cooked in a clay pot over firewood, it was heavenly.

The room was not well lit and the wooden rafters under the tiled roof looked suspicious, particularly after villagers told me that snakes and scorpions often scurried up there and fell on unsuspecting victims. My room was not in the madiga- wada but quite close to it, some fifty yards away. The owner was a Muslim who lived in Ibrahimpatnam town. I was glad that I did not have to rent a room from a reddy who would surely disapprove of my work.

Paul introduced me to his colleagues in the organization, Water Development Society, encouraging them to accompany me as I went around. Shankaraiah, Buggaiah, Ramulu, Gnaneswari, Sathyavathi and several others were part of his team. The first three were local villagers and continued to work with me in the area. Shankaraiah was from Cheeded, a kilometre

Buggaiah of Jalalmiyapalle holding Paul Diwakar's child, Anand, with Shankaraiah to his left

away from Jalalmiyapalle, Buggaiah from Jalalmiyapalle, and Ramulu was from Hasmatpura near Manchal. Shankaraiah and Buggaiah had some years of schooling but Ramulu was self-taught. One of his legs had to be amputated after an accident and he moved around on crutches. In some years, we managed to arrange a Jaipur Foot for him. With this well-designed, rubber-based prosthetic leg, not many people noticed that he was differently abled. Shankaraiah today is active in mainstream politics and has served as the sarpanch (chief) of his village. Buggaiah joined the Shramik Vidyapeeth with Shantha Sinha but died very young. Ramulu continues to serve as a mediator between the people and the government in the area. Sathyavathi went on to set up her own NGO, Reeds, and her biography, *Sathyavathi: Confronting Caste, Class and Gender*, was written by Vasanth Kannabiran and published in 2015.

For someone like me who had visited villages only for specific reasons such as a meeting or a wedding, it was a sharp learning curve. I was willing to suspend every belief and learn things anew. Wherever we stopped, I was full of questions, both for the people with me and the people we met—why did they say this, what did they eat, why did they eat what they ate, how did they work, who beat his wife, what were their wages, what was the interest on loans, what was their relationship with the reddy landlords, why did they pity the brahmin priest and so on. Life in the village was interesting, colourful and vibrant. People had ample time to explain everything I wanted. Even waiting for a bus had its charms. What would have been vexatious in the city was natural here. At the bus stand, I met scores of people who had all the time in the world to talk. The bus never came on time. Sometimes it didn't turn up at all. I learnt not to look at my watch when I was in Ibrahimpatnam and to think more heedfully about the world I was entering.

Food, for instance. I often skipped breakfast, had lunch only as late as four in the evening and sometimes went to bed at two in the night. Sometimes, someone would ask us to come to his village, and when we went there, the person would be missing. You asked a question and the reply was about something totally different. Everybody was late for everything. When they said morning, it could mean any time between 5 a.m. and 12 noon. No one in Ibrahimpatnam took offence at my constant questioning. There was an endless number of people willing to talk.

There were no mosquitoes. The villages were relatively

clean as the hilly terrain provided adequate drainage. There were so many plants and birds to ask about. I came to learn what one did to avoid snakes, scorpions and leeches and several other creepy-crawlies. To venture out at night, one had to carry a stick. It had to be tapped frequently on the ground to warn snakes that humans were approaching. Rafters had to be cleaned regularly, they said, to avoid scorpions and other poisonous creatures falling down when you slept. When crossing paddy fields or streams, one had to look out for leeches. The most terrible things, however, were the hen lice. People often kept their poultry (and sometimes even the cattle) inside their huts. If the hen had lice—tiny creatures you could not see with the naked eye—we not only had a sleepless night, but carried the bug with us for more sleepless nights, unless we fumigated our clothes and bedding and bathed in hot water.

Everywhere we went, there were rocks with picturesque names—mekalagutta (the rock with the face of a goat), nakkalagutta (the rock with the face of a fox), kondengulagutta (because it was inhabited by langurs), bollonigutta (where the rocks were white), and the commonplace devunigutta (a small idol on top of a rock). There is even a basavugutta, a corruption of Bhaisahab, named after a Muslim mystic. There were huge outcrops, sometimes miles of sheer rock as in the Rachakonda terrain, fifteen kilometres from Ibrahimpatnam. Fields were few and far between, and these were usually of jowar or castor, which meant that after October they were bare and cattle grazed on them. The occasional goatherd or shepherd looked at us inquisitively as we walked or cycled by. I had all the freedom to relieve myself behind a rock or a bush, and sometimes even sneak a smoke. I was a desultory social smoker. I couldn't smoke in Ibrahimpatnam publicly, but I cheated whenever I could.

People quite frequently asked me what my caste was. This was one of the first questions posed everywhere. I caught on quickly that the dakkali, a sub-caste of the madigas, were considered the lowest in the hierarchy. So I said I was dakkali. Since people had heard about Cyril, they countered, 'Your husband is a reddy.' 'Yes,' I'd reply, 'but I was born dakkali, we don't practise caste, so if you give me food and allow me into your home, you should do so for all dakkalis.' I never came to know if they found out that I was born a brahmin, but it did not matter after the first few months. I had identified with them by that time.

Going to the toilet was a major problem for me. Men went to a particular open place and women to another. None of the houses where I stayed had a toilet. You picked up a lota and went wherever you were directed. In some homes, it was the only lota in the hut, often doubling up as the drinking lota. I was relieved when plastic bottles came into vogue in the early 1990s. Fortunately, unlike in the coastal Andhra area, where there is no place even to shit because the land is so fertile, expensive and low-lying, Telangana villages usually have a lot of open scrubland. Women's and men's shitting areas are clearly defined. Shitting in the open was not considered shameful. Women accompanied me, squatted on their haunches, and told me their stories. After a point, I had to shout at them to leave and allow me privacy. Over the years, when I became well known, women thronged in the mornings to shit with me. Many were probably protective of me. Defecating in the open was the social norm, considered a part of wholesome rural life, a time of socializing with friends. I never got used to this and preferred to flee to the few houses that had a closed outdoor toilet. Christians among the madigas almost always had outdoor toilets, so I began preferring the Christian houses.

The government did give money to build toilets but since these had to be built close to the house, people did not take up the offer. The idea that defecation was something you did close to or within your home was anathema across castes. It was not until the late 1990s when the girls of this area became educated and daughters-in-law demanded toilets that these began to be built.

In 1984, Cyril worked actively with Shantha Sinha when she was in the Shramik Vidyapeeth under the aegis of the University of Hyderabad. The Shramik Vidyapeeth had adult education as its mandate and Shantha extended this to child labour. The organization began work among the poorest of the poor in the villages around Hyderabad. Earlier, in 1981, Shantha's family had established the Mamidipudi Venkatarangaiya Foundation, named after her grandfather, a much feted educationist and historian. When she left the Shramik Vidyapeeth, MVF was the chosen vehicle to pioneer work in the eradication of child labour—work for which she went on to receive the Magsaysay and Padma Shri awards.

In 1984, our home in Hyderabad was the HBT office in Chikkadpalli which had four small ten-by-ten-foot rooms and a tiny six-by-four-foot kitchen. We occupied one of the rooms. Salaha was housed nearby in another house. Our office–house was always bustling with people dropping in at all times of the day and night.

As I spent more and more time in Ibrahimpatnam, and as the novelty began to wear off, I longed to return to Hyderabad and often cheated by turning up at home unexpectedly. I returned home for a day or two once in a fortnight, and when there were festivals or curfews I stayed behind in Hyderabad. There was a lot of drinking during festivals in the villages and I was warned not to move around at that time. When in

Ibrahimpatnam, I longed for conversations about books and politics (as we understood them at the time). I found myself craving for better and familiar food. During my time in HBT, I frequently invited myself for meals at middle-class homes all over the state and had the best of all cuisines. In Rayalaseema, even if I had to leave early in the morning to catch a bus or a train, I wouldn't miss a meal of hot dosas with freshly prepared country chicken at the home where I had stayed the night. When I was in coastal Andhra I was treated to varieties of egg-based dishes, and in Telangana people often made mutton. In the middle-class homes, there were a range of pickles, and for every meal there was at least one cooked vegetable accompanied by curd.

In the villages of Ibrahimpatnam, the staple was jowar roti and chilli chutney, sometimes the hamsa variety of rice with maybe some seasonal broad beans. The lambada thanda—as a nomadic tribal colony is called—had roti with khova (cream) though. The poor got all their calories from jowar or rice. I could eat only a limited quantity of cereal and longed for different varieties of vegetables, fruits and meat. Sometimes, I sneaked a bit of chikki, peanut-jaggery brittle, in my bag when I left Hyderabad. Over the years, even when we visited Ibrahimpatnam town and taluka headquarters, our breakfasts were invariably limited to a cup of tea. Sometimes this included meals in hotels that served stale puris and dal. The area didn't even have a small hotel where one could eat rice with dal and vegetables. In time, some eateries did open, but since I was always accompanied by someone, I felt a little vain and stupid wanting to indulge my cravings by eating at a hotel, especially when everyone else was so stoic.

I recall a visit to Nomula, a village close to Ibrahimpatnam, where after a meeting I was housed with a poor widow. She gave me roti and wept that she had nothing else to serve, not even chutney. Still, she mixed up some jowar flour with chilli powder and salt, and boiled it in water to make a soupy gruel. Over the next few years, jowar disappeared as the staple. When the N.T. Rama Rao government of 1983 began providing subsidized ration rice at two rupees a kilo, the households in the region moved away from jowar, and rice became the staple.

With time, I learnt to shit in the open with a lota, and take a bath outdoors with my clothes on. The constant movement, walking and cycling also made me ravenous. I began to enjoy the hot food, even if it was just rice with chilli chutney. It took me some time to learn the Telangana dialect, and for a while I was blissfully unaware of its nuances. For instance, they used the term 'dengadam'—fucking—as a natural prefix or suffix for almost any given verb or noun. Dishonouring a debt was 'ega-dengadam', 'debt-fucking'; something was not simply 'nonsense', but 'fucking nonsense': 'dengudu kootalu'; they didn't just 'go away' or 'leave', they 'fucked off': 'dengeyi'. Instead of saying 'he left the field at five', they said 'he fucked off at five'. Till I understood what 'dengadam' and its variants really meant, I used it freely too. The legendary 'people's IAS officer' S.R. Sankaran, who mentored me, also took to this word unwittingly. In one meeting in Gungal in 1985, Sankaran, as secretary of social welfare to the government, had come with the Ranga Reddy district collector G. Sudhir, and was enquiring with the bonded labourers who went on about 'appu ega-dengadam', fucking the debt. Sankaran, who earned a name for earnestly enforcing the Bonded Labour (Abolition) Act of 1976, taking the cue from the workers, repeated the phrase, unaware of the red faces of the other officials present.

10 Maximum work, minimal wage

I sorely missed my friends when I was in Ibrahimpatnam: our long discussions about radical politics, books and culture, and just simply hanging out doing nothing. I wanted to tell them all about the exciting work I was embarking on, and the things that were happening every day. Bottling these up for a week or more was difficult, so I began writing for the current affairs weekly *Mainstream* which regularly published my articles. I did not know anyone there nor did they know who I was, but my first effort, a portrait of an activist who worked for our Sangam, called Bandi Sriramulu, was published in 1985. After that, it was smooth sailing.

On one of my visits back home, I attended a workshop organized by Cyril and his lawyer friends from Salaha, about the Minimum Wages Act and bonded labour. The Bonded Labour (Abolition) Act was passed in India in 1976 during the Emergency. It was the brainchild of the civil servant S.R. Sankaran, who had become quite popular in Andhra Pradesh. The precedent for such a law was set as early as in 1948 with the Minimum Wages Act that stipulated a bare minimum wage for all categories of work in India. It was left to the states to fix the actual wages, and these were revised from time to time. Wages were also set based on the kind of region and economic activity of a place. In Andhra Pradesh there were three zones: canal irrigated, dry irrigated, and dry areas. Cities and canal-irrigated (wet) zones had the highest wages, and dry areas like Ibrahimpatnam had the lowest.

Salaha held frequent sessions for activists from NGOs and dalit organizations, and I found myself at one such event towards the end of 1984. I was on a brief visit and keen to return to Ibrahimpatnam. I wasn't really interested in the proceedings. But something in the discussions lit a spark. They were talking about the possibility of organizing people to demand their minimum wages. I immediately remembered all my discussions with the people in Ibrahimpatnam. Hadn't they been telling me how badly they were paid, and how they always fell into unpayable debts? Shouldn't I take the discussions at this workshop back to them? The minimum wage for unskilled agricultural labour was supposed to be eight rupees a day in the Ibrahimpatnam zone. But the women here were getting as little as half a rupee in the off season. Returning to Ibrahimpatnam, I began talking to people in the villages about minimum wages, buttonholing them whenever I could.

By the time I moved to my new place in Gungal, I already knew Shankaraiah through Paul Diwakar. One day, Shankaraiah took me to his village, Cheeded, which was just a kilometre away from Jalalmiyapalle. Shankaraiah had long resented the authoritarian domination of the CPI(M) in his village. They had never spoken of minimum wages. Thinking that it would upset the apple cart, he invited me to speak at his village about the act and what could be done to implement it. Cheeded was a small village consisting of about a hundred and fifty households back in 1984. One evening, I walked down from Jalalmiyapalle to Cheeded and found myself holding an informal meeting of about twenty agricultural labourers. Most of the people in attendance were madigas, but there was also a considerable representation of telaga (oil presser) labourers. Shankaraiah asked me to speak about the Minimum Wages Act and the Bonded Labour (Abolition) Act. After I spoke, laying out the act, why it had been passed,

At a meeting in Ibrahimpatnam in the 1980s

and how it could be implemented, the agricultural labourers began murmuring among themselves in amazement. Some spoke out loud. While some said that government's laws were insane and impractical, others mused that it was indeed possible to ask for more. Prices for everything—rice, jowar, oil, transport, beedis, clothing—were rising; why should their wages be static? They discussed which landlord would prove intransigent or troublesome. They asked why the CPI(M), despite calling itself a party of the working class, had not raised such issues. I was amazed to find the next morning that the agricultural labourers had decided to strike work. Perhaps this being Shankaraiah's village was the reason for their taking the bold step. They trusted him and his friends.

The striking labourers sat in the centre of the village for three days. I didn't know what they hoped to achieve with this, nor did I understand their strategy—what purpose did it serve just sitting about idly? I sat with them; they sang songs, chatted and told passers-by why they had struck work while I spouted what I had learnt in the Salaha workshop. What the striking labourers were asking for was far less than the minimum wage—eight rupees a day—prescribed for agricultural work in the semi-arid zone 3 (to which this area belonged). At that time, the women labourers were paid two rupees a day and the men received three to four rupees. The farmhands (the jeetagallu who were always men) got three kundedu, about two rupees a day. We had heated discussions over three days. Landlords and rich peasants came over to argue with us. How were they to cultivate if, apart from increased fertilizer and pesticide costs, and reduced price for agricultural produce, they had to bear increased labour costs. I asked them to give up agriculture or fight with the government for their own demands but not exploit labour.

On the third day, the farmer–landlords came for negotiations and the wages were raised (not yet to the prescribed minimum wages though). Women now got three to five rupees, men six to seven rupees, and farmhands got three to four kundedu per month (roughly sixty to eighty rupees).

During the strike we had several long discussions about the many problems that affected agricultural labourers. Given my ignorance, they were happy to share their problems with me. One of the major hindrances for unity among the labourers, I gleaned, was the practice of bonded labour. The agricultural labourers complained about the farmhands who were often tasked with breaking strikes. If the farmhands join us, we will be invincible, they said. Much of the long-term regular farming was done by the jeetagallu, in effect bonded labourers. They were paid three kundedu for adults, and about half a kundedu for a child labourer who grazed cattle. If they wanted cash instead of grain, the adult wage was Rs 100 per month, even though the minimum wage had been set at Rs 500 per month at that time.

The labourers often took loans. The reasons could vary— ill health in the family necessitating treatment at Hyderabad, a wedding, purchase of a small plot for cultivation or for the building of a house, or even the wish to switch landlords, in which case the original employer had to be repaid his loan. The loan could range from Rs 1,000 to Rs 3,000, sometimes free of interest, sometimes with interest. These loans were negotiated at Ugadi, the Telugu new year marked by the harvest season. The need of the landowner, the farming expertise of the labourer, and the labourer's own need dictated whether the loan was interest-free or not. Once they were bound to a landlord because of the loan, it was understood that they had to work regularly—the loan was deemed an advance payment against wages. So they did not join the agricultural labourers' strikes, and instead helped in ending them. Apart from a monthly wage, which was often paid at the end of the season after a part of the loan was deducted, they were also given a pair of chappals, a gongadi—a coarse woollen shawl—and some tobacco. This was not because the landlords were generous. The jeetagallu had to start the irrigation motor before dawn and were often bitten by snakes. They also had to sleep in the fields when the harvest was ripening. A newly married jeeta could barely spend the night with his wife. I heard a story of one Alwal Reddy, the landlord in a village called Polepalli, some thirty kilometres from Ibrahimpatnam, who forced his farmhands to sleep near his wells at night making up some work or the other and then summoned their wives to his gadi—the fortress or mansion of the dora.

The farmhand could not strike. Neither could he leave his landlord unless he had fully paid back his debt. This being next to impossible, the only option if he wanted to leave was to tie himself to another employer and get him to repay the loan. This meant bondage to a new master. They were eternally bonded, some bondages passing from father to son to grandson.

Soon after the victory at Cheeded, where the landlords relented quickly since they didn't want to prolong the matter, we set our sights even wider. One of the first causes we took up was that of Buggaiah, a madiga from Gungal. Buggaiah was found dead after he had been electrocuted on the borders of a landlord's field. The landlord had electrified his fence to protect his crops from wild boars. The madigas of the village suspected that Buggaiah had been thrown against the fence and murdered. We forced the police to register a criminal case, organized compensation for the widow, and a job for her in a social welfare hostel for girls.

In the meantime, Salaha printed pamphlets and attractive posters giving details of the Minimum Wages Act and the Bonded Labour (Abolition) Act. These were distributed across the state among NGOs and activist organizations, and we made full use of them in Ibrahimpatnam. In this we were assisted by the staff of Paul Diwakar's NGO, Water Development Society. They were helpful in answering my myriad questions, but also apprehensive and I soon discovered why.

Landlords and local CPI(M) leaders went around asking after the upstarts who dared spread such incendiary propaganda. The landlords said they would beat up anyone found pasting posters and distributing pamphlets. Under pressure, the staff at Water Development Society ceased support; they were also rebuked by their managerial officers at Hyderabad. Landlords and politicians were complaining to the top brass of WDS in Hyderabad that their staff was fomenting revolution in Ibrahimpatnam. Of the existing WDS staff, Shankaraiah and Buggaiah remained with me, while Gnaneshwari and Satyavathi moved on. Since WDS was an NGO, and received foreign funding, the CPI(M) had a field day in claiming that our movement was a dangerous, foreign-funded imperialist mission sent to destabilize India by creating a rift between peasants and labourers. WDS soon closed its office in Ibrahimpatnam and, ironically, its ten-acre property was bought by Manchireddy Kishan Reddy, who was to emerge as our bitter enemy. He laid out a residential colony on the land and renamed the new colony as Bhoopal Reddynagar, after his father.

The minor success in Cheeded led villagers from elsewhere to come to Shankaraiah, Buggaiah and me, asking us to visit their village. Since I stayed in Gungal, there was a meeting every day in the madiga-wada there. The three of us began visiting the villages where we were invited. We spoke about the two acts—the Minimum Wages Act and the Bonded Labour (Abolition) Act—and the necessity of agricultural labourers to unite if their lives were to improve.

We now had to get the jeetagallu to stand with the agricultural labourers. The practice of jeetam in Ibrahimpatnam clearly violated the provisions of the Bonded Labour (Abolition) Act, 1976, which made it obligatory on the part of the tahsildar to release all bonded labourers and scrap their debts. The persistence of institutionalized bonded labour after the passing of the act was illegal. The tahsildar and the police were given powers to initiate criminal proceedings against landlords who had bonded labourers in their employ.

We listed out all the bonded labourers in the village. This was not easy. Many of them shied away if they saw their names being entered, this mere listing was seen as provoking the rage of the landlords. We explained the process of filing petitions before the revenue authorities, in this case, the tahsildar at Ibrahimpatnam. There was not a single signature in the first few petitions we drew up in Gungal, Nallavelli, Mondigourelli and Gaddamallaigudem—all the labourers having affixed their thumbprints. Initially, the jeetas struck work demanding their rightful minimum monthly wages of Rs 135. When the landlords refused to pay this, we filed a number of petitions under the Bonded Labour (Abolition) Act in the first week of December 1984 before the tahsildar. The petitions were filed by the bonded labourers themselves with Shankaraiah, Buggaiah and me accompanying them to the offices.

▶

Gaddamallaigudem was a village inhabited largely by the

kurma community that tended sheep. It was barely a kilometre from Gungal, the epicentre of our activities at the time. We passed it every day on our way to other villages. Villagers from here initially appeared at our meetings in Gungal. Besides, some Gungal landlords owned land in Gaddamallaigudem and the Gungal bonded labourers knew the Gaddamallaigudem bonded labourers well. All the bonded labourers of Gaddamallaigudem were from the kurma community. The village was important in that it slowly led the kurmas and other Backward Caste people of Ibrahimpatnam taluka to join us. Unlike the madigas, the kurmas were timid and reluctant to come forward in the initial stages. Word of mouth from their relatives was important to them and they did not wish to engage in open meetings with people from other communities. When the Gaddamallaigudem bonded labourers joined us, word slowly spread among their relatives in other villages in the taluka. Most of the bonded labourers in the other three villages were madigas with a smaller but significant number of telagas, mangalis, chakalis and malas.

The labourers then made representations to the Ranga Reddy district collector at his office in Hyderabad. This prompted the Ibrahimpatnam tahsildar to conduct a public enquiry at the gram panchayat offices in the villages. He was furious that someone had bypassed him and complained to a higher authority. The open enquiry, conducted by the tahsildar within fifteen days at the gram panchayat office, set off a backlash and prompted many labourers to retract their demands. They were being pressured on multiple fronts—the village sarpanch and the patwari, an array of big landlords in the gram panchayat office—all haranguing them to back down. Some were too frightened to even appear before the tahsildar. But the few who remained steadfast, about ten to fifteen per village, gave testimony and were formally released. The release notification under the Bonded Labour (Abolition) Act was issued on 10 January 1985.

This was an important event in building self-confidence among the people. Earlier, getting the labourers to the government offices was not easy. People still remembered the time when their fathers and mothers ran away when they heard that a tahsildar was visiting. Traditionally, at least until forty years before the present incident, the main task of the tahsildar was to collect taxes; and then he would take his pick of fowl, goats and women. Over the years, several welfare programmes were introduced by the government, and people were forced to go to the offices. Ration cards, caste and revenue certificates and such paperwork—all of these became hugely important. But the poor never dared to go without a pairvikar, the village lobbyist who navigated them through the process for a commission. Usually, one of the younger sons of a landlord played this role. Over time, educated men from other communities entered the fray as pairvikar. When I was living in Gungal, the dalits there used the services of a baindla (a category among the madigas) youth for their jobs with the local government.

Early in my Ibrahimpatnam years, I heard of a fearless mala leader, Bandi Sriramulu of Nandiwanaparthy, a big village three kilometres west of Yacharam. An ex-armyman, he accompanied fellow dalits to the police station and the mandal office. He was a pairvikar, but someone who did not fear difficult officers or cases. Curious, I sought him out. Sriramulu's father Ramaiah was a bonded labourer in Nandiwanaparthy. Illiterate and orphaned, he was picked up and enrolled in the nizam's army. After the Indian Army took over, Ramaiah returned home in 1948 to graze cattle. To the

west of the village, there is a large Onkareswaraswamy temple
where a monolithic nandi sits opposite the shivalingam in the
sanctum. The village acquired its name from this nandi.

A drama was being held in front of the temple one day. As
usual, the dalits squatted on the ground while the reddys and
brahmins sat on the steps of the temple. Bandi Ramaiah too
sat on the steps. The police patel screamed at him, 'Don't you
have eyes? The patels are present here.' Ramaiah replied, 'If I
am an untouchable, the gods should make me disappear before
your eyes.' He refused to get up and the entire gentry walked
off in a huff to report the matter to the police. Knowing that
Ramaiah had worked in the army, they did not dare to thrash
him then and there. The sub-inspector did not think that the
act deserved a thrashing and let things be. The incident passed
into village folklore. Ramaiah's son Sriramulu was educated
in the local village school. One day, Sriramulu carried lunch
to his father working in the fields. While at it, he fetched water
from the nearby well of a savarna. When he was thrashed for
his impertinence, the boy ran to his father, weeping. Ramaiah
then jumped into the well, clothes and all, shouting, 'If I am
an untouchable, all this water should disappear.' This incident
too became part of folklore.

An incident in 1971 shaped Sriramulu's future. In a hotel
run by a caste Hindu, there were fourteen separate tea glasses—
the seven glasses for the malas were marked yellow and the
seven for the madigas marked red. For six years, Sriramulu took
the glass of tea served to the malas, threw away the tea each
time, and paid up. One day, his mood changed. He drank
the tea and broke all the fourteen glasses. When he asked for
another cup of tea, he was told there were no more glasses. He
then snatched the tea served to a reddy and drank it. A group
of caste Hindus caught him and thrashed him. In the ensuing

fight, Sriramulu took a burning log and smashed all the tea glasses in the hotel. More reddys gathered and beat him with cycle chains and sticks. They threw an unconscious Sriramulu into a disused house. On hearing this, Ramaiah did not go to his son. Instead, he went to the hotel and set it on fire. When a reddy tried to remonstrate with him, he chased him up to his house and beat him too. Only after this did he go to see his injured son.

Three years later, Sriramulu joined the Indian Army. In his ten-year service, he worked as a bulldozer driver in Bangalore, Nagaland and Chandigarh. He returned to the village to join the CPI(M) but left it when the party tried to drive a wedge between a pair of lovers—a kurma girl and a Muslim boy. In 1985, Sriramulu joined us as an active member.

Much of the work at the Sangam involved training our people to walk straight in, take a chair if one was available, and ask what was needed without fear. No more standing with folded hands, no more scratching the head, betraying ignorance or a sense of inferiority, no more sidling behind doors. We gave them specific instructions about how to deal with difficult individuals. When they went to the revenue officer's headquarters and asked for a pahani copy or a caste certificate, the official often asked, 'Why should I give this to you?' The labourers were taught to reply, 'Why should you not give it to me? If you show me that there is some such rule, then I will go away. Otherwise, I will sit here all day.' If the official said, 'Get out,' they were to reply, 'This is not your house, this is a government office and I pay to run it. You are a servant of the government, and I am part owner of this building, not you.'

In the course of time, I noticed that several youths stopped wearing the traditional pancha (a dhoti wound between the legs and usually fastened above the knees) and instead wore trousers when they became leaders. They explained that when they wore trousers, the mandal staff gave them a level of respect they did not when they wore the pancha. This made me think back to my late teens when I wanted to wear trousers and shirts. Back in the 1960s, my family flatly refused. I bought myself a book on sewing, and taught myself to stitch my own trousers. They definitely weren't the best fit but I wore them all the same.

The first set of petitions and official releases which came out in January 1985 paralysed the landlords. The farmhands had been told by the administration not to go to work or repay their debts; instead, they were free to labour for anyone for a wage. They were also given Rs 250 as initial relief by the tahsildar. This was to be supplemented by rehabilitation worth Rs 4,000 in two months. We did not quite understand the value of this rehabilitation initially and allowed the block development officer to purchase buffaloes for the released persons. Very soon, we found that this backfired. The released bonded labourers were taken to a shandy far away, shown some cattle and asked to purchase these. Many of the released labourers were not used to dairy work, caring for buffaloes, milking them and selling the milk. In a short while, the buffaloes were either sold or died.

The farmhands did not quite celebrate this initial victory; perhaps they could not believe that things were moving in their favour at last. There were also a few incidents when landlords got their erstwhile bonded labourers beaten up and demanded that they repay their debts. Rabbani of Nallavelli and Gurram Janga Reddy of Mondigourelli were two of the biggest landlords who took to perpetrating violence. We gave representations to the police, and when the landlords were actually summoned to the police station at Yacharam, the villagers were awestruck. Both Rabbani and Janga Reddy had to visit the police station for three successive days and promise the police that they would desist from intimidating their erstwhile farmhands. The situation at the police stations had been pathetic before this incident. Back in 1984, no non-reddy civilian even entered the police stations at Ibrahimpatnam and Yacharam. Panduranga Reddy of Cherlapatelgudem at Ibrahimpatnam and Madhukar Reddy at Yacharam held sway over the police stations. Panduranga Reddy was the younger brother of erstwhile panchayat samiti president and strongman Yadgiri Reddy, and went around the villages with a rifle slung on his shoulder. He was the pairvikar at the police station for all non-reddys and perhaps for most reddys too. The actual petitioners sat outside the station, handed over money to Panduranga Reddy (or Madhukar Reddy), affixed their signatures on whatever petition he wrote, and waited outside while he went in. Police constables told me that for the last twenty years or so, until 1985 when we entered the scene, all FIRs were penned in the handwritings of these two gentlemen.

The summons of Rabbani and Janga Reddy coincided with the visit of revenue authorities to the villages, who gave a release order to each of the bonded labourers along with the promised relief of Rs 250. There were eighty released bonded labourers in all. With this, the situation quickly changed. Those bonded labourers who had not testified in the first instance now came forward in droves to ask for a second chance. We filed repeat petitions. Bonded labourers from other villages joined in.

At this point, we began facing problems with the

CPI(M). This party had an entrenched vote bank in many Ibrahimpatnam villages. Most of the landowning and rich peasant reddys there belonged to the CPI(M). Govardhan Reddy of the CPI–ML New Democracy group (a breakaway faction of the CP group), then a student in the PDSU (going on to become one of its leaders), also came from Rangapur, one of these villages. Both the CPI(M) and Govardhan criticized me for holding meetings only in the madiga-wada—the ghetto of the madigas—and for setting up labourers against peasants. Why did I not hold meetings in the main villages, the ooru, they asked. Why was I wary of the villagers (by which they meant caste Hindu peasants)? The peasants were also poor, they said, why did I set up labourers against them? Peasants and labourers should live in harmony, we were told. We should demand subsidies in fertilizer and seeds, and ask for redemption of interest on loans: all this talk of higher wages will ruin the farmer–labourer alliance, they said. It was clear to me that the madigas would not feel free to attend meetings in the main village. They were wary, and would not open up. It made sense to meet them in their own territory. I was also sure that there was nothing wrong in agricultural labourers demanding their constitutional dues. Landless labourers were not responsible for the plight of rich (or poor) peasants, nor did the onus of the revolution rest on their shoulders.

Through all this, Bojja Tharakam was a constant support, attending meetings, mobilizing for fact-finding committees and speaking at public gatherings. Along with him were K. Nagaiah, J.B. Raju and Prem Kumar. Nagaiah worked in the state government and was active in several dalit welfare associations, as was J.B. Raju who worked for All India Radio, Hyderabad. Prem Kumar who worked in a public sector undertaking was active in its SC welfare association and was a major leader in the Ambedkar Yuvajana Sangam.

At the outset, the authorities moved quickly in the villages where we presented petitions first, but after some time there was a lull. This was because of resistance and pressure from the landlords and local politicians. The pressure was covert and we did not know much about it. We dealt with the lull in two ways. Salaha organized a fact-finding committee to enquire into the non-release of bonded labourers and gave copies of the report to senior officers and the press. We also organized teams of reporters to visit the villages, to interview the bonded labourers and file their stories. S.R. Sankaran, then secretary of social welfare to the government, was proactive and toured Ibrahimpatnam with the Ranga Reddy district collector. Once again, the government machinery started moving.

The press was an effective tool at our disposal in those days. In the villages, the newspaper was like the Bible. 'Paperlo vacchindi'—the newspaper said this—a phrase that established the truth. Politicians also worried about what was reported in the press. Like others in that time, reporters too had a heart and they walked distances, went without food, and suffered the heat, if they were moved by the plight of the poor. We built up a good rapport with the press. Many of the stalwarts of today started off as cub reporters then. G.S. Vasu was a young reporter in the *Indian Express*, Stanley Theodore and G. Venkateshwarlu of *The Hindu* were greenhorns. The well-established seniors included T. Lakshmipati, R. Akhileshwari and R.J. Rajendra Prasad. Akhileshwari wrote regular stories about the women she met on her visits to Ibrahimpatnam in the *Deccan Herald*. I made periodic rounds of the newspaper bureaus and made good friends with reporters. I had stories to tell and they were great listeners with a heart to help.

With such publicity and optimism, more people in other villages developed confidence in us and came forward. Sangams, small collectives, were formed in each village. Spontaneously, each sangam started its own revolving fund—leaders said that this was one way to maintain unity. The funds in each village ranged from Rs 2,000 to Rs 4,000. These were used for meetings and helping former bonded labourers who were in financial distress. In some villages, the sangams began running chits.

Shankaraiah, Buggaiah and I now began visiting other villages when invited. When I asked the villagers what I was supposed to do, they said, 'Just come. We'll look after everything.' I was often led somewhere, asked to sit in a meeting. They asked me to tell everyone what the law was. After I said my piece, they took their decisions. Slowly, these meetings began to resemble the caste meetings or panchayats of the madigas. Other castes were there too, but the madigas dominated the gathering. Meetings were always held in the madiga-wada. I felt that this was a good thing since the madigas were the least privileged in the village, and may not feel comfortable outside of their own areas. Anyway, madigas made up the majority of the agricultural poor. Madiga caste leaders (kula peddalu) were present to legitimize the gatherings. But they did not take the dais. These were usually people whose names were called out by others. Somebody would say, 'Kishtaiah, you are the man for this,' or 'Chandramma, everyone listens to you.' Sometimes the nominated person backed out, pointing to some overwhelming personal responsibility for a grandson or a granddaughter, cattle that needed grazing every day or simply old age and painful bones. These meetings also had many women. Some were curious to meet me, many came to sit with me and counsel me, sensing that I needed guidance. When the women thronged around me, the men initially shooed them away, telling them not to bother me. I slowly began resisting this and welcomed the women and their questions. I was totally drawn into their warm embrace. They surrounded me when I went to sleep, when I went to shit, when I walked from village to village, and during meetings. During mealtimes, they disappeared miraculously to eat in other houses and not overburden the house where I was asked to eat.

The women who actively participated in the meetings were mostly in their late thirties. They had finished raising their families and settling their children in marriages. Most had grandchildren. Although some were widows, most of those who came forward had husbands who did not object. Some were talkative, garrulous even, some were calm and sedate; all of them were vivacious and beautiful, brave and compassionate. They were quite articulate and could hold their own in any crowd.

One such woman was Elimineti Chandramma from Yacharam. Her husband had died when her two children were babies and she had raised them single-handed, working as the village sweeper at a meagre monthly salary of twenty rupees. 'I did not yield to any man,' she announced proudly to me when we met for the first time, before telling me her life's story. It took me many months to understand the import of what she had said and how difficult it was for a single madiga woman to raise her family and retain her self-respect and identity. Her experiences lent her an unusual maturity and she was always called upon for advice. When the Yacharam bonded labourers struck, it was Chandramma who went to the landlords to inform them how and why the jeetas had struck, and present the charter of demands. Yacharam was an important village for us and we held many future meetings there. Chandramma sat by me for most of these affairs, quietly guiding me, shushing me when she thought prudent and pointing to something I had missed. She explained nuances when they were beyond me.

Chandramma was a most beautiful woman, about forty years old. Her face was lined but serene and smiling. She was lithe in body and graceful beyond compare. She was gentle but could be short when necessary. A ready smile, a generous laugh and twinkling eyes marked her. As our work expanded and led me to more distant villages, I did not meet Chandramma as often as I had earlier. One day, I heard that she had committed suicide. She had had a quarrel with her son with whom she lived and hanged herself from a rafter at night. It was a busy time for me with the agitation for land peaking in Jabbargudem. I was extremely troubled—was there any meaning in what I was doing when I hadn't had time to spare for Chandramma? I wonder about that even today.

Bacchamma of Pethula was another of my self-constituted guardians. Far more vociferous than Chandramma, she was at the forefront of every argument, whatever be the composition of the crowd. Her husband had worked in the railways and so she was privileged among the madigas with a settled monthly income and pension. She was one of those who walked with me to surrounding villages where she had relatives to harangue into joining our union.

The woman I loved the most was Gattu Ramulamma whose framed photograph I retain on my desk. The sheer beauty of the lines of that aged face stuns me even today as does the wise yet sharp gaze of her eyes that pierces through you. She was the oldest among the women I knew. But first a word about her son, Gattu Basha, the leader of the madigas in Eliminedu village that faced the most powerful and wicked Bhoopal Reddy. Basha was one of the sharecroppers whose share was denied to him after the bonded labourers of Eliminedu struck work. One of his brothers had repudiated Basha's debt, so Basha's crop raised over three months stood forfeited to the landlord. Basha was among the more militant people in Eliminedu. He never hesitated to jump into the fray and he was just as careful to assess the situation. I travelled on the pillion of his cycle on many occasions when we had to reach some place quickly, and there was no bus. He moved like the wind. He was slim yet sinewed. Narrow eyes set in a watchful face. A goatee beard that matched his sharp and pointed talk. His was one of the families that suffered enormously due to the Jabbargudem land struggle but he never complained. Basha was pivotal in keeping the quarrelsome Jabbargudem madigas in line, sharply reminding them that they had gained land while the Eliminedu madigas had suffered for them.

Basha's mother Ramulamma was totally free of household responsibilities, and attached herself to me, accompanying me to other villages. Her children had great-grandchildren, that is, she had five descendant generations. Girls had their first child when they were thirteen years old, so a young woman of twenty-six often had a grandchild. Ramulamma could count a descendant in every village we visited. She told me of the hard times she had faced. She was married young like everybody else, but her husband had died early, leaving the young widow to raise the children by herself. She remembers sieving freshly picked paddy fields to pick up leftovers like the voddla pilli, the tiny weeds that infest paddy, to cook for her children. Lacking clothes, she often stitched sacks together for a sari. Yet, she said, she never gave in to the lust of another

The woman I loved the most was Gattu Ramulamma

man as widows often did to support themselves. Her hair was still black and she could thread a needle with ease.

Ramulamma was old enough to often forget things. Apart from advising me how to dress, how to talk, how not to get angry, and how to view complex village affairs, she sometimes forgot whom she was talking to and would tell me about Gitamma, the young woman who walked about the villages to support the madigas. Who doesn't like hearing nice things about oneself?

Chandramma, Bacchamma, Ramulamma and several other women were my mentors in Ibrahimpatnam. They took the time to explain things to me and argued about what was the right thing to do. On one occasion, the daughter-in-law of a reddy household in Peddathundla committed suicide by jumping into a well. It was rumoured that her husband was complicit in allowing his father sexual access to her. My blood boiled and I was all for running to that village, talking to and mobilizing women of the village against the father-in-law. 'No,' said our women. 'Leave well alone. We cannot help those women unless they repudiate their men. If we interfere, the reddy men and women will unite and beat us up.' We argued and argued but I always heeded their advice.

In the early days, it took little to shock me. Stark poverty stared at me in some households. People would point to a house and say, 'The hearth in that home has not been lit for three days.' What did the children of that house do? Neighbours called them over and fed them. Neighbours tried to send over food, but not so often as to offend the family's dignity. I attended weddings where the bride brought only a mat, one brass lota and a few aluminium vessels, and one pair of clothes as katnam (dowry). Guests were served rice and pacchipulusu—raw tamarind soup with chopped raw onions and green chillies. I observed weddings with keen interest, watching those who attended, the clothes they wore, the baindla priest who conducted the rituals, the curious children who thronged the space, and those who watched me.

11 Stripping the master of his whip

The villagers were uniting. The three of us, Shankaraiah, Buggaiah and I, were working well together with enthusiasm. We needed to take this forward. We couldn't function loosely any more—we needed an organization, we needed to call ourselves something, we needed to present ourselves to the state as a legal entity, we needed a platform to represent ourselves to those outside our constituency, we needed to think of ourselves as something more than our individual selves.

In March 1985, we registered the Ibrahimpatnam Taluka Vyavasaya Coolie Sangam (the Ibrahimpatnam Taluka Agricultural Labourers' Union) or ITVCS as a trade union with the labour department. Amongst ourselves, we simply called it Sangam. We did not want to be an NGO, and a trade union was the right fit. A trade union that represented agricultural labourers and could take up questions of wages, forced work and compensation.

It was not an easy process. Any entity needs rules, a charter and a manifesto. I drew these up in consultation with Cyril, Buggaiah and Shankaraiah. When we first made the rules as we thought sensible, the department clerks at the labour office refused to register the union. We had to finally allow them to draft the rules as they saw fit (and even pay them a bribe). In its first meeting, sometime in March, the union followed the formal rules of electing office bearers (Shankaraiah was the president and I the general secretary) but our general body meetings were really village meetings. Everyone attended and elections were by general consensus. They became like an extension of a meeting presided over by the kula peddalu—the caste elders. When we enrolled members, each got an identity card, proclaiming their membership to ITVCS, their name and registration number. The card was an important part of their identity. They showed it everywhere—when they went to the mandal office or the collectorate. They were more careful when they went to the police station, because showing the card there often meant a beating.

Soon after we registered the union, N.T. Rama Rao's Telugu Desam Party government announced the formation of the mandal system on 25 May 1985. The mandal revenue office is unique to Andhra Pradesh: each district is divided into several administrative units called mandals, and the MRO is vested with the same powers and functions as were tahsildars of erstwhile talukas, including magisterial powers. NTR also abolished the post of the hereditary patwari. The patwari now became the village assistant, and continued in the post on pay scales fixed by the government. Each village assistant now looked after five to six villages. The erstwhile Ibrahimpatnam taluka was now divided into the five mandals of Ibrahimpatnam, Manchal, Yacharam, Maheswaram and Kandukur.

Our focus at this time was in Yacharam, but we had work in all the other mandals too. The mandal system proved more people-friendly when compared to the tahsil system. The tahsildar was a powerful man ruling over a large area. He was a gazetted officer, and that term had a powerful connotation to everyone. Gazetted officers are executive/managerial-level public servants and their authority to issue an official stamp comes from the president of India or the governors of states. The new mandal revenue officer could be a gazetted officer, but most often was not. The newly appointed MROs were usually young men (and less often, women) who had not yet learnt how to terrify poor people with a look, or less. Before, people from far-flung villages had to spend two days to visit the tahsil office because there was no bus for them to return to their village the same day. Now, a mandal office visit could be done in a day.

By June 1985, ITVCS had four full-timers—Shankaraiah, Buggaiah, Ramulu and myself. The three of them received Rs 450 per month (plus actuals for travel), while I had a Sruti fellowship of Rs 500 per month. Sruti is a Delhi-based non-profit running fellowship programmes since 1983 for young activists in the age group of twenty-five and thirty-five. I never drew any income from ITVCS or HBT from 1984 to 1998 and paid for my Gungal room myself. Our total monthly budget was about Rs 2,000. We had little travel expenses because we cycled or walked. We were fed by villagers so there was little other expense. In 1988, I became an Ashoka fellow and received a princely sum of Rs 3,000 every month from 1988 to 1992. The fellowship is given for what in NGO-speak is called 'social entrepreneurship'.

Things were happening at a rapid pace at that time. Wages were rising, I was part of this euphoric movement, but nothing was in my hands. I was a symbol. People saw me as an instrument. Such a beginning proved good for me. Decision making had not been given to me, so I did not have to exercise control and was never burdened by it in the days to come. Programmes were never decided in small meetings of a few worthies. These were taken only in big village meetings where the entire population of the poor turned up and where intense discussions and quarrels took place. Some sessions lasted hours, meandering towards irrelevance. But a consensus emerged miraculously out of the seeming confusion. It took about four years before I truly became part of the decision-making process. Till then, I was always asked to shut up by the local leaders.

The perceptions the villagers had of me never bothered me while I was there. They liked me, I liked them. Never again did I have to pay for a meal. I was invited to eat in every madiga house. In some years, when I became a 'leader', some madiga leaders, particularly Mantri Ramulu of Manchal, tried to get me to dress and posture in a certain way—like Indira Gandhi. I was too far gone in a general rejection of propriety. I used to wear salwar kameez in the beginning, and had long plaited hair and a small bottu (bindi) on my forehead, without jewellery of any kind. The villagers saw that I spoke authoritatively to the higher officers (the tahsildar or the circle inspector of police) in English; I was not deferential to them. They concluded that I came from some privilege. They saw that I was kind to them and especially concerned about their women and children. I did not sit on a chair when others sat on the ground. I did not eat what others did not have on their plate. I followed their instructions in most things. I was mostly listening and asking. They adopted me and took me into their hearts. In India, we have the mother/goddesss–prostitute binary categorization of women. I too was slowly assigned the matronly role.

Back then I was still a quiet, background character, and the movement spread far by the sheer will of the people. Several new villages filed petitions under the Bonded Labour (Abolition) Act. In the meantime, we did not wait for the MRO to release the bonded labourers; we encouraged them to stop work themselves. This led to considerable outrage on the part of the landlords who demanded their money back. Quoting the law, the bonded labourers refused to both repay the loan and return to work. As a consequence, they found it difficult to get regular work. Many families made it thanks to their wives' earnings. Several labourers had to seek employment in other villages.

Throughout this period, we held a number of meetings and demonstrations, both at the mandal level and at the district collectorate. The MROs reacted differently in different places. Most of them pleaded ignorance of the act and so I had to carry printouts that I could hand over. They said they only followed the copies of laws given to them by the government. Some contested the occurrence of bonded labour saying that since the labourers were given monthly wages, they could not be bonded. One MRO on an enquiry in a village went to the extent of threatening the labourers with arrest if they continued to boycott work.

Such bullheadedness meant that we had to seek relief from a higher authority. We filed a writ petition in the high court, asking it to direct the authorities to enquire into the petitions that had been submitted by the bonded labourers. The government machinery was again forced to move. Our reporter friends again came to our rescue, publicizing the events widely.

While this was happening, we organized the labourers to file petitions for recovery of back wages before the deputy commissioner of labour. The Bonded Labour (Abolition) Act confined itself to releasing the labourers and providing rehabilitation while the Minimum Wages Act provided for the recovery of back wages if the wage paid was below the minimum. Further, those cases where particular MROs did release labourers from their illegal bonds were helpful as evidence in claiming the back wages. Women of the villages who used to work in the landlords' courtyards or houses as domestic labourers for a pittance were also mobilized to file recovery petitions, calculated on the basis of the time spent daily and the actual amount received. According to law, the onus of proof is on the employer who has to be able to prove that he or she has maintained records, paid minimum wages and so on. If the landlord could not prove (by means of registers and salary slips) that he was paying the minimum wage, the jeeta could be awarded the difference in wages of six months to one year. When this became clear, many landlords were open to compromise.

Registration under the Trade Union Act entitles the union to present its case directly through the affected worker or through the union representative without the mediation of a lawyer. This has been utilized by all the organized trade unions in the urban sector. The organized trade unions, to give them their due, have transformed the arena of the labour courts into a comparatively people-friendly one. Workers and employers were provided similar benches to sit, the office was open to workers and their representatives at all times, and the staff did not patronize or abuse workers. I do not know if this practice continues today.

Our proceedings in the labour court in Hyderabad initially, and later in Ibrahimpatnam, were hilarious. As an official (general secretary) of the Sangam, I was entitled to participate in the proceedings and serve as an advocate. The landlords were represented by a high-profile lawyer called Satyaveera Reddy. We filled the benches provided in the court, while the landlords preferred to stand, sometimes for hours, because they could not bear to sit next to the labourers. The landlords' lawyers could not, unlike us, be present at every hearing thanks to their preoccupation with other civil or criminal cases where they got most of their money. In time, we requested the court to have its proceedings in the Ibrahimpatnam inspection bungalow which was more accessible to the labourers. Here, hundreds of our villagers were able to attend and the landlords had to pass through rows of jeering women and men to get to the court.

In most hearings, the landlords tried to prove that the labourers in question had not worked with them, and we argued the opposite. We asked the landlords how much land they had, how many labourers they engaged to cultivate it, and most importantly, to show their registers of employees. Labour laws make the maintenance of registers mandatory. The landlords could not show how they cultivated their land and had no registers to show the name and number of labourers under their employ. I barely followed any of the expected court decorum since I didn't know any better. The landlords' advocates were always outraged by this, while the mild deputy commissioner of labour, Madhusudan Reddy, who presided over the hearings, could only advise me; he seemed to be sympathetic to our cause. I was particularly unruly and freewheeling where examinations-in-chief and cross-examinations were concerned. I often rattled the landlords with targeted questions.

As per the Evidence Act, 'examination-in-chief' is conducted upon a witness by the party that calls the witness for giving evidence; the examination of that witness by the adverse party is called 'cross-examination'. The labourers were equally unruly when they were examined, during both examinations-in-chief and cross-examinations. Added to that, their language was not refined. They used 'dengadam'— 'fuck' and its spectacular variants—frequently, stunning the landlords' advocate into silence. Madhusudan Reddy gently remonstrated with the witness but this happened so frequently that he simply gave up after a point.

Our witnesses recounted a number of incidents to prove that they had worked with the landlords in question, leaving no doubt in anybody's minds that the landlord's stand was fraudulent. Never had the reddy advocates been forced to tolerate such forthright madigas. After a few sessions, the advocate of the landlords resigned his vakalat in disgust, refusing to argue cases against yokels. The landlords were now unrepresented, and no advocate was willing to risk his self-respect in such an unruly court. This led many of the landlords to then start compromising. We won in all the cases that were not already compromised through out-of-court negotiations. Several thousand rupees exchanged hands, with the labourer profiting this time. We later went on to file workmen's compensation cases too and won spectacular victories. All accidents—snake bites at the well, collapse of a house during construction, accidents during work—were covered under the archaic Workmen's Compensation Act of 1923. All in all, the labour court was a wonderful place.

We also tried hard to get the labour officers to do their actual job of inspecting the shops and fields, enquiring about the wages and timings, filing cases and seeing them through. Each assistant labour officer had about three mandals under him, but with no provision for secretarial assistance, stationery or transport. While most labour officers were happy to collect their 'monthly' from the shops, some were proactive. We got them to file cases under the Minimum Wages Act and ensured that they had stationery and help in moving from place to place.

If you consider the actual material gains from today's standpoint, our victories may appear small. However, to us, they meant the world was changing, the ground beneath us was shifting. In an undated note from June 1985, I mention the following as our accomplishments:

Amount recovered [back wages facilitated by the labour department]: Rs 17,880
Bonded debts written off: Rs 61,220

Relief for bonded labourers released by government:
Rs 20,700 (@Rs 500 each)
Rehabilitation @ Rs 4,000 each = Rs 3,00,000
[implies seventy-five bonded labourers released till
that time]

Since most of the jeetas and agricultural labourers were
madigas, the attitude of the majority of the other marginalized
castes was one of passive solidarity. They admired the way we
fought the landlords. They were watching and waiting to see
who would emerge stronger—the madigas supported by the
Sangam or the reddys.

We filed petitions with the revenue authorities and the
police to prosecute the landlords employing bonded labourers
and not simply stop at the fulfilment of welfare measures.
At this, the landlords of Yacharam and surrounding villages
filed a petition in 1985 in the Andhra Pradesh High Court,
challenging Section 12 of the Bonded Labour (Abolition)
Act dealing with the prosecution of those keeping bonded
labourers. Justice Sardar Ali Khan passed an interim order
staying further prosecutions under the act and this was vacated
later by us. The same year, on 25 July, the Ibrahimpatnam
taluka panchayat samiti passed a resolution voicing concern
over the fallout of the implementation of the Bonded Labour
(Abolition) Act. The resolution, in a reference to ITVCS,
said that some extremist forces were at work, dividing the
farmers and the labourers. The samiti resolution warned
the government that if the bonded labour business was not
reviewed, it might affect agricultural production in the area
as farmers were finding it increasingly difficult to engage any
labour for their operations. Samiti president Yadgiri Reddy
went on record to claim that 90 per cent of the cases were

bogus. The landlords led by Yadgiri Reddy and the district minister went in torn clothes to chief minister NTR to complain about our work and tell him about their distress and that they were being forced to cease agricultural operations. This was publicized widely in newspaper reports. During NTR's tenure, he had designated one minister for each district to supervise and monitor both government and TDP activities. On a visit to Cherlapatelgudem in early 1986, the district minister and minister for labour P. Indra Reddy, who was active in the PDSU between 1973 and 1975 and had gone to jail during the Emergency, told labourers who were on strike for higher wages, 'You must not ask for minimum wages in the dry areas. All demand for minimum wages should be made only in irrigated areas.'

Such foolishness meant that I spent most of my time in Ibrahimpatnam, returning to Hyderabad once in a rare while. In September 1985, when I was back in the city one such time, something happened which was to cast a blight on my life for several decades. Stree Shakti Sanghatana was a feminist group in Hyderabad that started in the late 1970s and continued till the late 1980s when it split into two different NGOs—the Anveshi Research Centre for Women's Studies and the Asmita Resource Centre for Women. Several of its members were my friends, including K. Lalita, whom I counted as my best friend. I had known her from my university days. She, Cyril and I had stayed together during the Emergency and also after 1980 when we returned to Hyderabad from Ghaziabad. Though I was in agreement with their politics and was friends with many of its members, I had been on the fringes of the feminist group, both because I was busy with HBT work and I was uncomfortable with the group's insistence on discussions only in English and on problems concerning educated women.

Still, we had cordial relations and I worked with them on the book *Savaalaksha Sandehaalu*, a Telugu version of *Our Bodies, Ourselves* in 1984 and 1985.

On 21 September 1985, Lalita called me up to say that she was coming to our house to 'demand' an explanation from Cyril about two issues, only one of which was discussed that day. Stree Shakti Sanghatana wanted the leading feminist Marxist writer, Ranganayakamma, to write the foreword to the Telugu translation of the book *We Were Making History: Women and the Telangana Uprising*, and she had refused to do so if HBT was to publish it. Ranganayakamma's grouse was with the George Reddy Book Trust, which Cyril headed. He had refused to send some copies by airmail to the US on her request, of the Telugu translation of *China Since Mao* by Charles Bettelheim (of France's New Left), which she had translated and GRBT had published. Often the most trivial matter can rouse great passion. Ranganayakamma and GRBT had agreed to six author copies. When she wanted the six copies shipped abroad, Cyril asked her to bear the expensive postage. We all worked on shoestring budgets. She refused. GRBT didn't send the books, and the relationship between Ranganayakamma and GRBT soured and ceased. Ranganayakamma conflated the GRBT with HBT, which I headed, and refused to write the foreword for *We Were Making History*. Angered that Cyril's earlier fracas was causing problems for them now, Lalita wanted answers.

I told Lalita that she could neither 'demand' an explanation nor would Cyril give one if demanded. She said she was coming anyway. Inampudi Rambabu, who headed an NGO in Chintalapudi that worked with adivasis to help them retrieve land from coastal Andhra settlers, and I were at home with Cyril. When Lalita arrived, late morning, after some perfunctory conversation, she did what she had come to do: demand an explanation. She was not satisfied with Cyril's reply and asked him what kind of a Marxist he was. He said he didn't claim to be one. Hot words ensued. Lalita was aggressive in tone and language, 'You have to give me a reply,' she demanded in a raised voice. Cyril asked her to get out if she was just going to keep haranguing him. She refused, saying, 'It is Gita'a house, you get out,' and turned to me to ask, 'How can you live with such an animal. He should be put into a mental asylum ....' Wham! Cyril threw her handbag at her. In turn, she called him a bastard. At this, he called her a whore. All of us rose, Rambabu and I to restrain Cyril. Lalita got to her feet and shouted at him. He threw a chappal at her, and they continued to abuse each other. In the melee, he kicked her.

Thereupon, Rambabu took Cyril out of the room and I took Lalita to another room where we sat for about twenty minutes. I tried to console her. I specifically asked her if she had been hit by the things Cyril had thrown wildly towards her. She said no. We promised to meet each other later in the evening. And so she left.

That afternoon, Rambabu, Cyril and I went out to clear the air. Rambabu and I were late for some reason and Cyril was the first to get home by dusk. He was greeted by ten members of Stree Shakti Sanghatana accompanied by Lalita, sitting on our doorstep. He asked them to come in. They entered and within a minute, they fell on him: they threw water mixed with chilli powder into his eyes, and beat him with sticks and broomsticks. They broke the light bulbs and the glass cut him further. We reached home while all this was happening. Vasanth, one of the women from the Stree Shakti group, turned towards me dramatically and said, 'Here is one more blow for you, Gita,' and struck Cyril with a stick. As they left, they trashed the moped Cyril and I rode, slashing the seats and breaking the handlebar. This was even more upsetting; many of them were salaried women with cars and rich husbands. We had purchased the moped with hard-earned Rs 4,000, a huge sum for us in those days.

Over the week, the canard was spread that Cyril had been beating me and the SSS was 'saving' me. After that, some mutual friends, Kancha Ilaiah and Narendranath convened a meeting with them which Manohar, a Salaha member and a lawyer, also attended. A compromise was worked out. Shortly, all ten accompanied by Ilaiah and Naren came at a fixed time to our house, sat on a bench, and said, 'We are sorry for what we did.' Cyril replied, 'I am sorry for what I did.' That was all that was said, and they left immediately. I did not enter the room but stood in the inner doorway. I wanted no part in this charade. Lalita was my best friend in the morning but was no longer the same by evening. She had brought down a mob to attack my husband and ransack my house. My own friends had come into my house and done unspeakable things without a word of warning to me.

From 1985, for more than a decade, the necessary political correctness of supporting newly emerging and aggressive feminists ensured that our long-standing friends were divided into two groups. The majority supported Lalita; Cyril was dubbed as a violent maniac, Gita, a doormat. Many of our ex-comrades had joined NGOs and Lalita's wealthy husband Vithal Rajan had fostered many of them. No one asked me what happened. We were not invited to get-togethers when friends came from outside and not even to weddings. Within the space of a day, I had lost many of my friends. This troubled me enough for me to discuss it with my Sangam colleagues and some villagers at a meeting in Gungal to get a sense of what they thought. My friend Shantha Sinha also attended the meeting. They commiserated and this helped me to calm down. Over the years, some of the husbands of these women apologized to me, which left me baffled. Their wives hadn't, and the husbands were certainly not responsible. What were they apologizing for?

This incident impacted my marriage in several ways. I felt Cyril's humiliation deeply—here was a man who had stepped into knife fights with ABVP cadres even when overwhelmed in numbers, but who had stayed his hand when my friends attacked him. He could have hit them all back within five seconds, but did not do so because it would have worsened the situation. Whenever I met any of them, usually for work, he used to say, 'They attacked me mercilessly as if I was their enemy, yet you meet them.' In 1993, when two of them wished to visit me after my first and only child was born, he agreed silently but stepped out of the house for the duration of their visit. Till he died, he could never understand why they did what they did. The one word 'sorry' had not assuaged his grief and humiliation.

As long as Cyril was alive, this matter did not trouble me as much as it does now, because it was something that primarily concerned him. He had a short temper, was often rude, and had certainly behaved badly with Lalita. But what wrong had I done to invite the attack on my house and my subsequent boycott? How could my feminist friends come to my house, not behave as guests should, and attack my partner violently? What was the burden of my own feminism on my dead husband? What kind of friendship was this and what kind of human beings were they to abandon me in a matter of a few hours? I had virtually no family—they were my family and they had done this to me? The issue continues to remain the elephant in the room. When I began writing this book, I brought it up with two of them, who apologized, but refused to discuss it.

Our larger circle of friends never referred to this incident and it was quietly buried away. Cyril and I had never revealed the details of the incident to them, and all they knew was that Cyril had struck Lalita for no reason. I continued to meet the women of this group after 1998 when they had work with HBT. I became close to Veena Shatrughna after she helped me out of post-partum depression. I slowly forgot the episode but after Cyril died in 2016, the bitterness in me resurfaced though our larger circle of friends is embarrassed about the fault line among us. Forget the past, they say; they tell me to move on. I did not include this episode in the first draft of this book, as I thought that this embarrassing pain should not be spoken about. But if I could write about my sister being beaten by her husband, and about the Naxalite group to which I belonged and to which some of my dear friends still belong, why should I conceal the part of the hidden history of the feminists of Hyderabad which impacted my life so dreadfully?

12 The Sun who bled on the fields of Karamchedu

Working in Ibrahimpatnam and seeing the arrogance of the landlords had not prepared me for what happened in Karamchedu in 1985. When I opened the newspaper on 18 July 1985 and saw the headlines, "Six dalits chased and axed to death in Karamchedu", I was shocked. Karamchedu is among the bigger villages in Chirala taluka of Prakasam district. It is home to Daggubati Chenchuramaiah, father-in-law of N.T. Rama Rao's daughter, Purandeswari, who later became a minister in the Manmohan Singh–led cabinet in 2009 and joined the BJP in 2014. Karamchedu and the villages around it are dominated by the kamma community. They form the agrarian gentry and are the dominant caste in coastal Andhra, where they own most of the land, even though they have migrated in large numbers towards the interior and southern regions of the Indian peninsula, both to newly irrigated areas and to the cities. They occupied key political and economic positions in undivided Andhra Pradesh and continue to dominate the sectors of agriculture, real estate, healthcare, cinema, television, newspapers and information technology in both the Telugu states.

On 16 July, a kamma youth, Pothini Sreenu, washed his buffalo near the steps of the water tank that dalits used for drinking, dirtying the water. A dalit youth, Katthi Chandraiah, standing nearby, upbraided Pothini Sreenu who reacted by beating him with his cattle whip. A dalit woman, Suvartha, who had come to fetch water, saw the incident and asked Sreenu, 'Why are you beating him?' Infuriated at this, Pothini Sreenu aimed his cattle whip at her. She raised her water pot to resist the blow. This act of simple resistance led to the kammas uniting to attack the madiga colony from all sides, destroying their property and chasing them into the fields to attack them with sticks, axes and spears.

That day, we heard a first-hand account on the telephone at Tharakam's house where we had gone as soon as we heard the news. The dalits had fled en masse to the nearest town Chirala, which was eight kilometres away, where they took refuge in a church and were fed by the local dalits. One of these locals immediately telephoned Tharakam and told him what had happened. Katthi Padma Rao from Ponnur was the first to reach Chirala and meet the stunned victims. My first visit, two or three days after the massacre, was a learning experience. Tharakam and Cyril were with the others in a closed space, talking with the victims to prepare the case. The Karamchedu people were in the vast church compound. Some stayed with their relatives close by. This was not the time or place for me to ask questions. Men had been killed, one of them brutally, by twisting a spear into his groin, women had been raped and scores of people had been brutally beaten up. Groups of people were sitting about quietly, sometimes talking, sometimes still. There was wailing from some groups. I went to the place where the church opened to the road and found lorry after lorry rolling in with rice and provisions. Talking to those accompanying the lorries, I found that they were dalits from other villages and towns, some of them as far as two hundred kilometres away. They did not know any of the Karamchedu dalits but had come here and brought the provisions in solidarity. I knew of left solidarity, but that was a kind of cultivated solidarity. This dalit solidarity stemmed from the accident of birth. For the first time, I had an inkling of what Ambedkar's mission had created among the dalits.

Salaha organized a fact-finding mission within a week

and I was a part of this. This was the first fact-finding mission for the incident and Salaha published its report immediately. Others in the team were the independent and radical communist leader Kolla Venkaiah, Prof D. Narasimha Reddy, Shantha Sinha and R. Akhileshwari. The small booklet, *Karamchedu 1985*, was the first publication on the massacre and is a widely cited source. It was because Kolla Venkaiah was with us (he was a kamma) that we even got the kammas to talk to us. They denied all knowledge of the incident. We met the local dealer of Enfield Bullet motorcycles and learnt that there were about four hundred such bikes in Karamchedu. The kammas were wealthy. But it was not as if the madigas of Karamchedu were poor, especially considering the standards in Ibrahimpatnam. There was a tahsildar among them and several government employees. Why did the developed coastal areas which benefited from the Green Revolution see such extraordinary violence perpetrated on the dalits?

Part of the reason is that when N.T. Rama Rao came to power, kamma arrogance rose to incredible heights. When N.T. Rama Rao visited the victims of Karamchedu at a hospital with fruits and flowers, he was not allowed by the dalits to address them. Veeramma of Karamchedu who saw her son get beaten up said, 'Ayya, after you became the chief minister, they made us their targets. We are now shattered, our families are broken, and drowned in blood.'

In the 1960s, the old feudal ties were broken, and there rose a new market-oriented class of agrarian kamma gentry, which enriched itself during the process of agrarian development and diversified into a wide range of non-agricultural economic activities opened up by the overall economic development. This class could not tolerate any dissension or challenge from the labouring castes, particularly the dalits. At the same time, dalits were participants in economic development; their children were getting educated, employed, and exposed to different environments where caste did not matter in the ways it did in the village. Dalits were not willing to stand by getting insulted and humiliated day after day. Kammas, who could not tolerate the slightest dissent from dalits, now saw a brewing change in social relations. The slightest 'provocation' saw them respond with terrible fury.

Reportage on the Karamchedu killings saw new ground being broken. Caste, not class alone, was highlighted. For the first time, the Telugu press declared that 'kamma' landlords had assaulted and killed 'madiga' labourers. The issue of caste was centre-staged and those who sidestepped it with classical Marxist jargon were hauled up. The PWG was criticized roundly for releasing a pamphlet headlined, 'Landlords attack Karamchedu Harijans'.

From the Chirala church compound, the Karamchedu victims shifted to four or five newly erected tent houses called shibirams which became the primary centres of the dalit protest movement. It was called Vijayanagar, the city of victory, in defiance of victimhood. The tents were not intended for individual families, but were large structures where everyone stayed together in a rare demonstration of continued solidarity. They ate from a community kitchen, and slept together at night. These large tents remained till the Andhra Pradesh government conceded to the demands of the dalits and granted them housing units here along with a rehabilitation package for the whole community.

Tharakam and Cyril made several trips to the Vijayanagar camp. I accompanied them on some occasions when I had less work in Ibrahimpatnam. While they were busy preparing the legal case, I moved around in the camp and visited different households. I spent time with Duddu Sulochana who was raped and lost her husband Ramesh; with Alisamma, a key witness in the case (who died mysteriously a year later); with Tella Jedson's family and with Bhagat Singh who later married Sulochana. Even in such turmoil, they were large-hearted, brave souls. They faced a terrible enemy and did not flinch.

We collected money and provisions for the Karamchedu dalits and some members of our Sangam visited the camp at Vijayanagar to hand these over. We visited in batches, each batch having nine to ten members from the Sangam. Never having visited the coastal areas, Jogu Jangamma and Elimineti Chandramma, with whom I went, were amazed at its prosperity. At the same time, they were shocked that such atrocities could occur unchecked. They said they were poor but such an outrage never occurred in their villages. It is true that Telangana has never seen the kind of mass atrocities that the dalits of the coastal area are subjected to. The reasons could be many: the lack of a rapid rise in agricultural productivity and the accent on market relations that the coastal areas saw; the effect of the series of militant peasant rebellions such as the Telangana peasant revolt of the 1940s; a lack of unity among the reddys, unlike the kammas. The madigas and the reddys of Telangana have a closer relationship than one assumes. The reddys often call the madigas their younger brothers. The reddys dominate the village space only because of the physical strength they derive from their madiga underlings.

The movement in support of the Karamchedu dalits went on apace. The Dalit Mahasabha was formed in September 1985 at a meeting in Chirala to give shape and structure to this new movement. A 'Chalo Chirala' call was given and three lakh people from all over the state converged here. I had never seen such a massive gathering before, a gathering that spoke in one voice. When the great poet and singer Gaddar inaugurated the meeting with his new song, '*Dalitapululamma, Karamchedu Bhooswamulatone Kalabadi, nilakadi Poruchesina, Dalitapululamma*' (We are Dalit Tigers, my dear, tigers that bravely stood up and fought the Karamchedu landlords), I had goose pimples. The meeting saw the stage reserved exclusively for dalits: no savarnas, howsoever sympathetic, were allowed on the dais. So also with the Dalit Mahasabha; no savarnas were allowed to become office-bearers, they could remain ordinary members.

The Karamchedu carnage changed the face of Andhra Pradesh subaltern politics. Dalits and other marginalized communities strode forth to occupy the canvas of subaltern politics confidently. Other actors like the various left parties and factions now had to face the questions related to caste upfront. There could be no more hiding or evasion. That this took place at a time when the powerful kammas were consolidating their hold over the state through N.T. Rama Rao and later his son-in-law Chandrababu Naidu was not a mean feat. The press at that time was largely controlled by the kammas with the largest circulated Telugu daily, *Eenadu*, helmed by Ramoji Rao, as the most powerful voice. The large publishing houses (Visalaandhra Book House, Prajashakti Book House, Ashok Book Centre, Navodaya Publishers, Sri Raghavendra Publishers) too were controlled by them, as was the sizable Telugu-language film industry. Manufacturing, real estate and the hospital sectors were all in their domain. That the dalit movement could grow in the face of such entrenched opposition speaks of the mood of the times. This movement became the backdrop for our own work in Ibrahimpatnam and lent mighty strength to it. At no time did I feel that our struggle—whether it was the larger dalit movement in Andhra Pradesh or our own small movement in Ibrahimpatnam—was leading nowhere. We may have been losing battles, but we were winning the war. We were sustaining ourselves and changing our destinies.

Prior to Karamchedu, my own focus on the madigas of Ibrahimpatnam was hazy. I felt that meetings must be held in the madiga-wada as they were the least privileged and poorest in the village. But Karamchedu and the discussions around it brought a class–caste perspective to me. And this wasn't merely about tokenism or carrying out some ritualistic performances. From 1985 onwards, we circulated Ambedkar texts translated into Telugu, we mobilized our people to attend the several meetings held in Hyderabad to commemorate both his death and birth anniversaries. We celebrated Ambedkar Jayanti every year in both Ibrahimpatnam and Yacharam. We also encouraged the educated youth of this area to attend Ambedkarite meetings in Hyderabad and elsewhere to help build solidarity with similarly inclined people. I was not yet reading Ambedkar seriously. I virtually read nothing at all between 1984 and 1992. After all, where was the time? To me, work in the field was all that mattered back then, not theory.

13 Breaking bondage with one rupee a month

By 1985, the basic organizational structure of ITVCS was beginning to set itself. The bedrock of the union was its full-timers. These were young men, aged between eighteen and thirty-five, who had been educated up to the high school level and mostly from the madiga community. Shankaraiah and Buggaiah were the first to join. Shankaraiah, a telaga, is an inquisitive man with great insight. He stayed till the end with the Sangam and was its president all through. He continues to be active locally and served as sarpanch of his village, Cheeded, in recent years. Buggaiah, a mala from Jalalmiyapalle, worked with us for a short period and went on to join the Shramik Vidyapeeth when Shantha headed it. He was sharp as a tack, but there was criticism from madiga youth that he did not encourage them. I brushed these aside at that time and only understood the import of these early criticisms later after the Madiga Dandora movement for categorization of sub-castes came up in Andhra Pradesh. Buggaiah died an early death in 2013.

Pandi Maisaiah, a madiga from Cherlapatelgudem was illiterate when he joined us and went on to learn to read and write and pass the class seven board exams. He had five daughters; he kept having children since he wanted a son (he did have two later), and we often teased him about this. He was quite sociable, made quick touchdowns in villages, and was one of our active and well-liked colleagues. Pandi Maisaiah and I were the ones who invariably had police cases on us. He died in 2018 after a paralytic stroke. Kunti Ramulu, a madiga from Hasmatpura, is a natural activist. Crippled in one leg after a lorry accident, he lived by his wits and made his living as a pairvikar till he joined us. His limp—kunti in Telugu—became his first name. After he went to Jaipur and had a Jaipur Foot fitted, he walked without his stick. When he wished to escape from a difficult situation, he would lift his trouser leg and say, 'Look! I am lame!' Ramulu was the mediator among us. Whenever there were differences between Sangam members, he eased the tensions. He was popular among women and older folks because he explained issues simply and clearly. All in all, the group was full of cheerful, happy young men. They were cautious but were glad to be part of and lead an initiative to change the world around them, particularly to dethrone the hated reddys.

Many youths joined us to work in an active capacity and some went on to work full-time. Gandu Narasimha, a madiga from Meerkhanpet, joined us after his village took up the question of land rights. He was clear-headed and eloquent, and rose to become an important leader in the Dappu Collective which was founded in 1996. The dappu is a leather drum made and played by the madiga; its name is derived from the simple dap-dap sound it produces. Traditionally, the dappu was used for village announcements (called dandora) and was an instrument of communication from the rulers (kings/landlords/modern governments). From being an instrument with a ritually sanctioned role, by the mid-1990s, the dappu marked its presence at all political meetings with the rise of the Dandora movement (and the Madiga Reservation Porata Samiti that demanded the sub-categorization of reservation). The Dappu Collective had about a hundred NGOs as members with a particular focus on dalits. Jogu Krishna, a madiga from Yacharam, was extraordinarily gifted in music and dance. Affable and jolly, he was liked by everyone. There were others who worked for short periods—Ramachandraiah, a madiga from Gungal, Baindla Ramulu, a madiga from Meerkhanpet, Yacharam Anjaiah, a madiga from Jabbargudem, and more.

Most of the full-timers drew their salaries from the non-formal education programmes we had set up. They doubled up as supervisors in this initiative. The NFE programme had meagre government funds to provide education for children who had been freed from bonded labour. For the others, we raised money from well-wishers in Hyderabad. Most continued to live in their own villages but spent at least three nights a week in some other village. Except for Shankaraiah who rode a moped (and later Lingaiah when he joined us), the others made do with public transport and walking. Before they joined, some of them wore the traditional pancha. Once they became full-timers, they switched to trousers.

The everyday working structure of ITCVS was loose. All decisions were taken in the open meetings in madiga-wadas. The Yacharam madiga-wada led the others, by example, in sheer numbers and in the leadership potential among the youth. In the years to come, Eliminedu and Pulimamidi madiga-wadas played key roles. Organizing a democratic vote was not really difficult—it meant that none of us full-timers led the discussions, we encouraged the others to speak and lead. Both the full-timers and the people were vocal and decisive. For most local decisions, the people and their leaders always had the final say. This was the only way to go about things, since it was the people who bore the brunt of repression, both from the landlords and the police. Both women and men sat in these meetings and thrashed out all issues. There was no voting or show of hands. For any decision to hold, it had to have unanimous support. This meant night after night of long discussions. If anyone opposed a decision, we had to

The president of the Sangam, Shankaraiah, with Gandu Narasimha to his left

re-examine the subject, and we did. Every decision meant that the world around us changed a little more and change always came at a price; so we were careful.

There were, of course, times when we took decisions within our core group of full-timers. This was done in closed-door meetings mostly held inside a house in the madiga-wada. We discouraged others from participating in these because delicate matters like someone's disturbing love affair or truancy, and sometimes even misappropriation of funds, could not be discussed in public. We also discussed our internal work division, our own problems, and any question that we needed to clarify among ourselves before an open meeting.

The Sangam never had difficulties in determining who was to lead any given activity. Natural leaders came forward and others did not oppose them. The bigger problem was

trying to convince someone that they could be a leader.
We never had any female full-timers other than myself. To
tell the truth, I did not consider myself a woman while in
Ibrahimpatnam. It was my city-bred self that marked me as
different in the village. The entitled savarna person that I
was, I had to disregard my womanhood if I had to be of any
use to the agricultural labourers. I had to transcend gender.
This construct collapsed in a crisis, as you will see—when
neither my class nor my outsider status protected me. Most
of the time there were women who actively roamed with us,
staying on for weeks together, but usually they returned home
after a point. Both the madigas and our full-timers actively
discouraged taking on women as full-timers. They said that
this would lead to widespread rumours of affairs amongst us.
This meant that women's sexuality was monitored. Apart
from this, women who were even slightly educated tended
to be young and shy. The natural leaders among the women
were the older matriarchs and since they were totally illiterate,
it would have been difficult for them to help people with
paperwork. But always, and in all ways, women were the
better, more militant leaders and they had total integrity.

We did not seek political affiliation with any group, but
we were friendly with many—most of these were the leftwing
groups of the region, from the CPI to the ML factions. All of
us met with leaders and cadres of all groups.

I raised funds for ITVCS from friends in Hyderabad.
Someone gave a hundred rupees a month, someone else
gave fifty. We were never short of money when we needed
it since we were frugal and spartan. I did not want to register
a society or take foreign funds; I was averse to the idea of an
NGO. Maybe this came from my leftist distaste for NGO
work coupled with my own puritanism. I knew that what

we were doing was bound to be controversial and I did not want any accusations that could be easily avoided. Recall how the NGO Water Development Society was attacked for doing political and activist work while receiving foreign funds and they had to quickly shut shop. Since the Sangam collected a membership fee of one rupee per month from its members, we always had enough money to cover the expenses of our usual meetings. The biggest expenditure was during public meetings when we needed a shamiana, a dais and microphones. Any food provided at the meeting was contributed by local villagers. Later, when we got some more funds through our education programmes, we were even able to maintain small office spaces. These consisted of one small room. Because our neighbours liked and respected us, we could use the open space around the room for small meetings too.

By 1987, Karunakar Reddy, a patel from Eliminedu, also joined in campaigning actively with us everywhere and even ate with us. Earlier in 1984–85, the non-dalits who joined us quietly slunk away during mealtimes and ate at some relative's house. Even the malas did not eat in a madiga home. In a few months, these people were pulled up and asked to join us when we ate. We spoke openly about caste. All our full-timers were madigas with the exception of Shankaraiah and me. In villages where we worked with non-madigas (some villages were almost exclusively kurma or telaga or mala), we never had any issue with our madiga full-timers eating and leading there.

Those who wanted to work full-time always came forward on their own. They were usually people who did not have the kind of obligations in the village that would tie them down. Whenever there was a need to expand into villages that were repeatedly inviting us, Sangam full-timers easily found another person to work full-time. The full-timers never drank in the villages we worked in. If they wanted to drink kallu (palm toddy), they went to the villages beyond Maal—where we were not active—and drank there.

Some full-timers did not deal ethically with people's money on occassion. They took loans from the community chit funds and were probably not refused, given their important role in the organization. Some collected membership fees and did not remit these. They collected the official amount of Rs 311 from people as a contribution for a housing loan application, but did not remit this to the government. These were troubling developments, but we did not yield and asked them to return the money.

Our work was now really shaping up and had acquired a structure and direction of its own. We full-timers met at least once a week, if not more. Though there were no phones, word-of-mouth communication was effective. Buses travelled up and down, and if we needed someone, we sent word with a person headed that way by bus. Often the message was relayed from village to village till it reached its final recipient. We travelled separately because there were many villages to visit. In my third year in Ibrahimpatnam, I was barely using the cycle because I was often accompanied by others who did not have cycles. We walked or bussed. I continued to maintain a home at Gungal, but I rarely got to spend two nights in a row there. I would reach a village by evening, attend a meeting after 8 p.m., have dinner there, sleep over, and leave for a nearby village by dawn. Late evenings and mornings were about meeting an extraordinary array of people from grandmothers to curious members of the Backward Classes to young boys. An early morning meeting, followed by brunch, and I would take the bus to Ibrahimpatnam or Yacharam, attend to office work at the mandals, return to Gungal and stay over till it was time to leave for another village.

I only went to Hyderabad when I needed to have papers deciphered by Cyril. My sling bag had a set of clothes, a towel, soap, paper and a pen. I disliked going to Ibrahimpatnam town because I had no bathroom there. In later days, we had an office, but the office had no bathroom either. Attending court or a dharna was a nightmare because I had to hold my bladder till late in the evening when I could get to the outskirts of a village or a deserted road. Working on *Where There is No Doctor* and *Our Bodies, Ourselves*, I knew that holding pee led to urinary infections, and I had had my own battles with chronic urinary infection. So I learnt to pee behind deserted houses in the town. We women stood guard over each other and warned passers-by to keep away. This lack of prudery stood me in good stead in the years to come. I was never embarrassed to stop to pee anywhere. On fact-finding missions or trips to villages, I always boldly asked for a bathroom or a deserted place and peed. On road trips with friends or acquaintances or in public buses, I would ask the driver to stop and take the bus to the kerb.

The news of our struggle against bonded labour spread to neighbouring areas, not through the printed word but because people had relatives across the region (and beyond). This prompted visits to our Yacharam office by people from far-off areas like Medak (150 kilometres away), Mahabubnagar (120 kilometres) and Nalgonda (ninety kilometres). They brought with them horror stories, some of them beaten black and blue, some bent double because rocks had been placed on their backs for days together to get them to repay their debts. At this stage, neither any of my union colleagues nor I had begun travelling outside Ibrahimpatnam taluka. The work here kept us fully engaged. But we helped them write petitions and told them how to approach their local authorities. This, however, was no substitute for mass action and mobilization. I never heard back about what happened to these unfortunate farmhands.

Most of our activities then were centred around the Yacharam mandal, which lay to the north of Ibrahimpatnam, and east of Kandukur. Yacharam had a large number of madiga families, many of whom served as lower-rung government employees. There were people working in the electricity department, in the department of telecom, and those commuting to the city to work as ward boys in government hospitals and as Class 4 employees in different government institutes. Perhaps they were financially more secure, perhaps they were associated with the dalit welfare associations in their parent organizations; whatever the case, they welcomed us with open arms. We could make free phone calls—no small matter when there were no cellphones, no public telephone booths and where no phone-owning reddy would allow us access to his phone. The telecom employee called us to the telephone pole and charged the call to a reddy; we were given free access to electricity for our public meetings. Food was another essential that the people of Yacharam gave us generously. We rarely had to eat outside on our visits to the village.

In most of the big meetings we held throughtout Ibrahimpatnam, members of Hyderabad's civil society were a mainstay. Bojja Tharakam frequently attended our press conferences and addressed questions relating to police torture and harassment. Over time, innumerable fact-finding committees were organized and these had people from all possible groups—leftists, feminists, Ambedkarites. Others who spoke at our meetings included B.S.A. Swamy, Suravaram Sudhakar Reddy, Professor G. Haragopal and Volga. Swamy, a Backward Class rights activist and lawyer who hailed from the powerful goud caste, was to become a high court judge. Haragopal is an orator from the radical left camp and taught at the University of Hyderabad. Volga is a Telugu writer, previously associated with the ML movement, but had made a path-breaking dissociation with the far left in the early 1980s towards feminism. We even had the Bahujan Samaj Party leader Kanshi Ram at one election meeting. At that time, Bojja Tharakam was in the BSP and he helped in getting Kanshi Ram over. The latter was actively touring the state to estimate BSP's chances in the assembly and Lok Sabha polls.

In Ibrahimpatnam, speaking at the village-level meetings was not a problem for me. I spoke as and when the need arose. But I found myself completely tongue-tied in the bigger public meetings. I had this overwhelming feeling that I was too ignorant to speak. I truly was ignorant, anyway. I always refused to get on the stage. Another reason for my reluctance was that I often found many of the middle-class speakers to be long-winded, talking as if they loved the sound of their own voice, with incredibly repetitive speechifying, unable to speak simply about the subject at hand.

▶

As our movement grew, the landlords started pushing back harder. But the people were now emboldened, and in a mood to defy injustice. On 19 July 1986, the bonded labourers of Eliminedu struck work. This was a major victory for us—this was where the tyrannical Bhoopal Reddy ruled with an iron fist and a gun. In his day the man was nothing more than an ill-tempered landlord brandishing his rifle as he went about. Today, his family holds huge political sway in the region. Besides holding more than a thousand acres of land, the family owns fleets of buses and lorries, and even operates petrol bunks. Bhoopal Reddy's son, Manchireddy Kishan (Krishna) Reddy, has held three consecutive terms as the MLA of Ibrahimpatnam from 2009 till the time of my writing this, changing parties from the Telugu Desam Party to the Telangana Rashtra Samiti in 2018. People call him 'nakka', or hyena, the quiet scavenger. The hyena did all his business in a smooth-tongued manner without a gun.

His uncle and Bhoopal Reddy's brother, Raghunandan Reddy, had raped a woman from the washer-people's community in the early 1950s and a police case had been registered—a miracle in those times. Raghunandan Reddy was acquitted on appeal, thanks to some slick work by his lawyer, Bonala Krishna Rao. Bhoopal Reddy and his five brothers were the sons of a reddy peasant who had some twenty acres of land to his name in the days of the last nizam. The communist peasant movement enabled the old patriarch to acquire much more land through terror when the Muslims fled, so that by the early 1980s, this family controlled about twelve hundred acres of land just thirty kilometres from the capital city of Hyderabad. The six brothers had complete control over the three villages of Eliminedu, Madapur and Jabbargudem. One brother was the chairman of the cooperative society, another controlled the forest resources, the third was the village patwari, the fourth was the police patel, the fifth the sarpanch. Their sons continued the tradition, by consolidating the family's hold over Ibrahimpatnam after 1985 when the erstwhile panchayat samiti president and strongman Yadgiri Reddy of Cherlapatelgudem passed away. Of the younger generation, one brother was the village headmaster, another was the village usurer, and they were also the principal agricultural employers in the village.

The family owned the sole petrol pump in Ibrahimpatnam in the 1980s. They had several rice mills, and all the fat government contracts—for road laying, electricity cables, building government offices—went to them. Kishan Reddy's cousin and Raghunandan Reddy's son Venkatarami Reddy was the leading advocate in the munsiff court in Ibrahimpatnam. Kishan Reddy's sister was married to Yadma Kishta Reddy, the powerful independent MLA from Kalwakurthy who later joined the Congress and was elected as MLA again from that party in 2004. They were related by marriage to every leading reddy family in the area and had their tentacles spread everywhere—from high court judges to high-ranking officials. The family was ruthless when it wielded power—a driver of theirs who was suspected to have robbed a watch was tied to a tree and thrashed; labourers who plucked fruit from their orchard met a similar fate. Their decades-long fight with the people of Jabbargudem village over two hundred acres of government land is known all over the erstwhile taluka.

So when the bonded labourers of Eliminedu struck work, it was momentous. In the afternoon of 19 July 1986, they took out a peaceful procession around the village raising slogans for minimum wages. A group of landlords, among whom were the chairman of the local cooperative bank, and a practising influential lawyer, fell on the tail end of the procession with sticks and stones, attacking infirm old men who were lagging behind. A scuffle ensued, and over twenty labourers and a handful of landlords sustained injuries. Anjaiah, the sub-inspector of Ibrahimpatnam police station who tried to intervene, was roundly cursed in filthy language and a blow from a big stone caused him to suffer six stitches on his scalp.

There were five or six policemen on duty, but none of them lifted a finger against this outrage on their officer. No less a person than the assistant superintendent of police drove down to Ibrahimpatnam from Hyderabad to accept the 'arrest' of the landlords as they filed into the station late in the evening while the groans of the injured filled the air. The landlords were then escorted to a guest house in the city, so that they did not have to suffer the ignominy of staying overnight at the local police station. In the morning, the magistrate let them off on personal bonds. Sub-inspector Anjaiah (who incidentally belonged to a Backward Caste) was transferred within a couple of months to another station. The charge sheet too was never filed. Whenever we went to enquire about this, we were asked to file a private complaint. One can imagine the situation had the roles been reversed and it was the agricultural labourers who had beaten up the landlords and the sub-inspector.

The next day, the bonded labourers were summoned by the landlords and were threatened that if they did not repay their debts, they would face dire consequences. When they stood strong, a social boycott was proclaimed on them. Dalit sharecroppers were prevented from harvesting the crops which had come close to ripening. The Manchireddy family summoned all the other reddys and told them that a fine of Rs 500 and five beatings with a chappal would be administered to any reddy family that associated with the dalits. Privately, the reddy farmers with smaller landholdings assured the dalits that they did not want to enforce the boycott but were afraid of the Manchireddys.

Our representations to the mandal revenue officer, to the revenue development officer and the collector from July onwards were like leaves in the wind. The sufferings of the dalits were well reported in the media by reporters who visited the village. The RDO and the additional superintendent of police of Ranga Reddy district, Chandrasekhar Reddy, also visited the village, but were unable to ensure that the sharecroppers were paid their dues. Meanwhile, Ashok Rao, the assistant executive officer at the Scheduled Caste Welfare Corporation who was to have enquired into the bonded labour petitions, gave two dates for the enquiry but never turned up. Subsequently, he conveyed his refusal to enquire on the grounds that the District Planning Board was apprehensive of 'bogus petitions'. As the high court had already, in an order on 9 April 1986, directed the collector of Ranga Reddy district to dispose of all pending petitions, we sent a contempt of court notice to the assistant executive officer. We staged a day-long dharna on 23 October in front of the Zilla Parishad office in Khairatabad, in Hyderabad, which is behind the *Eenadu* office, the largest-selling Telugu daily.

Uniting the Eliminedu madigas had been an uphill task for us. Manda Swamy, once sarpanch of the village when the seat was reserved for SCs, was their leader and he was with the Congress party. As a madiga, he approved of us and was friendly with me, but as part of a larger political entity led by landlords of the region, he was wary of our movement and held the others back. The Eliminedu madigas knew that they faced the most powerful reddy landlords in the area and naturally had to be careful where they threw their lot. But with their attempts at boycott, the Manchireddy landlords ended up forging a complete unity of all madigas of the village, something we had not been able to do for so long. It was no longer just the bonded labourers who suffered the boycott. The sharecroppers and the agricultural labourers realized that everyone was in it together. The madigas organized sieges on the landlords' houses in Eliminedu for ten straight days from dawn to dusk. Women were in the forefront and the Manchireddys could not even step out lest they faced the anger of the women. Armed personnel of Andhra Pradesh Special Police tried to remove the agitators in vain. It was an epic dharna. The women spat at the policemen and jeered at them. Songs and slogans rent the air and no landlord could move about freely on the streets. In the end, they came to private agreements with their sharecroppers, paying them their dues.

Our women sang wonderful songs in the meetings and dharnas. They could sing for hours, making up endless rhyming lines on the spot. The leader sang a line, others joined in the refrain and an entire story unfolded in the improvisational back and forth. I sat for hours listening to them, marvelling at their incredible creativity. It wasn't just that they sang well, they matched rhythm with beautiful stories and ever-evolving melodies, that were collectively made up in the moment.

After the Eliminedu struggle was resolved, a delegation from the CPI(M), led by their leader K. Krishnamurthy, visited the village, met the villagers, and released a press statement condemning the violence of the landlords. They didn't stop at that: they condemned the partisan attitude of some 'destructive forces'. These included dalit organizations, the NGO Aware (headed by a Malayali, P.K.S. Madhavan—many other NGOs in Hyderabad in the 1980s were also led by Malayalis), and 'the wife of a Hyderabad advocate, who had registered a trade union of agricultural labourers'. Their point was that we were creating a rift between 'Harijans' and 'non-Harijans'.

By this time, I had become more proficient in Telugu, to the point where I could write bold, effective, and often provocative pamphlets in the language. Whenever we had a demonstration against the local MRO, the heading of the pamphlet read: 'Chettu meeda konga, MRO (so-and-so) donga' (The monkey on the tree, the MRO is a thief). Where my Telugu failed me, I asked Bojja Tharakam to write the pamphlet. We brought these out for every event that happened. Every strike, every incident in a village, every atrocity, saw an immediate pamphlet which was circulated in the thousands. Ramanamurthy of Anupama Printers in Hyderabad was an unfailing friend who attended to all our printing needs free of charge.

As the bonded labourers in village after village repudiated their debts and struck work, landlords began taking precautionary measures. Some landlords took the signatures of their bonded labourers on promissory notes. Abhileni Jangaiah, a velama landlord from Nayanampalli village, filed a suit in the Ibrahimpatnam munsiff court in 1985 for the recovery of money taken by a bonded labourer on the basis of a promissory note. The matter was successfully defended by our lawyer who argued that the amount paid was a bonded debt and had to be extinguished by virtue of the provisions of the Bonded Labour (Abolition) Act.

In the same village, when the bonded labourers repudiated their debts, the landlords refused payment to the dalit women labourers working for them. This again was retribution on the madigas for failing to comply with the feudal norms. Twenty women faced the wrath of the landlords. When even meeting the ministers of labour and social welfare did not yield fruit, they filed petitions with the deputy labour commissioner, demanding payment of their wages. History was created when the district labour commissioner, Madhusudan Reddy, ordered recovery of the wages of the women from the landlords in 1986. When the landlords did not pay, we approached the munsiff court for execution of the order in 1987. But the munsiff magistrate did not act for a whole year. In 1988, the desperate women then approached the district judge. Soon, a letter from the district judge went to the munsiff magistrate enquiring why no action was taken. This shook the magistrate

up and he deputed the bailiff to recover the amounts by
seizing the properties of the landlords. What happened next
was like a film script. Some landlords locked their houses up
and disappeared; others locked the bailiff inside a house for
several hours. Eventually, the properties of five landlords were
seized—an unheard of act. Ibrahimpatnam was shaken up.
Never in the last thirty years had the property of a landlord
been touched, certainly not of the reddys and velamas, even
if they had defaulted to the tune of lakhs of rupees to the
cooperative banks or for their revenue taxes to the tahsildar.
Most of the landlords were rattled enough to deposit the
amount with the munsiff magistrate, and this eventually
was given to the women. It was a long struggle spread over
eighteen months, but our success was worth it. It was a fitting
reply to the taunts of the landlords who had said 'What can
you women do?'

In another case, a bonded labourer, Malla Reddy, filed an
application with the mandal revenue officer at Yacharam for
release from his landlord Viji Reddy in Choudaripally village.
This incensed the landlord and he seized a cow and two calves
belonging to Malla Reddy. On top of that, he got the latter
to sign a note that said that cattle had in fact been sold to Viji
Reddy. Malla Reddy had a bit of a mental disability, and so
his wife, Yashoda, took up the issue. She filed a case against
the theft of cattle, and the matter went to court. The evidence
was stacked against Yashoda since Viji Reddy had the signed
slip from Malla Reddy. Viji Reddy didn't even want the
animals really; he just wanted to teach the upstart labourer
a lesson. In the end, the compromise reached was that the
cattle would be kept at the police station and Malla Reddy
was given the responsibility of feeding and looking after it. I
remember frequently walking past Viji Reddy's mansion on

the road from Choudaripally to Yacharam and hating him because he had caught us in a bind. Since he lived outside the village, social boycott did not bother him. Besides, he carried a licensed gun and people were afraid of him. Malla Reddy lived in a small hamlet of Yacharam called Mogullampu; he and his wife were adopted by the madigas of Yacharam as soon as they brought their case to the Sangam. They advised, supported and followed the family in every move. Malla Reddy and Yashoda, in fact, permanently moved to the madiga-dominated hamlet in Yacharam the next year.

Eventually, we filed a case in the high court and got the cattle released; but we had to deposit some money in the Ibrahimpatnam criminal court to get this done. We lost the money but it was a big moral victory for us. When the cattle were freed from the Yacharam police station, they ran about all over the village in joy, confined as they were for close to a month. Their mad stampede proclaimed the victory of Yashoda and of the Sangam. We did not have to take out a victory procession as we usually did.

As we pressured the courts to enforce the Bonded Labour (Abolition) Act, hundreds of children were released from their cattle-tending jobs. It was difficult to admit them to formal schools—they had missed much of their schooling and couldn't be placed with the children of their own age group. In the beginning, we got the children admitted to the government-run hostels for SCs and BCs in Ibrahimpatnam, Yacharam and Medpally. But these were at capacity in no time, and we looked elsewhere. They went on to fill up the social welfare and residential hostels in all of Ranga Reddy, Mahabubnagar and Nalgonda districts. The procedure at that time was fairly simple. The caste certificate of the child and income certificate of the parents had to be submitted to the hostel warden.

When the wardens objected to so many children coming from Ibrahimpatnam and Yacharam, we went to the higher authorities and found D.R. Garg, the commissioner of social welfare, to be helpful. 'Get as many children as you can and we will find a place for them,' he assured us.

There were many agricultural labourers who took great interest in educating the children, and not just their own. There was one man, Mekala Galaiah of Kappapahad village, who borrowed a home guard's uniform, and went around the villages telling parents who still sent their children to work that he was making a list to send to the higher officials, and that they would be jailed if they didn't comply. He told children that if they ran away from the hostels (as they frequently did) their parents would go to jail. Galaiah regularly visited the various hostels where our children were housed, met them, took their feedback and relayed messages from their parents in the villages and the other way around. He nagged us to pay attention to the problems the children faced—like violent teachers, bad food, neglected scabies, lack of books, and the unavailability of free trunks and bedsheets that were to be given to the students at the start of every term. We took all these complaints up with the authorities.

Many of the children completed their schooling, only some joined colleges, but all of them became leaders in their villages. Madari, the present headmaster of the upper primary school at Nallavelli, was a bonded labourer in his village of Kothapally. We sent him to a hostel at Medpally near Yacharam, and after he finished schooling, he joined as a non-formal education teacher with us and studied his way through graduation and a teacher-training course. Kandukur Ramachandraiah became the sarpanch of his native village, Nanaknagar, and later the zilla territorial pradesh committee member, overseeing the work of the mandal development office. Gudugundla Narasimha of Kishanpalli also joined as an NFE teacher with us and later became the upa-sarpanch (elected deputy chief of the village panchayat) of Maal, an important village nearby.

After seeing the tremendous response to our education initiatives, the Sangam began NFE schools under a meagre scheme of the Central government which funded such projects. NFE was introduced on a pilot basis in 1977–78 for out-of-school children between the ages of six and fourteen, who had remained outside the formal system owing to socio-economic and cultural reasons. It was initially limited to ten educationally backward states with a focus on urban slums, hilly, tribal and desert areas. The NFE syllabus was devised by the Department of Adult Education and the students were helped to write the seventh and tenth board exams. The teachers did not require a college education, nor a teacher training certificate. The programme was really a substandard system of education for the poor and unreached. Government funding required a society and I registered Cheyutha as a society for this purpose in 1986. Cheyutha means 'a helping hand' in Telugu. The founder members of the society were the banker O. Diwakar Reddy, lawyer C.V. Mohan Reddy, agricultural scientist Dr Choudhary, Dr A.K. Vasudevan and I. All of them are my friends. Since we envisaged Cheyutha for developmental activities, we registered it as a society so that we could access funds and programmes from the state and the Central governments. We joined the NFE programme of the Department of Adult Education of the Government of India and started twenty-five schools. These were evening schools with a part-time teacher who was given a modest stipend of about Rs 150. There was much enthusiasm in the

Sangam for the schools. Parents sat outside the evening class to ensure that the teacher was present and active.

I must mention that we failed to revamp the functioning of the various government schools in the area. They did improve and attendance (of teachers) picked up remarkably, but there were too many structural constraints. A school usually had just one or two teachers, and one, and sometimes both, were deputed frequently for census enumeration, election duty, training workshops and the like. Every time we went to the district education office to complain about a particular school, we found that the teacher in question had actually been called out on official work. We also found that monitoring officers were non-existent. One monitoring officer was in charge of five mandals, rendering his work non-viable.

Teachers' unions, even those of the left, were not helpful and tended to protect erring teachers. Ibrahimpatnam was controlled by the United Teachers' Federation of the CPI(M). While they protested strongly against punishment for absenteeism or submission of false certificates, and lobbied for transfers, paying bribes all along the way, they were apathetic about improving teaching standards in schools and ignored the habitual absences of teachers. Often, teachers were active farmers, realtors, chit fund operators, rice mill owners or benami contractors who absented themselves from school with impunity; even in such cases they were unfailingly supported by the unions.

As word of our work spread to other mandals, agricultural labourers came to us, asking us to spread the movement beyond Ibrahimpatnam. This prompted landlords in Telangana to complain about us to politicians. Chief minister N.T. Rama Rao even asked S.R. Sankaran, then principal secretary of social welfare, who the tigress in Ibrahimpatnam was that he was supporting. When Sankaran explained what bonded labour was, NTR told him, 'In that case, my ministers too are bonded labourers.' NTR's ire descended on Sankaran who ended up taking a long leave in 1986–87. It was in this period, when he was on leave, that he, along with six other IAS officers, were kidnapped at Gurthedu by the PWG. By then he had completely fallen out of favour with the big politicians. Sankaran never blamed me, but several of his colleagues said that it was his support for my work that had led to his current state. He continued to face serious pressure from the government. The then Tripura chief minister, CPI(M)'s Nripen Chakraborti, sought him out, and Sankaran joined as chief secretary to the Tripura government.

All said, our work in Ibrahimpatnam was well within the frame of law. Even if they wanted to, the police could not treat us as they did the ML movement. The media and courts were also favourable to us, but I was learning that little would come from petitioning the government. In fact, enquiry officers began routinely telling us that no bonded labourer could be identified since the landlords were declaring that they had never given any loans to the labourers working under them. The good thing was that we took certified copies of this declaration and used it when landlords harassed labourers for repayment of the debt. This was how labourers released themselves—they repudiated the debt, stopped their bonded work, and were free to offer their labour to anyone who paid them. The landlords could neither recover their money nor file cases against them. Of course, bonded labourers were also deprived of the relief and rehabilitation that was rightfully theirs.

We filed petitions for prosecutions of the landlords as an added step to keep them from harassing the labourers. The vexed landlords then started filing petitions on behalf of the bonded labourers working under them, promising them a share of the money from the relief and rehabilitation that the government usually provided, all of which legally belonged to the labourer—Rs 500 as relief, and Rs 4,000 as assistance for rehabilitation. This led to a bizarre chain of events where all kinds of people, including government employees—a total of about five thousand people—filed petitions claiming that they were bonded labourers. A lot of people falsely ended up getting relief and rehabilitation payments, which was then shared between the pairvikar, the landlord and the pretending labourer.

Janardhan Reddy, brother of the Ranga Reddy district TDP president Mula Bhaskara Reddy, was presented to officials as a released bonded labourer. In Dabbedguda, 238 individuals were officially released from bonded labour though the voters' list indicated an adult population of only 222. Bonded labourers were listed as masters and vice versa in the released bonded labour lists. Tea shop owners, newborn babies, employees in Hyderabad, schoolchildren, all were now being named as bonded labourers—the landlords and their agents had gone berserk. Most of the releases were happening in the Kandukur mandal. One day, we learnt that government relief money was about to be disbursed secretly by officials at a hotel near Lemur, a few kilometres from Kandukur on the Hyderabad–Srisailam main road. We were furious and began planning to expose and stop this. If these bogus releases continued, labourers would also continue to be in the grip of landlords. We procured the official list of bonded labourers from the mandal revenue offices of Kandukur and went from village to village to do our own enquiries. We also invited leading journalists like Amarnath Menon from *India Today* to accompany us on these surveys. It was not an issue to procure the information because we gave no indication that we would use or expose this. We filed another writ petition in the high court in 1986, submitting startling details of the bogus releases. The media gave this wide publicity. The court passed an interim order for enquiry. False releases were stopped and the MROs began procedures to recover the sums that had been doled out.

Through all this, we were constantly confronted by arguments from groups like the CPI(M) that farmers were in no position to pay better wages. We were told that farmers were in a crisis themselves. The party leaders knew that it was a politically incorrect stand, so they did not articulate it publicly. But the cadres often berated us with this argument. In the beginning, we politely told them that each section has to look out for itself and that the agricultural labourers were at the bottom of the pile. The constant haranguing made us less than civil. I argued that farmers should stop farming and fight militantly with the government if they were so badly off, and that agricultural labourers were not responsible for their problems. The reddy farmers of Ibrahimpatnam owned all the real estate in east Hyderabad and were not in need of any help. It was clear as day that they comprised the well-to-do ruling class: there was no limit to their greed, all they wanted was more and more and more. Were the rich farmers of Karamchedu not worried that they had no airport in their village, and that people from outside had to motor down from Gannavaram airport to Karamchedu to visit their relatives? The CPI(M) had no logical argument; all they cared about was their constituency of middle and rich peasants.

There was no dearth of pompous privileged folk trying to tell us how we were taking things too far with our movement. I often met government officials of all hues who talked in this vein—from the tahsildar and the sub-inspector of police to the commissioner of social welfare and the deputy inspector general of police. I tried hard not to fight with all of them at the same time. I often drank tea with them and heard what they had to say. Most thought I was misguided, and were raring to teach me about reality. Responses when I went with petitions to them varied. All of them knew of the rampant low wages and the high-interest debts that perpetuated bonded labour. The more liberal officers, while deprecating the practice, said: 'Well, it is less here than it is in Shahabad (another mandal in Ranga Reddy district, or they cited some other remote place). Maybe you should not be so harsh. Maybe you should go there and organize the farmhands.' Another said, 'We can't release everyone, you know. The government doesn't have the funds. And imagine the political turmoil.' Those who were more conservative said, 'Who asked them to take the debt in the first place? You have to repay what you borrow.' Some even said, 'Actually, we officials too are bonded labourers of the minister!'

Then there were the police. At this stage, skirmishes with them were rare. One incident remains in my memory though. Narasimha Reddy, a constable, caught Shankaraiah alone on the road once when the latter was going from Gungal to his village Cheeded, pulled him by his collar, and threatened him, 'The villages here have been ruined because of people like you. If I see you tomorrow outside your village, I will finish you.' To protest against this, we sat in a dharna outside Ibrahimpatnam police station, shouting slogans, till the circle inspector Balakrishna Reddy came out and apologized on behalf of the constable. Apart from this, there was no other incident. I think that I stumped the police just as I stumped the landlords. A young woman who spoke English, was at ease with top officials, and stayed in villages on her own without the cover of a political party or an NGO, was rare at that time. It is also possible that intelligence officials had vetted me and cleared me of any continued association with ML groups. If I had been a man, I would have been dead by this time. This was one of the few occasions where it helped to be a woman.

14 Slogans that severed feudal fetters

By the end of 1985, the fledgling Sangam that had started out in the four villages of Gungal, Nallavelli, Mondigourelli, Gaddamallaigudem, all in Yacharam mandal, had spread to many villages in the nearby mandals of Ibrahimpatnam, Manchal, Kandukur and Maheswaram. Yacharam continued to be our centre, but we set up another one at Ibrahimpatnam as it was better connected by bus and had a major shandy. This angadi had people coming from as far as fifty kilometres away to trade their wares. Shepherds walked their cattle for two to three days to reach the fair.

I had now begun travelling outside my comfort zone of the four villages which were the pivot of our activites. I found Ibrahimpatnam and Manchal different from Yacharam. As these areas were close to the city, property rates were higher, and there were more settlers from outside. Villages in Yacharam mandal rarely had people from outside except for government servants and everyone knew everyone and their ancestors. In Ibrahimpatnam and Manchal, people were also more suspicious and slower to take opportune decisions. They vacillated, were often fence-sitters and we sometimes found whole villages turning tail after just one major open meeting. Maheswaram and Kandukur had a larger acreage of fertile land. The villagers here did not migrate as much for work elsewhere, and people were not as quick to unite as in Yacharam. We activists often sat and wondered over the peculiarities of each region. The local Sangam full-timers were even more parochial than me and often said that we would never get people to organize here.

Kandukur was nearly forty kilometres from Ibrahimpat-nam and thirty kilometres from my room in Gungal. This meant that, sadly, I had to reduce my cycling. There were more people around me, and they took me to their village by bus or on foot up to five kilometres. These trips lasted up to three or four days. I was also staying in my room in Gungal less often. Slowly, the cycle went back to Shantha's house.

While we were still testing the waters in Kandukur, we received urgent pleas for support from Talakondapalli, a mandal in the adjoining Mahabubnagar district to the south-west of Ibrahimpatnam. Villagers from here had been attending the Sangam meetings in Ibrahimpatnam since 1986 and wanted us in their villages. They had relatives in the villages we worked in and, by 1987, these relatives began pressuring us to visit the villages in Talakondapalli mandal.

Talakondapalli is nearly seventy kilometres from Ibrahimpatnam and thirty kilometres from Kandukur, the latter being the last mandal of Ranga Reddy district. As you turn off the highway to Srisailam past Kadthal, you encounter vast areas of shrubbery. The area is dotted with tiny lambada hamlets. As the soil is poor and rainfall low, much of the land is used for grazing, with herds of sheep and goats dotting the landscape. Bonded labour touched the lives of villagers here more intensely than we were used to in and around Ibrahimpatnam. Some of the villages in Talakondapalli mandal were Cheepununtala, Talakondapalli (after which the mandal was named), Chandana, Matukupalli and Sangaipalli. In their enthusiasm to get us to their villages, the madigas had already started an organization called Self-Released Bonded Labourers Union. This was led by Pothuganti Narasimha and other leaders, who were working on organizing bonded labourers before we began visiting these villages in early 1987. Since the reputation of our Sangam preceded us, hundreds of people gathered in the madiga-wadas. Compared to our early days in Ibrahimpatnam, mobilization here was easy since it appeared that the local madigas had already decided that they wanted to end bonded labour and hike labour rates. Calling us was all about getting some outside help to sustain their decision.

Entering these new villages of Talakondapalli was a bit embarrassing and comic, especially since I was at the centre of the goings-on. I was accompanied by the leaders in a procession with a band of sannai and dappu players (bugle and drums) and hundreds of people marching behind us, raising slogans such as 'Vettichakiri nashinchali' (Down with bonded labour exploitation), 'Vyavasaya Coolie Sangam zindabad' (Long live the agricultural labourers union), 'Kaneesa vetanalu amalu cheyalu' (Implement the Minimum Wages Act), 'Aakilu ookedi raddu cheyyali' (Stop forcing madiga women to sweep your courtyards), 'Dorala dourjanyam nasinchali' (Down with the oppression of the doras), 'Police zulum nasinchali' (Down with police repression). It embarrassed me no end but I understood it to be a show of strength for the madigas.

Poverty in the Talakondapalli villages was stark. The harijan-wada, as it was called then by the madigas, was full of thatched huts. There was not one pucca dwelling. (Peculiarly, the area where malas lived was not called harijan-wada—the term 'harijan' was synonymous with madigas.) The children were in rags. When I entered the huts, I found them bare. A rope tied across the length of the hut had a few clothes and a bontha on it. A bontha is a stitched sheet made out of old clothes. A neatly folded mat stood in a corner, and the kitchen was a raised mud platform about a foot high with a couple of vessels on it. Wages were lower than in Ibrahimpatnam. In contrast, the landlords had palatial mansions that stretched across acres.

Early in 1987, about five hundred bonded labourers in the five Talakondapalli villages petitioned the MRO to release them from bonded labour. Though these villages came under the administrative control of one mandal, they were served by different police stations—Amanagal on the state highway and Velijal in the interior. In May 1987, they struck work, declared themselves free in the absence of prompt government action, and refused to serve their 'masters' any longer. The MRO of Talakondapalli refused to conduct enquiries saying that the bonded labourers were working on 'monthly wages', it was only a question of a violation of the Minimum Wages Act and it was the duty of the labour officer to enquire into this. Following this, on 27 August that year, Pothuganti Narasimha, the leader of the Self-Released Bonded Labourers Union, and a few others were arrested by the Amanagal police and severely beaten up. They forced him to sign a statement which said that he was not a bonded labourer and that the system of bonded labour was not prevalent in the area. Later, he was produced in the Kalwakurthy court and released. But the brutalities continued.

In October, four children of self-released bonded labourers of Matukupalli were forced by the landlords to do 300 sit-ups when the cattle they were tending strayed into the landlords' fields. Then, in November, six labourers were beaten up in Sangaipalli village and a woman's mangalasutram snatched away by landlords for their involvement in the revolt. FIRs and counter-FIRs were filed the same day. The Velijal police sub-inspector threatened to set fire to the harijan-wadas to force the bonded labourers to attend to work. In Talakondapalli village, the mandal headquarters, one landlord smashed the pots of a group of madiga women when they went to draw water from his well. This was during a time when the village was facing acute water shortage and the madigas were the worst hit.

The pattern kept repeating itself. The powerful wanted to snuff out every whiff of revolt. On the instigation of the landlords, the MRO ordered the auction of the crops grown by the madigas of Matukupalli on kunta sikham land—which is a government-owned pond that has dried up and become fertile land fit for cultivation. Owing to this vindictive action, they had to pay Rs 1,855 to bid for their own crops. I was finding it difficult to contend with this continuous oppression. It was extremely troubling to see the people suffer so much. We had no support for these five villages from the villages around them; our centre in Ibrahimpatnam was some seventy kilometres away; we had no quick legal help either since the courts were even further away in Kalwakurthy, some ninety kilometres from Ibrahimpatnam. Salaha was already too stretched and could only spare part-time service of one lawyer for the Ibrahimpatnam court. We found a sympathetic lawyer in Kalwakurthy, but how long could we depend just on him? Could we take this up at all? Did the expansion of the Sangam make sense at all? Wasn't it leading to meaningless suffering for the people? I was so overstretched.

The officials of Mahabubnagar were most uncooperative. When I met the superintendent of police A. Sivasankar with a complaint, he said that he swore only by the Indian Penal Code and that it was written in the IPC that a strike by agricultural labourers was illegal, hence the arrests. He said that I should be arrested for disturbing the peace in the villages. Indeed, I was arrested in a case in which the FIR actually stated that I had led a strike by agricultural labourers in Sangaipalli village in 1987—and they actually claimed that this was illegal and contravened the provisions of the IPC. I went to the senior advocate Padmanabha Reddy with the FIR and the case was quashed by the high court. There were several such 'illegal' and nonsensical cases filed by the police against me all over the area and Padmanabha Reddy had most of them quashed. I was often targeted as the chief accused by the police; they were clever in exploiting the vulnerability of the local dalits. The FIRs read 'Gita Ramaswamy and others' and during the course of investigation, the police could insert new names and arrest anyone if there was not enough counter-pressure from us in the form of protest demonstrations and petitions to higher authorities.

Slowly, as the self-released bonded labourers in Talakondapalli stuck to their guns, the issue subsided. The administration took no steps to support them. But the landlords realized that the madigas could not be cowed down and now preferred conciliation. A wave of bonded labourers releasing themselves swept over the entire mandal of Talakondapalli. The landlords lay low, hoping that the tide would pass. If they did not resist this wave, the dreaded agricultural labourers' union would not enter their villages.

The Sangam continued in these villages though we did not expand to newer villages. We formed the Mahabubnagar Zilla Vyavasaya Coolie Sangam in 1987 with Pothuganti Narasimha as president, D. Chennaiah of Sangaipalli as vice-president, D. Narayana as joint secretary and D. Balakishtaiah as treasurer. I was general secretary. There were two women in the managing committee. The Mahabubnagar Sangam was registered on 8 December 1987 though we had applied for it some months earlier. Men and women from these villages and those around them also meet me now to tell me that they were teenagers when we had organized in those villages and that this changed the face of the villages. Wages rose exponentially, madiga children were withdrawn from cattle grazing and sent to school, and people no longer feared landlords as they did before. The paper tigers stood exposed.

Another unexpected responsibility that fell on the Sangam's shoulders, as it grew in prominence, was in helping young people who fell in love and found it difficult to marry because they belonged to different castes. These young people belonged to the area we worked in. We spirited them out of the place, got them married at the temple town of Yadgirigutta, about eighty kilometres away, and worked quietly on the caste elders in their respective villages till there was peace and they could return. There was not a single incident of violence when inter-caste marriages were arranged and these happened frequently. I understood Babasaheb Ambedkar when he said that intermarriage is the only way to break caste.

One case was that of Padma, a mala girl from Nallavelli village. After her father died, her mother, a member of our Sangam, moved the family to Maal, a small town close by, and put up a hut on the roadside. We had helped thirty malas of Nallavelli to get house site pattas in Maal in 1986, and this family was one of them. Padma taught at the NFE centre here and fell in love with Mangali Jangaiah, a local youth belonging to the mangali (barber) caste. The couple were warned on one occasion by elders of both the castes, but they continued to meet. When they came to us for help, we asked Padma how serious she was. She said, 'I will not marry anyone but Jangaiah.' Jangaiah also wanted to marry her but when we firmed up plans for a registered wedding, he disappeared. Apparently, his brothers had warned him that they would disinherit him of his share of the family's agricultural land and threatened to kill him if he married Padma. We finally found him at his relative's place in Begarikancha and convinced him

The inter-caste marriage of Padma with Mangali Jangaiah arranged by the Sangam in Ibrahimpatnam in 1986

to stand bold. Padma's mother was also dead set against the marriage, so there was a lot of talking to and fro.

We took the couple to the registrar's office at Ibrahimpatnam. A big procession accompanied them from the bus stand all the way to the office in town. We printed a pamphlet about the rights of young people in love and the evils of caste and distributed this in Ibrahimpatnam town, Maal and in the villages where the Sangam worked. Some five thousand rupess were raised from the shopkeepers of Maal, who were sympathetic towards the young couple. With this we bought a gold mangalasutram for the bride and new clothes for the couple. No one from either family attended the ceremony. Months after the wedding, relatives on both sides were reconciled. Padma now works as a clerk in the Medchal MRO's office and has children. Jangaiah passed away a few years ago.

In another case, a madiga girl, from Indiranagar in Gungal, had an affair with a member of Kotha Das's gang. Kotha Das was a famous gangster in the Malakpet area, a suburb in the old city part of Hyderabad. We took the madigas from Gungal to Golnaka in Hyderabad where we sat with the gang and hammered out plans to get the couple married. At the time, I had not known about Kotha Das's notoriety, and was high on our own strength. Later, I wondered—how did we dare to pick up a quarrel with a rowdy city gang? I was surprised that we could work out a compromise with them so easily. Working on this book, I asked Shankaraiah who had accompanied me to this meeting: 'Why did they allow us a say at all?' He told me rather shamefacedly that there was a story that I carried a pistol in the sling bag I had with me on all occasions. This rumour sprung up because of my previous Naxalite associations and because people couldn't believe that I could be as bold as I was without a gun. Shankaraiah and my other colleagues did not actively disabuse people of this notion, and Kotha Das and his gang believed that this crazy woman carrying a gun could well use it.

Our duties were not just restricted to uniting lovers. We also had to help couples who were having troubles in their relationship. There was the case of Eedaiah, a voddar (stone cutter) who ran a hotel in Maal. His daughter was married to a man from Malkisgudem who spent all his earnings on drink. As her natal family was earning a decent income and could feed her, the girl frequently ran away to Maal to stay with her parents. Her husband disliked this. The parents, concerned about the bad situation, approached every political party leader to resolve the problem. When at last they came to us, we suggested a compromise. The girl knew how to run a hotel as she had learnt this from her parents and was already working there anyway. Why not help the couple run a hotel in a village other than Malkisgudem or Maal, so that the youth could avoid the drinking sessions with his friends and the couple could also avoid the shadow of the girl's parents? They set up a hotel in Vinjamuru on the Srisailam road and are still running it successfully.

These were small victories, but they helped in uniting people and giving us the courage to take up larger issues. The smaller causes gave me more pleasure because the results were soon visible in the affected people's lives. They cemented our connections with the madigas and helped me understand their lived experience. For the first time, I understood the tortuous links between the sexes, the intricate family relationships that governed daily lives and how far we could stretch them to arrive at a solution that works.

15 Hunting down the hunters

The Sangam would have swiftly expanded its operations on the question of wages and atrocities by landlords, to Mahabubnagar on the south and Hayathnagar and Choutuppal to the east, had another set of events not overtaken us. We had now earned the confidence of the madigas and other marginalized communities of Ibrahimpatnam. From 1986, they started urging us to take up matters of land rights and entitlements, given how they had been cheated out of land ownership. Our union had not planned on getting involved with the land question; we reckoned that our remit was limited to issues of wages, work entitlements and compensation.

But people started bringing bits and pieces of paper to us. When I visited villages, men and women waited for a long time till after a meeting and then approached me with documents they had preserved for decades. Others whisked me away to their huts, where a dented old aluminium trunk was carefully opened and papers were pulled out from a plastic bag by the light of a flickering oil lamp. 'Read this,' they said. 'I had this land which was taken away from me.' 'My grandfather signed some paper for a pot of toddy.' 'My mother was a young widow, and we were evicted from our land.' 'My father was given a patta certificate but never got any land.' And so on. The papers were old and in poor condition—yellowed parchments kept untouched for years in plastic folders; they were written in old-fashioned Telugu, and worse, used old Telugu numerals (which I was to learn to read). Sometimes, there was only one page of a court paper with the operative part torn out or indecipherable. There was no one around to explain to me what this was all about.

In 1986, the Sangam's members were the poorest of the poor and largely uneducated. By 1987, after we emerged as a strong force in the four mandals of Yacharam, Ibrahimpatnam, Kandukur and Maheswaram, a few individuals from among the middle peasants who were educated and conversant with land records became close to us. We categorized middle peasants as those who did not go to work on other people's fields, but worked on their own. They too had issues with landlords because they were frequently short-changed when buying land, paying taxes, and when pattas had to be made in their names. The patwaris and landlords always tried to cheat them. Previous battles with reddy landlords had embittered them. These small and middle peasants, mostly non-dalits, belonging to the Backward Castes, helped me understand how important land was, the laws and rules governing the ownership and use of property, and how landlords always cheated the poor in these matters.

The problems brought to us were varied. Typically, the story was this: Poor people cultivated what they knew was government land to which they were rightfully entitled. Government land could only be cultivated and assigned to a landless poor person, with priority given to madigas and malas. When they cultivated government land, they were recorded as possessors, hence had the first right of assignment. Then an outsider stepped in with a piece of paper, claiming that the land was sold to them by the local landlord. Another scenario was when people knew that the landlord had land in excess of the land ceiling (which was set at fifty-five acres per adult male in the dry regions of Telangana in 1973) and had placed it in benami names—in the names of people who were their relatives or farmhands, and who would not contest the entitlement, but understood that it was only a paper transaction.

Then there were protected tenants (this is a concept peculiar to the Telangana region and the law was enacted in 1950 after the armed peasant rebellion led by the communists) who had been evicted over thirty years ago and their descendants still harboured hopes of recovering the land. Another concern pertained to the land that had been assigned to poor people by the government but was not shown in the field in actuality; people suspected that this was because such land usually adjoined a landlord's property, who wanted to occupy it himself. Even the fertile land belonging to local temples was cultivated by landlords when poor people should have been given the first preference in this regard. The land that was gifted to the poor under the Bhoodan Act of 1952 was still being occupied by landlords. Such issues were common in Telangana.

Then there were the less common ways of usurping the poor of their land. After the Muslim landlords fled rural Telangana during the terror of 1948, many villages saw the bona vacantia land—a Latin term used in legal discourse for property left without any clear owner—being taken over by the landlords. There were also many plots that had not been marked out on government maps or in revenue records, called bedakhala land—these also went to the landlord. All in all, the landlords were greedily slurping up any little pasture they could find, expanding the size of their properties to obscene limits.

The initial hard work of deciphering the bits of paper that were brought to us was done by Cyril. He stayed up several nights, reading and rereading the papers, trying to make sense of them. By morning, he had a set of questions for me to research for him. I then returned to the village and questioned the villagers, or went to the mandal office, or the ceiling records office, or the Ibrahimpatnam court, wherever it was I had to go, to try and get supplementary papers. Much of this work had to be done by me because the records were in English and my Sangam colleagues were not able to read the language well enough. Besides, more doors opened for me than for them. Sometimes when I lost interest or was exhausted, Cyril kept at it, pushing me to get him the relevant details so that he could build up a case. Initially, I baulked. This kind of digging into archives was new to me and the learning curve was steep. Besides, I had enough work on my hands with the fledgling trade union. Pincered between the desperate villagers and a determined Cyril, I plodded on. I did not know where all this hard, lonely work was leading us.

ITVCS took up its first land case in 1986, in Jabbargudem. Here, the villagers claimed that 150 acres of government land had been usurped by the powerful Manchireddy Kishan Reddy, who was later to become the MLA of the area for three terms.

Jabbargudem is a hamlet in the village of Thimmapur which was part of Kandukur mandal. It is just over a kilometre away from Eliminedu, which is in Ibrahimpatnam mandal, and the two villages have many dealings, marital or otherwise. Most of the land in Jabbargudem was owned by the Eliminedu reddys, particularly the Manchireddy landlords—so the two villages had a stronger relationship since they shared a common oppressor. I noticed that, through the year, a group of four madiga men from Jabbargudem had become a constant fixture in all of our meetings. In the beginning, they sat in the last row, came up to me after the meetings, exchanged pleasantries and left. The group included a wizened Yacharam Buddajangaiah as its leader, who was accompanied by Yacharam Buggaiah, Yacharam Pullaiah and Bairupula Jammaiah.

After many casual encounters, I asked them out of curiosity why they came to our meetings, and they replied, 'You talk of labour and wages. We have 150 acres of government land in our village which we are not allowed to cultivate. Help us.' I told them that we would support them in any activity. But they didn't want our support, they wanted our active involvement. After this, they kept following us for three long months, attending our meetings all over the taluka, sitting quietly as they did, until we agreed to get involved. My accession also owed to my ignorance. As they say, fools rush in where angels fear to tread. My colleagues in the Sangam, who lived in the villages and knew the ramifications of the land question, watched me silently, not pressuring me either way, and that was that.

Yacharam Buddajangaiah was the madiga leader of Jabbargudem during the confrontation with the patels. He was a dwarf of a man with bright eyes and a sharp tongue. He was not a brave leader and every time there was a bust-up, he disappeared and hid in some hut in Jabbargudem, and we had to go looking for him. He protested loudly every time we pulled him and insisted that he accompany us. I could never understand how Buddajangaiah became a leader in his village, but loved hearing him talk. In our clashes with the revenue authorities, he could talk their heads off, alternating between dramatic pleading, sorrow and anger. Long after I left Ibrahimpatnam, I met Buddajangaiah again in 2002. He said this about the old days, 'Our jagirdar had twenty horses and our job was to feed them every day. Their stables were behind our huts. The jagirdar's family used to come for the Dasara festival, stay for a week or so, and leave when the sitaphal, custard apples, ripened. They drove down in their motorcar via the Mangalpalli–Patelgudem road, and we had to beat the dappu drums as they entered. We didn't do just vetti, unpaid slave labour, for the landlords. We were also the vetti servants of the jagirdar. We worked without food or money. We had to draw the water, dig wells, sow groundnuts, plough and plant sugar cane—all this was vetti. Everyone else got wages ranging from two-and-a-half to five rupees per week, but we got only two annas. That itself was a great treasure.'

The principal matter in Jabbargudem was this: Manchireddy Kishan Reddy's father Bhoopal Reddy, the rifle-toting landlord, claimed to have purchased 107 acres from Azeezunissa Begum, wife of the Thimmapur jagirdar Mohammed Abdul Sattar, in 1953. He even had a document to prove this. He used this same document to claim yet another 107 acres of government land. In the village, the madigas and other poor people contested this, saying that they had been cultivating a part of this second plot of land for decades and that it was an important grazing pasture for them. In 1967, the joint collector proclaimed his findings on a petition by the dalits and ruled that Bhoopal Reddy was claiming two different plots of 107 acres on the basis of a single document of sale from the jagirdar's wife. Bhoopal Reddy's claims were categorically dismissed and the joint collector ruled that one of the properties was government land.

But Bhoopal Reddy filed cases against the government— two writ petitions in 1969 and one writ appeal in the high court in 1971, against the joint collector's rulings. Both were rejected, one in 1971 and the other in 1974, and he was advised to go to a civil court against the government. He did not do this, probably fearing that he would not win. Instead, he took the easy way out by filing an injunction suit in the Ibrahimpatnam munsiff magistrate's court in 1971 against his weaker opponents—eighteen poor families of Jabbargudem.

Index

Encroachment made by
Side Patledars

● Encroachment made by
Patledar of S. 17 at 173
and 168 to 169 as per
Shet was issued and
incorporated in Map.

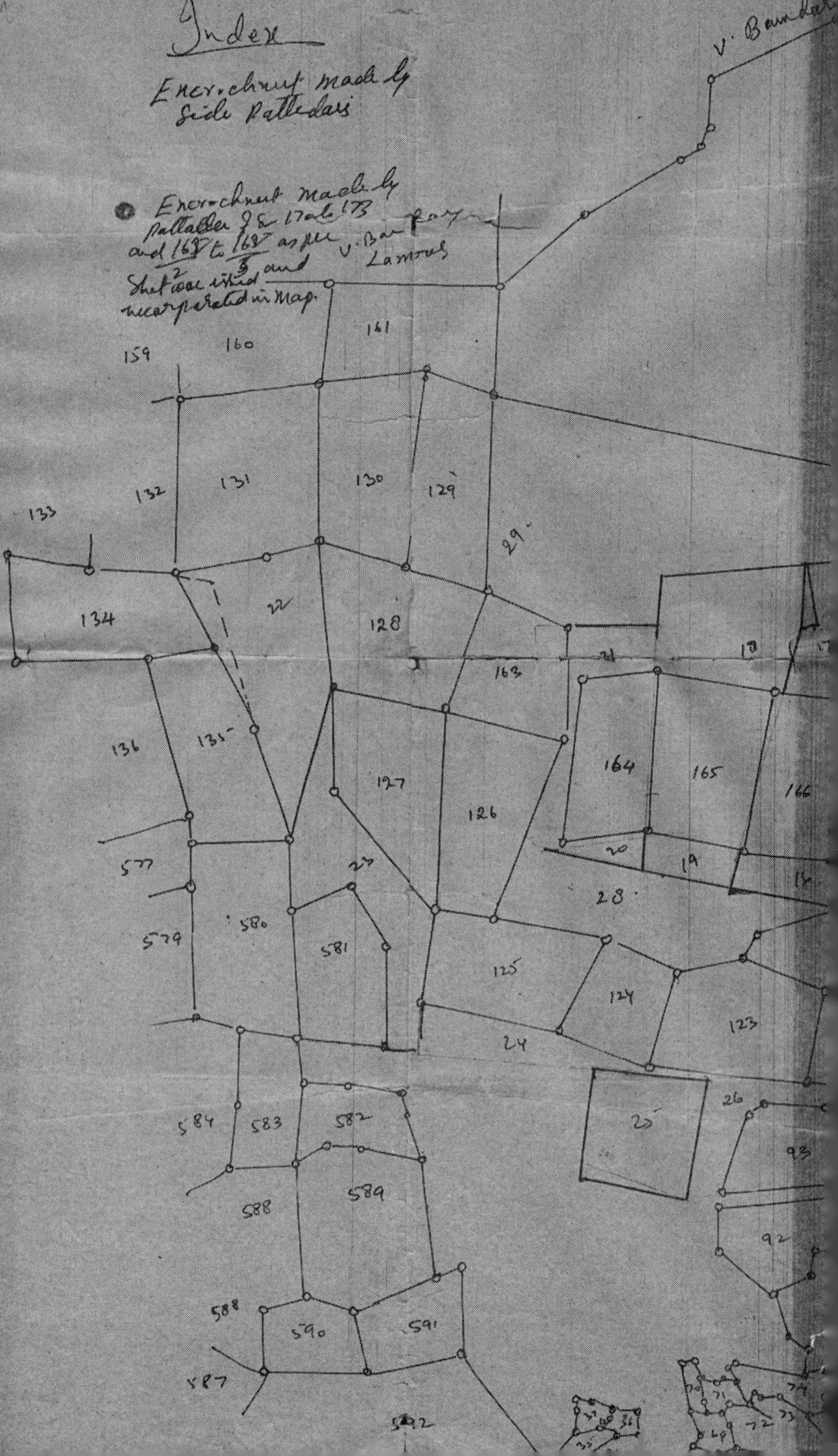

V. Bankar

V. Bankar Pavv
V. Bau
Lamrus

159   160   161

133   132   131   130   129

29

134   22   128

163

136   131   127   126

577   22

579   580   581

584   583   582

588   589

588   590   591

587

592

164   165   166

20   1A   1A

28

125   124   123

24

25   26

93

92

74
70   71
72   73
69

A survey map of Jabbargudem, a hamlet of Thimmapur

Filing an injunction suit against the state requires more exhaustive work since the state possesses all the relevant papers unlike poor villagers. Again, if there is a determined officer or collector in charge of the case, it is not easy for the landlord to fight against this powerful enemy. In most cases, poor people lose on all counts—papers, advocate, hearings in court, and ultimately justice. Bhoopal Reddy won his injunction suit in 1975. Buddajangaiah recalled that the patels had a lawyer who was paid Rs 3,000 and the madigas had a lawyer who was paid Rs 100. He remembers the tahsildar, a man called Saleem. When Saleem came to Jabbargudem to inspect the land, he met a glowering Ramulu patel (Manchireddy Ram Reddy, Bhoopal Reddy's brother). Frightened, Saleem left without doing what he had come to do.

Buddajangaiah thought that Saleem was a good officer as he had taken the trouble to visit the disputed area, and so he went to the city in search of him. He knew that a boy from a neighbouring village delivered milk to Saleem in the city. In those days, rich and important people in Hyderabad had fresh milk from the villages delivered to them every morning. Men actually pedalled thirty to fifty kilometres, some of it uphill, with two heavy cans on either side of the bicycle, to deliver milk to select households in the city. When Jangaiah met tahsildar Saleem at his house, he was told: 'Don't worry, your land will not go anywhere. They will never get the land. Go to the collector. Only he can help you. If I support you, will anyone listen to me? So what if I am the tahsildar. Only money speaks. If you have money, everyone will speak for you. He has crores of rupees. He can give me a thousand rupees. Can you give me anything? So wait until you meet a good man who will support you and you will win your case.' The implication was that while Saleem was a good man, he was not powerful enough to stand up to the reddys and too afraid to tangle with them.

In 1975, the dalits submitted an appeal to a higher court, the city civil court in Hyderabad, but lost that too. Bhoopal Reddy's path to establish control over the land was clear now, and the local government administration remained silent. This is a common subterfuge adopted by landlords to take control of government land, especially since the local revenue administration is apathetic and often connives with the powerful. Fake documents on old stamp papers are prepared, an injunction suit is filed against the mandal revenue officer in the local munsiff court and the government pleader is paid to absent himself. Often, to strengthen the encroacher's case, he gets a benami, that is, another person who's not the principal owner, to contest his case in a separate suit. The landlord wins this case. Once he gets an ex parte injunction in the suit against the government and also proves his right vis-à-vis the benamidar, he takes possession (after paying off the local police and media), and then continues his proceedings in the local munsiff court to make the injunction permanent.

The Jabbargudem dalits did not have any official or usable documents. They brought scraps of paper to me in March 1986. These included, for example, only the first page of a stamped agreement between them and Bhoopal Reddy. According to the dalits, an agreement was drawn up on stamp paper when they had a truce with Bhoopal Reddy. They were given the first, third and fifth sheets of the agreement whereas Bhoopal Reddy was given the second, fourth and sixth ones. They also had the pahanis (land records) of one year where ten of them were marked assignees. This was intriguing. I took the papers home to Cyril and we began the painfully long process of reconstructing the case. Cyril made up a diagrammatic map and marked areas (papers) that were absent and it was now my job to hunt for those.

I did this quietly. At the mandal office in Kandukur, I located a friendly face, told him what I needed when he was alone and pestered him until he gave me some of the papers. I frequented the houses of officials as early as at 6 a.m. I knew that I could catch them at home. In the office, even sympathetic officials worried that someone would carry tales to the landlords or to the MLAs and MPs if they showed me any papers. The wives of the officials were curious and sympathetic when I called on them so early in the morning. I had endless cups of tea with everyone working in the mandal office. One paper led to another and in three months, by May 1986, we had the whole case mapped out before us. The reconstructed case perfectly matched the stories of the oldest Jabbargudem warriors and we understood that poor people, when they are serious, always told the truth, but not in ways that everyone could understand. It was our job to interpret this truth in a language that the revenue administration and judiciary could appreciate.

The history of the struggle, before ITVCS stepped in, is fascinating. The ping-pong battle between the Manchireddy family and the hamlet of Jabbargudem saw regular destruction of crops. The Jabbargudem villagers never gave up the war even though they lost several battles. If the reddys sowed the crop, the villagers destroyed it. If the villagers sowed the crop, the reddys not only destroyed it but also got the police to arrest and torture the villagers.

Most of the madigas of the hamlet were bonded labourers of the reddys and it is a wonder that they managed to fight at all, given that they often had to ask the reddys for bus fare when they needed to go to court. In one compromise in 1978 after some of the madigas were assigned certificates on the contested land, the Manchireddy family agreed to share the land equally with the peasants. This could possibly have happened in 1978, when ten poor villagers were granted pattas over ten acres of this land by the government. Since the government had won the case against Bhoopal Reddy, it was free to assign the land to whom it thought fit, and some tenacious official had managed to get ten acres assigned to the landless poor. He must have been unable to do so over the entire land, possibly due to political pressure. After an agreement on a stamp paper was drawn up, the peasants retained the second page of the document, only to find that the reddys had reneged on the agreement the next year in 1979. They found that their half of the deed of agreement was now invalid. Then there were certain sections of the hamlet that regularly sided with the patel—some of them were economically dependent on the patel, some were lured by bribes, not to mention the internal dissensions. For instance, there was Yacharam Balaiah who worked closely with Bhoopal Reddy from 1978 to 1988.

The poor have limited means to fight powerful landlords. The system of justice in the civil courts is adversarial but not necessarily justice-friendly. The two advocates represent their parties' case or position before an 'impartial' person, usually a judge, who attempts to determine the truth only on the basis of the papers and evidence before them. The poor often cannot procure the documents that can help them in their evidence; they cannot trust lawyers either, because they usually belong to the dominant castes, and the poor have no social contact with them; fees cannot be paid due to lack of money; the language of the court cannot be understood. The courts rarely appreciate the concerns of the poor since it is usually composed of people from the dominant castes.

Our strategy, planned meticulously by Cyril, was two-pronged. We decided to take the issue back to the revenue courts and to the government where favourable judgments could be expected, given the nature of the case. Since Bhoopal Reddy had claimed victory through deceptive means and had not actually won against the government in the courts, we could go back to the government to demand that it implement its own final decision in the judgement of the joint collector in 1967. We had to maintain the unity of the village since this was crucial in fighting against landlords who had a strong local presence. At the same time, we decided on defensive action in the civil courts—this way we could use the different vested powers and jurisdictions of the civil and revenue courts. The civil courts, all the way up to the high court, had confirmed the injunction against the people, but the revenue courts had upheld the people's contention, and the joint collector's order of 1967 was uncontested.

In 1986, we encouraged the people to till the land. The landlords had already sowed castor in the fields. Possession is nine-tenths of ownership, Cyril never tired of saying this. After all, if the people wanted the land, they should fight for it in all the ways they could. This was easier said than done. The Jabbargudem villagers wanted land, but did not want to fight Bhoopal Reddy at whose hands they had been brutalized repeatedly. So we needed the help of people from surrounding villages and sent out a call. The response was magnificent. The brunt of the suffering of this land struggle was borne by the villagers of Eliminedu, but never once did they complain. People, most of them madigas, came from Kappad, Cherlapatelgudem, Madapur and from as far away as Dandumailaram, some twenty kilometres from Jabbargudem. They had been watching their resistance to the ruling gentry and identified wholly with their Jabbargudem brethren. It was early June and the cruel summer had passed. While we spent the days occupying the field, late evenings were full of song. The Jabbargudem women cooked food for all of us. When the Jabbargudem villagers pulled out the patels' castor seedlings and planted jowar, the patels brought goondas from Hyderabad to terrorize us. The goondas were stationed close to the fields but did not dare to move as we had mobilized close to a thousand people from the surrounding villages. The visitors stayed with us for four full days to protect the crops till the goondas left.

The administration took note of the situation that was unfolding in Jabbargudem and feared a confrontation between the landlords and us. After we had sown the jowar, the RDO of Hyderabad (East) imposed Section 144 on the land and took it over. Section 144 of the Criminal Procedure Code of 1973, which can be imposed by a magistrate-level official, restricts the 'unlawful' assembly of more than four persons at a place. It generally prohibits a public gathering. This worked in our favour. Though the RDO had imposed Section 144 to secure peace in the area, this one stroke removed the land from the possession of the landlords. Because the Jabbargudem villagers had sown the jowar, they got the crop too. The MRO appointed a contractor to reap the crop and the villagers had to pay the costs to receive it, but the victory was sweet. Jabbargudem soon became an everyday issue for me from 1986 till I left the area in early 1993. I visited the village much more than I did other villages. I knew every villager by name and I followed everyday events with great care. This was an important struggle. We had to win there and set an example, especially since it was in the control of the most rapacious and powerful man in the taluka.

We had finally unsettled the reddys from the land. After the first victory, however small, the going became much easier. We continued with cultivating the land and the court cases, but found time to also take up other issues. This small victory impacted the entire area. It was unbelievable to every person here, landlord or labourer, that Bhoopal Reddy and his family could be removed from the land. It now seemed possible that reddys elsewhere could also be divested of their illegal properties. From this, the poor people all over the four mandals took heart.

❯

I had heard of the Pulimamidi land—thousands of acres occupied by one reddy family. The Pulimamidi madigas and artisanal castes, which included chakali, mangali, kummari, kammari and golla-kurma residents, had come to the Sangam early in 1986, spoken of their land issue, and also participated in the sowing of the crop in Jabbargudem in 1986. As soon as the Jabbargudem papers were cleared, I began work on the Pulimamidi conundrum.

I have found that when landlords of a village are less powerful, the people are also strangely meek. When the landlord is powerful, people rise to great heights in resistance, courage and stamina. The village of Pulimamidi is located in Kandukur mandal of Ranga Reddy district, forty-two kilometres from Hyderabad. The 'Fairs and Festivals' section of the 1961 census report says that Pulimamidi was a forest infested with tigers and full of mango groves, hence the name ('puli' means tiger and 'mamidi' means mango). Over time, it became Phulmamidi—this was because there is another story that says that the place is named after the sour mangoes that probably grew here. (In Telugu, 'pulla' is sour.) Pulimamidi's people certainly are tigers.

The village lies on the border between Ranga Reddy and Mahabubnagar districts. It is one of the larger villages in the area with people of all castes as residents. The disputed land here was spread over a whopping 1,800 acres, far more than in any other village. Like many aristocratic Muslims, Shamshad-ud-doula, the jagirdar of the village, fled to the city after police action in 1948, and the patwari Kothapally Ramachandra Reddy who worked under the jagirdar as a clerk, simply wrote his name in the patta column and claimed ownership over all the jagirdar's land. Shamshad-ud-doula's son Azhar Hussain fought many civil and criminal cases to retrieve his family land, but nothing came of it.

Ramachandra Reddy's father Pulla Reddy came to the village from Kothapally village in Yacharam, in the first decade of the twentieth century. 'Potta chetulo pettukoni vacchadu,' said an old-timer (all he had on him was his bare stomach.) By the 1940s, all the watandari posts, like that of patwari (who maintained land records), mali patel (who collected land revenue) and the police patel (in charge of law and order), were with their family of three sons, of whom Ramachandra Reddy was the eldest. After he took control of the jagirdar's land, Ramachandra Reddy sold hundreds of acres illegally, transferring some 240 acres to a temple, and retained about 2,000 acres in his and his sons' names as well as those of many benamidars. Most of the land was rich, black cotton soil and Ramachandra Reddy brought in and settled many hamlets of kamma families from coastal Andhra on this property. The then chief minister Marri Chenna Reddy's daughter was married to Ramachandra Reddy's son. Besides, the daughter of Konda Ranga Reddy, the deputy chief minister of Andhra Pradesh from 1959 to 1962, after whom the district is named, was also married into this family.

Konda Ranga Reddy's son was Justice Madhava Reddy, who served as chief justice of the Andhra Pradesh and Maharashtra High Courts (1983–85); his grandson Konda Vishweshwar Reddy is a former member of parliament from the Telangana Rashtra Samiti representing the Chevella constituency, and he is also the son-in-law of Pratap Reddy, the founder of Apollo Hospitals. The media had reported that Vishweshwar Reddy was the richest member of the seventeenth Lok Sabha. Marri Chenna Reddy was the Congress chief minister from 1978 to 1980, and in the crucial years of ITVCS from 1989 to 1990.

The Pulimamidi land struggle had some precedent. The CPI(M) under K. Krishnamurthy had taken up the retrieval of land in the 1950s, but had not achieved anything substantial. The CPI(M) then had either withdrawn or the people had exhausted themselves. Since then, Ramachandra Reddy had refused to sell or lease land to the local villagers, probably thinking that this would bring them prosperity and then build a powerful opposition to him. The poorer the villagers, the tighter his control. This was one reason for his downfall—the villagers hated him. Whenever they went to him requesting to buy or rent land, he told them, 'Ooriki chese seva, peenigaki chese singaram—rendu vottide.' (Both service to the village and decorating a corpse are useless activities.) To dissuade the locals from coveting 'his' land, he brought kammas from coastal Andhra and lambadas from northern Telangana and got them to settle on 600 acres of the village land.

The locals were not going to easily forget the history of oppression under this family. Ramachandra Reddy's father used to place heavy stones on the backs of those labourers who owed him money, forcing them to stand with the loads for hours together in the blazing sun, until they agreed to hand over their meagre assets as repayment. Older women recalled how they were forced to work for him during the peak of harvest, forced to ignore their own little plots. 'Our payment for this work was a few grains of jowar thrown to us through an open window early in the morning,' one of them told me. One person in every family had to perform vetti for him. Shepherds had to supply kids free of charge, labourers had to bring in cartloads of wood, and every family had to perform some or the other kind of ritual service.

Since Ramachandra Reddy had illegally taken ownership of this large chunk of land, he had to conceal his wrongdoings cleverly after the first Andhra Pradesh Ceiling on Agricultural Holdings Act was passed in 1961, and again when the Andhra Pradesh Land Reforms (Ceiling on Agricultural Holdings) Act in 1973 was introduced, allowing for only fifty-five acres for one adult male in the dry regions of Telangana. Moreover, the Land Ceiling Act of 1964 had an important subsection: Section 50B that facilitated sale deeds on plain paper made between 1961 and 1969. The intention of the insertion of Section 50B was to dissuade landlords from showing excess ceiling lands as sold to benamidars and evade the first ceiling act. A landlord had to apply to the tahsildar whenever he was purchasing any property or had purchased any property in the past. After an enquiry into the 'genuineness' of the claim, the tahsildar validated the transaction with a certificate under Section 50B of the Act. This indicated that the buyer did not possess property over the prescribed land ceiling.

The work was cut out for us. We had to find out the benamidars and petition the collector to cancel the 50B certificates. Unearthing the records was not difficult because all the fraud was in one place—in one instance—800 acres of land had been transferred into the possession of Ramachandra

Reddy through fraudulent 50B certificates, written in one hand and all in one day. The then sub-collector of Ibrahimpatnam (East) closed the files. Ramachandra Reddy then got Janaki Rama Rao posted as the tahsildar of Ibrahimpatnam. Janaki Rama Rao, who had been posted in distant Mahbubabad taluka earlier, was considered an expert in the manipulation of papers to evade the Land Ceiling Act. He promptly reopened all the files closed by the sub-collector and issued 50B certificates for a record 600 acres in one day— 8 February 1975.

Ramachandra Reddy transferred 240 acres to the Cheekati Venkateswara temple in the village, but no villager knew that this land belonged to the temple as the leases were given by Reddy himself. A priest, Anjaneya Sharma, who lived in Hyderabad, was appointed to the temple by the landlord. The crumbling temple had never even had any festivities or pujas up to this point. At this time, Ramachandra Reddy's nephew Balakrishna Reddy was deputy commissioner in the endowments department. Even this department was unaware of the ownership of these lands until we brought it to their notice.

The MRO of Kandukur, Premsagar Rao, was particularly helpful to me. His being a Christian, perhaps of Scheduled Caste background, probably made him sympathetic to the underdogs. It was exciting to chase down the benamidars one by one. The dead records on paper were coming to life as we started tracking the faceless names. The records gave their addresses. Often, the person had shifted home, but I located them all. Govinda Raj, a prosperous doctor in Ramnagar, not far away, was dead and his two sons asked me to approach Ramachandra Reddy. One of them, Damodar Raj, lived close to our house in Chikkadpalli and was the chief medical officer in the Municipal Corporation of Hyderabad. There, the deputy commissioner was Pulla Reddy, one of Ramachandra Reddy's sons. The other benamidars were Syed Sirajuddin, Gulam Umar and Mohammed Sharmil Ansari—all of whom denied owning land in Pulimamidi, but clamped down when I asked them why they were listed as pattadars. Since all the benamidars were in Hyderabad, I did the searching myself.

The people of Pulimamidi were remarkably organized. It was as if we had found a ready-made army. Their leader was Salaiah, a young madiga, about thirty years old. He was the only leader I came across who was so young, although his hair had already greyed. Salaiah was calm and composed and knew how to keep the entire village together. I never saw him lose his composure. His right-hand man was Mangali Ramulu whom people feared because he was militant and fast on his feet. Sarpanch Srinivasa Reddy was a middling landlord who supported the poor. There was not a single family in the village that supported Ramachandra Reddy. There were no factions in the village, as in Jabbargudem, and that was a great relief. The village was an organizer's dream. They could implement any plan to a T. They were frightened of no one and only needed help where police were concerned.

With such unity, the people called the shots. In 1986, we organized a social boycott of Ramachandra Reddy's family. No milk was to be supplied to them, no barber was to shave them, no woman was to sweep, cook or clean in their house, no washerman or washerwoman was to wash their clothes and no person was to work on their land. They had seven poultry farms. One by one, these closed down, and except for one son, Linga Reddy, all left the village. This happened within a month of the boycott. What particularly irked them was that they had to shave themselves and watch their huge mansion detriorate because no one was cleaning it. Ramachandra

Reddy's brother-in-law, Bucchi Reddy (or Bucchaiah), had managed the land and the poultry farms for years. He was much hated by the people and left the village soon after the Sangam took up the land issue. They all left for Hyderabad where they, undoubtedly, had several properties.

Even before we began aggressive activities, like ploughing the land, we faced repression. This happened with the blessings of Chenna Reddy, who was not even the chief minister yet (his opponent N.T. Rama Rao held power at the time). In June 1986, we planned our first public meeting in the village. The lawyer-activists Bojja Tharakam and B.S.A. Swamy were to address the gathering. We had sought permission to use microphones from the deputy superintendent of police as well. Although we applied fifteen days prior to the meeting, the DSP refused to give a written refusal. 'Should I help you to go to court?' he asked. Apprehending refusal but helpless in the face of the lack of a written one, we petitioned the high court. Directions were given to the DSP to accord permission. I gave the DSP a copy of the order personally and took a receipt.

On the day of the meeting, as the public address system was being set up in front of the speakers on the dais, Circle Inspector Ganesh Rao took away the amplifiers. He had always been rude to me on prior occasions. When he was shown the high court order by the advocates in front of two reporters, he jeered at them, 'Are you going to defy the police? Do you want me to order a lathi charge and break up your meeting? Go, take your four thousand people and lead them crying and weeping to your high court!' We went ahead with the meeting without the mikes.

The advocates were shocked. 'How can these CIs and DSPs defy the high court? We will file contempt of court.'

Contempt was filed and endless days passed. I attended every hearing. The DSP came only twice. He doffed his cap before the judge and said that he hadn't seen the court order, that his clerk had not put it up to him and that he wouldn't dream of defying the high court. The judge let him off with an admonition.

Despite these setbacks, the villagers of Pulimamidi prepared to take their struggle forward. The Sangam began by preparing petitions to the administration—to the joint collector, who had the authority to cancel the fraudulent 50B certificates; and to the endowments department, to appoint trustees to the temple and lease the land to the villagers to bring income to the temple. The Sangam also rallied the lambadas who had been settled on the village land by Ramachandra Reddy. They had been brought here as lessees but had not received any receipt for the money they had paid, nor had their names been recorded in the land rights register.

16 Tattered documents, broken mirrors

With both Jabbargudem and Pulimamidi land struggles picking up steam, there was ferment in all the villages where ITVCS had a presence. People were now bringing papers and documents to us in droves. These included pahanis (the ownership record of a particular plot of land), protected tenant certificates, lavni certificates (certificates issued to the landless poor for use of government land that cannot technically be transferred) and fragments of court judgments.

The common term for legal papers in the Telangana villages was addam—mirror. They literally reflected a person's identity, security and status in life. People fished out tattered remains of old documents from their trunks to show me and ask if they had any 'balam' (strength). This lasted well into the 1990s and even happened in areas dominated by the Naxalites. I was surprised to find, on a visit to Mominpet with the local ML group later in 1990, people fishing out scraps of paper carefully preserved to ask this very question. In a region where ML groups were dominant, I did not expect such constitutional entitlements as land rights and land records to hold sway among the people. The poor have so few rights that they cling desperately to scraps of paper and meagre entitlements. This was one of the reasons why electoral boycott, as a policy, failed with the older generation. For those with other entitlements, especially the urban rich, casting their vote may mean nothing. (I for one have never voted despite trying to do all my work within the frame of law and democracy.) But to the village poor, it is a sign of one's worth. 'Am I a corpse that I cannot vote,' was the unfailingly constant answer when I asked people why they voted when all it brought them was a few rupees and a bottle of liquor.

The poor had no land before India's political independence. If they were lucky, they cultivated as tenants-at-will. Slowly, they began exercising their democratic right of adult suffrage, and the government launched populist programmes like Garibi Hatao: in this context there was growing sense of the right to own land. The Naxalite uprising in the late 1960s led to the Land Ceiling Act of 1973. But rich farmers evaded the ceiling by filing court cases on flimsy grounds. In Andhra Pradesh alone, some half a million pending cases pertaining to land ceiling were filed in the various courts from the munsiff magistrate's court to the Supreme Court. Hence, the Union government came up with the thirty-fourth constitutional amendment in 1974. This amendment placed most of the revised ceiling laws (of state governments) in the Ninth Schedule of the Constitution so that they could not be challenged in court on constitutional grounds.

As far as the government statistics go, redistribution of surplus land was happening at a healthy rate. In the early 1980s, government records indicated that 2,000,000 acres of land was redistributed. Whether this actually happened on the ground is of course doubtful. Nevertheless, I observed in Telangana the deep desire among dalits to take ownership of land as a means of empowerment. However, this yearning needed to be supported by 'papers'—it was precisely this form of legal sanction that inculcated in the people a tenacity to fight for land and entitlements. We realized this early during our struggle in Jabbargudem. The people who came to us were forthright and adamant about what was legally due to them. They prided themselves on accurately conveying the truth of the matter. But the reconstruction of cases in the institutional world of revenue authorities, courts and the police was painfully slow. To match it with the oral history of the case as recounted by people was like a jigsaw puzzle. We realized that we would not get access to revenue records if we asked for them openly. Even friendly MROs told us, 'This is the only gold we hold in our fists. If we open our fists, what will remain with us?'

The growing clamour from the people prompted Sangam activists to begin searching for land records in early 1987. We wanted to map the changes in the records of land relations from 1953, the crucial year in which a land survey of Telangana was done by outsiders, till the present day. Several entitlements that could have been granted from 1953 onwards had been denied. This included protected tenancy. Then came the ceiling legislations in Andhra Pradesh in 1961 and 1973. Here too the records would reflect a certain reality. We copied and examined the 1954–55 land records (commonly called the khasra pahani), the village map, the ceiling cases in 1961 and 1973, the protected tenancy register, the list of government land in every village in our mandals.

We tried a variety of techniques to get this information. We cajoled the most efficient pairvikar of the village to share his records with us; we had the patwari's agricultural work and housework boycotted by the village poor till he agreed to show us the pahanis; we drank endless cups of bad tea with petty officials of the mandal, especially the record-room keeper; we brought letters from universities and national institutes to show that there was an ongoing study for which accessing the records was essential; we identified rival factions of landlords, each of whom could give us access to the records in the hope of the other faction's downfall. My 6 a.m. house calls to the MROs so disturbed them that some even brought records home to get rid of me. Entire villages were mobilized for this effort and educated dalit youths were set the task of copying down the precious 1954–55 khasra pahani, tenancy records and the later pahanis. Maps were comparatively easier to obtain. We had to write an application with the name of some pattadar, the holder of the document, and hand it in with the requisite challan at the land survey office in Hyderabad, far away from the scheming landlords, and then drink tea with the official at the office to get things going.

We waited till we had information on some thirty villages before we went public. Early in 1987, we began matching the records with the maps. This involved walking around different plots of land, identifying the survey stones one after the other, noting where these were missing (or rather, removed) and mapping the extent of government land. We were accompanied by many of the madiga elders since they already knew how far the pasturelands extended. It was not that difficult to match the record and the map. We now had to get the government to verify our findings. It is the general practice for an interested party (someone who had a title deed or tenancy certificate to the land) to apply to the mandal revenue office or the survey office in the collectorate, pay the requisite challan, and then wait for the government surveyor to actually demarcate the land concerned. This involved many trips to the office, many days of fruitless waiting at the site and a hefty bribe to the surveyor to complete the work. Since in most cases we could not show the government an interested party (as the poor had neither pattas nor could claim to be possessors) we could not call the surveyor and had to do the work ourselves. On the ground, boundary stones define the limits of different properties. The map also lists several guddi gurtulu—natural and other lasting landmarks in local parlance, such as a dried-up stream, a banyan tree, an outcrop of rock, a stone for the goddess, a mosque, etc. We could follow these to lay the boundaries. Sure, this did not have official sanction and could not be claimed in any court, but it allowed us to understand the relation of land to paper and then substantiate our claims by other methods.

Before the summer of 1987, mass meetings were held in the villages, night after night, where the records were read out, with the older people sharing their own knowledge in order to validate the findings. The attendance ranged from two hundred to five hundred people. Practically the entire madiga-wada in every village and hamlet attended the meetings. There was pin-drop silence when the records were read out. People often demanded that a particular record be read loudly over and again, so that they could be doubly sure everything was in order. Those were exciting days for all of us.

By June 1987, the dalits of Pulimamidi, Maheswaram and Meerkhanpet had begun agitating for land entitlements in their villages with the backing of the Sangam. Soon, this spread to nearly every village of the four mandals of Ibrahimpatnam, Yacharam, Kandukur and Maheswaram. Everyone was now united in demanding land. It may have been twenty-four acres in Yacharam or three acres in Cherlapatelgudem, but there was ferment across the four mandals.

Meanwhile, the Jabbargudem struggle moved at a rapid pace. We continued to petition the district administration and demonstrate before their offices. In 1987, the district joint collector ruled categorically that the land belonged to the government and that Bhoopal Reddy had no right over it. The Manchireddys appealed to the high court, demanding that the labourers not be given pattas. They lost here too, the same year. The people were clearly winning and everyone's hard work had paid off.

Yet Jabbargudem proved continuously troublesome. It was

a small hamlet of about sixty households of which forty were madigas. Despite this, there were many factions here. The sixty households had sixty leaders. This lack of unity, or perhaps the lack of strong leadership, manifested itself on several occasions. This was known not just to all the full-timers in the Sangam, but was a standing joke among the madigas in surrounding villages. 'Never trust these Jabbargudem madigas,' they warned me all the time. 'They are habituated to the doras. Not only will they kick you, we will also get kicked.'

Just when we were winning the battles, Manchireddy Bhoopal Reddy summoned the villagers. I came to know that some village leaders had acquiesced and gone to meet him. I was so enraged that I called them to my Chikkadpalli home in Hyderabad. I had collected a few old chappals from friends. They did not ask why. I strung these together with a rope. When the six leaders (which included Yacharam Buddajangaiah and Yacharam Buggaiah; of the others I am not certain) walked into the room, I placed these garlands around their necks, one for each. I asked them why they had not discussed this in the open before all the villagers and then gone to the reddys. I asked them why they were betraying the people of their own village and those from other villages who had risked their lives to help them. I asked them if at all they could trust the reddys to whom they were going for negotiations. I asked them how many times they had been called for reconciliation in these last twenty years and then betrayed. I asked them how they could forget these bitter truths and run when summoned. I asked them how their own villagers could trust any leader after this. I asked them to tell me all this for the last time, and we would leave them alone to do what they wanted—negotiate with the reddys and drive their own bargain. 'Give us the word and we will leave you alone,' I said. 'Don't pull us down with you if you want to go and drown.'

They were remorseful and apologized profusely. I had them remove the footwear garlands as soon as they said they had made a mistake. When word of this reached Jabbargudem, the people were overjoyed that their cheating leaders had been taught a lesson. All my colleagues in the Sangam also felt that those who backstabbed the people were taught a good lesson. They were pleased. But I was troubled by what I did for many days. I had garlanded them with chappals because that is what the madiga elders did to recalcitrants from their community. I had always tried to stop this practice earlier, but now, I was indulging in it myself.

My own questionable actions aside, the villagers now stood united. There were no more private negotiations with the landlord. We continued to concentrate on Jabbargudem. The enemy here was more powerful than the Pulimamidi landlords who had the Congress strongman Chenna Reddy as their close relation. Although they lived in Eliminedu, the landlords of Jabbargudem were young and energetic, and had close links with other landlords in the village and in the entire area. The Pulimamidi landlords, on the other hand, lived in the city, thought they were the cat's whiskers, and kept aloof from the landlords of the area. This meant that the villagers were united and had a strong and confident leadership.

With the onset of rains in June–July 1987, the agitating villagers began ploughing the occupied land in Jabbargudem, Pulimamidi and Maheswaram. This prompted immediate police repression and hundreds of people were picked up, taken to Kandukur police station, beaten and charged with trespass and destruction of property. We usually managed to get them out on bail immediately, and so the police changed tack. They began arresting people late on Saturday evenings (since the courts were closed on Sundays), and packed them off to the Musheerabad central jail in Hyderabad. Surprisingly, the experience of jail was positive for most of them. Here, they met murderers and robbers who laughed at them for being arrested on such trivial charges. 'Kill a man and return,' they were told. So they didn't have to feel like they had committed a crime. Besides, they knew that we would arrange bail for them at the earliest.

Maheswaram was another flashpoint. This was the headquarters of the mandal neighbouring Ibrahimpatnam, and had a large proportion of bedakhala land—land that was unaccounted for and missing from all official records. For instance, there could be twenty-five acres of actual government land in a village, but an error in accounting could mean that only fifteen acres was reflected in official records. Such errors could be rectified by checking survey maps. In 1987 the people of Maheswaram argued that fifteen acres of such unaccounted-for land was being illegally cultivated by rich peasants. Led by Katikela Sattaiah, they occupied and ploughed the land themselves.

Eight women and nine men, all agricultural labourers, were picked up before dawn and severely beaten up on 21 June 1987 at the Maheswaram police station. Thirty-year-old Lakshmamma, Sattaiah's wife, suffered the most. She was hit on the stomach where she had recently had a surgery. When she pleaded with the police to spare her, the newly appointed sub-inspector, Mangipet Sarveshwar Reddy, instructed the constables to remove her clothes and show him the operated part. Only then was she spared. Reddy further threatened to parade the women naked on the streets of Maheswaram.

After the beating, the men and women were herded into a

lorry and taken to a police station in the city. As soon as I heard of the arrests, we tried to locate our people. Even a habeas corpus petition did not work, because the police kept moving them from station to station. I then approached the Ranga Reddy district collector, M.V.S. Prasad. When he questioned the superintendent of police about this, the latter said that nobody had been arrested. The collector then decided to visit Maheswaram himself—this was the only way he thought he could verify the police claim. Only then were the victims produced in the Ibrahimpatnam court and given bail.

At the time, Geetha Ramakrishnan, who organizes construction workers in Tamil Nadu, was visiting us in Hyderabad. Once the Maheswaram people were released, Geetha, Cyril and I went to Maheswaram to meet the women in their houses. We drove in from the Srisailam highway, one kilometre into Maheswaram village, up to where the police station stands at the entrance of the village. Immediately, Sarveshwar Reddy came out, brandishing his revolver threateningly. We were a bit shaken and stopped the vehicle at a roadside tea shop opposite the police station. It was a tense moment, we sat there drinking tea and all the while Sarveshwar Reddy glared at me, fiddling with his revolver like a Bollywood film hero. I was prepared for a rough encounter, but the moment passed.

We decided to file a private complaint—filed directly with a court—with the district munsiff magistrate of Ibrahimpatnam against the sub-inspector since his superiors condoned his actions. The incident was widely reported in Hyderabad newspapers and the government hospital in Maheswaram had recorded the injuries inflicted on the labourers in detail. When the private complaint was heard in the magistrate's office, the women showed the welts on their swollen arms and lifted their saris to reveal the bruises on their legs. The judge and the lawyers turned their faces away in horror. The case was then recorded and admitted as a complaint in the court.

Sarveshwar Reddy had to be summoned. The court issued summons six times from July to October through registered post, but the sub-inspector claimed to have not received it. The postman did not dare to record 'Refused'. He recorded 'Absent'. This didn't deter the Salaha lawyers. A court commissioner was appointed to serve the summons, but he too could not locate the SI despite two further attempts. The process was then sent to the superintendent of police of Ranga Reddy district for the SI's appearance in November 1987. This was received and the acknowledgement sent to the court, but the SI still did not show up. The complainants, on the other hand, appeared on every date of the hearing for they would never be afforded such high-handedness.

I then met the deputy inspector general of police, Anjaneya Reddy, known to be an upright officer, at his home. Later, in 1991, he converted to Buddhism and revived the Ananda Buddha Vihara Samiti. He set up the Mahabodhi Buddhist Vihara at Mahendra Hills in Secunderabad and the Buddha Vanam for cultural tourism at Nagarjuna Sagar on the banks of the River Krishna. I was taken to him by C.K. Narayan Reddy, co-founder of HBT, who knew him well. After I recounted what had happened at Maheswaram, Anjaneya Reddy turned to me and asked, 'Do you think we should give you the Bharat Ratna? This is what is bound to happen if you upset the prevailing law and order.' On hearing this I burst into tears. This was the first time I had ever wept openly in front of a police officer. I felt cheated. I had thought he was an upright officer and would be sympathetic. He turned out to be like the others. Looking back at this now, I see that this may not have been true. He was warning me that this was what I had to face. I was not to expect to be rewarded for taking on the reddys.

Sarveshwar Reddy was soon transferred, not as a punishment, but so that he did not have to face the opprobrium of a private criminal case against him. He was an ex-Naxalite, and had been an active member of the Radical Students' Union. He was suspended briefly from service when he approached the PWG owing to a dispute with his brother-in-law over dowry for his sister in the late 1980s. The PWG shaved one side of his brother-in-law's head—a great loss of honour for reddy landlords in Telangana—and beat him up. The man ended up committing suicide over this. In 2011, Sarveshwar Reddy was suspended again and was arrested on charges of possessing assets disproportionate to his known sources of income. As is the practice with the police mafia, he brokered land deals and forced pattadars to sell valuable land to him and his benamis at cheap prices. Most cases of this nature are quietly shelved, especially if the accused has plenty of wealth to distribute. Sarveshwar Reddy rose to the rank of additional superintendent of police by the time he retired.

We faced difficult situations in every police station. I had to attend to this every time our people were arrested and harassed. It was not easy for me to interact with the police during my work in Ibrahimpatnam. I tried to take recourse to the fact that we were doing nothing illegal, we were peaceful, we were helping to implement the laws of the land, but whenever I entered a police station, it was with some trepidation. I was entering the lion's den and never knew if I would come out unscathed.

This was because the police had been a real threat to my comrades. During the Emergency, I heard first-hand accounts of police torture. We met a comrade from Maharashtra who was arrested and brought to Andhra Pradesh for interrogation. At that time, Vijaya Rama Rao (later to become a minister in the TDP government) was in charge of anti-Naxalite operations under the Congress chief minister Jalagam Vengala Rao. Laxman Pagar, the comrade from Maharashtra, recounted quite calmly how he was taken to Vijaya Rama Rao who asked him to shout, 'Indira Gandhi ki jai'. When Pagar refused, Rao called two police officials, one to hold him down, and the second to cut half an inch of his tongue. Pagar even showed us his maimed tongue. In the same period, our friend Jampala Prasad was arrested and tortured. All the nails from his hands and toes were pulled out during interrogation. Jampala was declared dead in an 'encounter'.

Every time I entered a police station to help a landless labourer give a petition, I noticed that the sub-inspector had all the chairs removed and himself sat on the only remaining chair. Sometimes he ordered the removal after I entered to make it clear who had the authority. I learnt not to get rattled and also learnt not to sit even after being offered a chair. There was one circle inspector who always made a show of removing his clothes down to his underwear in front of me. This cheap behaviour led me to further detest the police. During one particularly brutal beating of the Jabbargudem villagers, the circle inspector asked each of them repeatedly, 'Does she fuck all of you? Is that why you listen to her every word? How good is the fuck? Do you think she will oblige me too?' I found this out only later. When I was talking to them about their ordeal, they were being unusually evasive. When I asked why, one young lad blurted out what had happened and the others shut him up quickly. I did not forget this for a long time. I think it shocked me so much that I had no language to interpret it for myself. As women often do, I wondered if I had done something wrong. I never discussed this with anyone, not even Cyril.

Not that there were no good officers. Although, for us, a good officer did not mean someone who did not beat our people. It meant someone who beat everybody, rich and poor, with the same stick, in the same way. Satyanarayana, who was the Ibrahimpatnam circle inspector in 1987–88 (when most of our police cases were in Kandukur and Maheswaram), was known to be such an officer. He was considered 'good' because he only took money when both parties were rich. When one was rich and the other poor, he did not take a bribe. When he was the circle inspector, the Sangam was relatively untouched. My colleagues often met him at the police station or his house for cups of tea. Another one was Bhadra Reddy, the circle inspector of Ibrahimpatnam from 1989. He did take the law into his hands, but treated both landlords and labourers equally, beating up both in equal measure. A police officer who arrested a reddy landlord became a hero in the taluka and was spoken of with awe. This is how I learnt that justice is relative, not absolute.

17 The Sangam was asked to solve every problem

By 1987, we were getting involved in a medley of activities ranging from militant land struggles, campaigning in elections, running schools and development programmes. Sometimes, it felt like there was no order in our lives. We were being pulled in different directions. Jabbargudem had stabilized, both because the Eliminedu madigas were firmly with the Sangam and because the government had removed Bhoopal Reddy from the land by imposing Section 144. In Pulimamidi, the landlords had left the village after they were boycotted, and people were readying themselves to plough the lands.

In March 1987 our work was interrupted by the local body elections. These were elections to the zilla praja parishads and mandal praja parishads, ZPPs and MPPs, created by the TDP government. People had a choice between the Congress and the TDP candidates, and in some places, the TDP ally, the CPI(M). All three parties had been opposing the wage and land struggles to this point, so I wondered why people supported them. We had meetings in village after village where we asked people what should be done. Did anyone want to contest for the post of MPP president? Should our people vote for a candidate who obeyed the dictates of the landlords? There was a guarded response from the madigas. None of them volunteered and quietly scouted for Backward Class candidates with some money who could contest.

Two people volunteered to stand in the elections. One was Erra Narasimha Goud (of the toddy tappers' community) of Nerepally for the Ibrahimpatnam Mandal Parishad Territorial Constituency. The other was Bandi Sriramulu, a mala, for the Yacharam MPTC. Sriramulu, the former army man from

Nandiwanaparthy, mounted a colourful and memorable campaign. He went from village to village with his small band of youth on bicycles. 'I am like one of you,' he told people. 'I have nothing to give you—no liquor packets, no money. But if I win, it will be your victory. I will give you a seat when you visit me at my office. You will not have to stand by the door and call out "Patela". Even if I lose, we will have made our point.' Over two hundred women campaigned for him for a whole day from dawn to dusk in a hired lorry, unprecedented at that time. Daughters of other villages married to the sons of Nandiwanaparthy, returned to tell their mothers, fathers, brothers and cousins: Sriramulu is our man. If you don't vote for him, we will snap our ties with you.

The Sangam members also supported a few sarpanch candidates in some villages, though we did not have polling booth agents and counting agents. We also decided to counter the culture of candidates offering money to people in exchange for votes. Instead, we asked people for money—our campaign, asking for a rupee and a vote, raised substantial sums for the candidates. But none of the Sangam members had any previous election experience, and nobody was able to win. Some of them (all independents) forfeited their deposits. Much later, I was buttonholed by old women in villages who said, 'I gave you one rupee and one vote. What did you do to get me my pension?'

Romantic notions of being able to negotiate one's way through electoral democracy disappear fast when working in villages. I found the elections to be a completely different beast compared to what I had done until now. The corruption, the chicanery, the bargaining—everything is out in the open. Everyone knows how much money is spent by each candidate and what sums are distributed to each caste elder.

5

The fights over money are also public because it is almost always accompanied by a liquor component. Slips of paper are distributed that can be exchanged for liquor at the local outlet. You can hear people complaining, 'You were given so much to distribute among us, but you gave us less.' 'Why were you given five hundred rupees and I only two hundred?' So now we knew that we could never win in the elections. We saw what kind of money was spent and how people's votes were bought. We also saw that people *expected* their votes to be bought—elections were the only time when they could question a candidate. But our experiences in the many defeats of 1987 helped us later in our struggles.

It did not matter that we were not successful in the elections. People trusted us where their land entitlements were concerned. Two other major land issues surfaced early that year—one in Meerkhanpet in Kandukur mandal, and the other in Dandumalkapuram in Choutuppal mandal, more than fifty kilometres away. Meerkhanpet lay ten kilometres west of Yacharam. As I write this, the village is abuzz with the news that Amazon is to set up a data centre here with an investment of Rs 11,624 crore. Back in 1987, it was a sleepy village. When the bus from Yacharam made its single trip towards Kandukur and stopped there in the afternoon, not a fly stirred in the village square. The three hamlets of Begarkancha, Thimmaipalli and Akulamailaram adjoin the village. While Meerkhanpet has people of all castes residing in it, Begarkancha is a small hamlet of telagas (oil pressers) and Akulamailaram has a preponderance of the sheep-grazing kurmas.

Akulamailaram was a surprise. In Ibrahimpatnam, the kurmas are known to be a peaceable community, but the ones here were militant and joined us with gusto. Their landlord was Lakshminarayan Reddy, father of the human rights activist, socialist and future Supreme Court justice B. Sudarshan Reddy. This man was cruel and a serial rapist. Once, in the early 1970s, when he dragged a young kurma girl to his house, the village rebelled. They caught him, freed the girl and beat him up so badly that he died. They cremated him by the stream near the village, collected the ashes and took it to the Yacharam police station to confess to what they had done. Several of them served life sentences of fourteen years. When they came out in 1987, they were not afraid of anyone. The criminals they met in jail had laughed at them for confessing to their crimes. But now they felt lesser to no one, and they spoke of how there was no place for morality in a caste-ridden society. They said they would fight shoulder to shoulder with the Sangam.

Begarkancha was home to one of my favourite persons and mentors in Ibrahimpatnam—Dilli Jangaiah. He belonged to the telaga caste. Much before the Meerkhanpet land struggle began in 1987, he was one of those who attended our meetings—a backbencher, watching and listening carefully. He could not be missed: tall and dark, and always accompanied by two or three telaga people. From 1987 through to 1993, he counselled me, researched about the new areas that the Sangam was entering, and gave sound advice. Begarkancha barely had ten households but I visited it often for the sheer pleasure of meeting him and listening to him talk about everything under the sun. He and his three sons had just three acres of their own, but they planted crops and worked their land with great passion. His land had some access to water, so he largely grew vegetables and coriander for the Hyderabad market. Visiting the market every second day with his produce, he became a keen observer of the Hyderabad wholesale market scene. He grew rice, millets and pulses for his household needs and there were always chickens clucking away in his courtyard. They also raised goats which one of the daughters-in-law or Jangaiah himself grazed. It always amazed me to watch this totally self-sufficient family that made do with three acres. It helped me to understand that land and access to water were critical for a household's survival and growth.

Dilli Jangaiah never hesitated to give me advice on issues he had opinions about. He considered things carefully before speaking up. He was patient in explaining the ramifications and never made short shrift of the many doubts that I raised. He brought me news of happenings in distant villages and political events nearby that could impact us. He also read the newspaper, heard news on the radio, and discussed political happenings with me, asking me for news and information not normally available to him. His curiosity and insight opened a different way of thinking for me. He was one of the few people who continued to meet me in Hyderabad long after I stopped work in Ibrahimpatnam. He was my self-appointed guardian.

Meerkhanpet village is closely linked to Hyderabad's Deval Shivji temple. This temple was in possession of 1,200 acres of land in the village and continues to be in possession of 928 acres even today. Normally, temple land is governed by the endowments department of the state which is responsible for the safeguarding of its land and assets. When it was in the temple's control, its trustees gave the land on lease to the villagers to graze their cattle. The telagas of Begarkancha hamlet were, and are, totally dependent on this land for grazing and cultivation and paid the temple rent. Vithal Reddy, a big landlord of the village, who was a patwari and former sarpanch, encroached on a sizeable chunk of the temple land and obtained an injunction order in the munsiff court against the pujari of the temple in 1961. He first took control of 200 acres, and then, on the strength of this injunction, he claimed ownership of a further 400 acres. Before this, the land had been used by cultivators and sheep grazers of the village. Now, Vithal Reddy began collecting rent from them. He also had the revenue records changed to have himself assigned as the pattadar.

In 1987, Vithal Reddy sold over a hundred acres of the land to industrialists and contractors from the Andhra region. The new owners then fenced the land in, and refused the villagers entry. This created a commotion in the village and they approached us. The Sangam had already released bonded labourers in this village, so we were known there. Dilli Jangaiah and pastor Boda Balraj came to me as their representatives. Balraj was a pastor at the Mennonite Church in Meerkhanpet when I met him in 1986. Unlike many others, he did not drink or smoke and was soft-spoken, patient and unflappable. He always argued for an ethical struggle. Balraj and Jangaiah together offered an unbeatable sounding board for some of our Sangam's riskier ideas and events. Thirty-five years ago when dalits did not want to educate their daughters, Balraj educated all five of his, each now a high achiever in her field.

Jangaiah, Balraj and we at the Sangam went through the papers, verified these with both the Deval Shivji trustees, the endowments department and the mandal revenue office, and confirmed that this was indeed temple land. The villagers and the released bonded labourers then broke the fences down and began cultivating the land. This brought the police out, and they arrested and beat up the occupying villagers. Some of them were charged with attempted murder, making it difficult for us to bail them out. Boda Balraj, the pastor, was pushed into a well. Pots of human excrement were flung into the madiga well. Vithal Reddy never appeared in person; he got all his dirty work done through his cronies in the village. Balraj was caught walking alone. Since he was a dalit person and because the attackers were also the same, no case was filed. The purchasers got the munsiff court to issue the now expected injunction order against the villagers.

The strange thing in all this was that the new landowners and we were both taking advice from reddy lawyers who were working in the same law firm in Hyderabad. The advocate we were consulting was the brother-in-law of their representative. The matter took an even more curious turn when Sudhakar Reddy of the CPI called me up and asked if we could meet. He was keen on a compromise as the people who purchased the land from Vithal Reddy had approached the CPI. After the discussion, Sudhakar Reddy understood that there could be no compromise and the purchasers dropped out of the scene. They no longer wanted to retain the land. For the first time, victory fell into our laps. The people retained the land and were recorded as cultivators. After repeated petitioning and dharnas, the joint collector cancelled Vithal Reddy's patta in 1988 and declared the entire 200 acres as government land. The rest continues to be temple land under the control of the villagers.

This was also the only village where the police were able to secure a conviction against me. There was one family of telagas in Begarkancha, a hamlet of Meerkhanpet, who had been attached to Vithal Reddy since long. They refused to join the struggle. Consequently, their fellow villagers had enjoined a boycott on them since 1987. They filed a case against me and the Begarkancha villagers in 1988 saying that I had instigated the boycott. That I supported the boycott was certainly true. It felt like a minor case and I did not take sufficient care. I was convicted in 1989 in the munsiff magistrate's court in Ibrahimpatnam and had to pay a fine of Rs 400, as did the other accused, one of whom was Dilli Jangaiah. We appealed against the conviction in the district court in 1989 through a good criminal lawyer, Challa Narasimha Reddy. But our appeal was dismissed, and I learnt a valuable lesson. Munsiff courts are very important in giving direction to a case. Never ignore the trial court. All that follows is built on the trial court verdict.

Discovering how to take on land struggles was a sharp learning curve. I had imagined that we just had to support communities of people in retrieving government land from landlords. Now, protected tenants began coming to us. What were we to do with them? These were individual cases, and they mostly belonged to Backward Castes with a sprinkling of madigas. How would taking up such questions keep the village poor united? Ours was an agricultural labourers' union and I was wary of the mistakes the traditional left had committed by getting small and middle peasants to join their unions and dominating them with their demands. Another reason was my proximity to the madigas, which led me to partly closing myself off to other communities. The madigas rarely had protected tenants among them. Would we be swamped with BCs and lose our primary constituency, I worried. It was Satyamma of Nazdik Singaram village who taught me what we could and should do with protected tenants. The madigas of the area also unequivocally supported BCs in their struggles against the landlords.

We had many protected tenancy cases. Section 32 of the Protected Tenancy Act (1950) says that protected tenants should be put back into possession of the land where they are tenants. The MRO is empowered to do so and civil courts have no jurisdiction over the matter. In fact, the MRO has the power to issue injunction orders protecting the tenants. But the revenue authorities never did any of this, and the pattadars approached civil courts with fictitious arguments to get a stay against the tenant. Every village saw people coming forward with tattered and torn PT certificates asking us if we could do something about it. While we started the paperwork of filing petitions for restitution of the tenant's rights, we mobilized the other villagers to support the PTs.

We successfully fought several cases under the PT Act. Eliminedu Muthyalu's case was one such. In 1954, when he was a young man of about twenty years, he had been cultivating, as a tenant, about sixteen acres belonging to Malla Reddy. After the enactment of the Andhra Pradesh Tenancy and Agricultural Lands Act, 1950, he was declared a protected tenant in 1956. Malla Reddy immediately evicted him; the landlord correctly figured that the piece of paper with Muthyalu gave him security of possession. Muthyalu's father died at that time. Burdened with family responsibilities and deprived of his livelihood, Muthyalu became a bonded labourer for a debt of fifty rupees. The wages were never sufficient to pay off the debt. Many bonded labourers shift from employer to employer, but Muthyalu remained with Malla Reddy for thirty years. In 1987, he still lived in the same thatched hut and had no earthly possessions. His young son was also put to work tending the master's cattle. When the bonded labourers got together to help themselves, Muthyalu was their vocal leader.

Muthyalu filed a tenancy recovery case at the MRO's office against Malla Reddy, repudiated his debt and stopped work. Malla Reddy came to his hut and took away the torn gongadi and battered sandals he had given him. Muthyalu never forgave him for this and refused to let him live in peace hereafter. He was vociferous about the injustice done to him—he spoke loudly and abusively at the MRO's office, at the tea shop and at the bus stop, till Malla Reddy had no shred of respectability left. The wives of landlords would say, 'Madigolla noru antha cheddadi, inkemi ledu' (No one has a fouler tongue than the madigas). Indeed, even local villagers refused to translate several of Muthyalu's colourful tongue-twisters for me. He filed a petition for restoration of his tenancy with the Yacharam MRO. With our help, he succeeded in getting his sixteen acres, forty years after losing it. It helped that the London-based son of Malla Reddy, while on a visit back home, persuaded his father not to contest the suit, part with the land, and move on with the times. When he came to Yacharam, he had his father call Shankaraiah. He asked Shankaraiah what the law said, and when Shankaraiah explained this and showed him the documents of protected tenancy, he told his father to leave the matter be.

Ravula Ramulu from Akulamailaram was another tenacious and silver-tongued protected tenant. He fought his own protected tenancy case for fifteen valuable acres and won all the way from the mandal revenue court to the high court. He is now a prosperous farmer.

Satyamma of Tatiparthi deserves a whole section to herself. She is the elder of two daughters of a golla family in Nazdik Singaram village, six kilometres west of Yacharam. Her father had no sons. He was the protected tenant of about four acres of land there, belonging to Pappu Subbaiah. Usually, whenever a tenant received a PT certificate, he was evicted by the landlord immediately because the certificate gave security of tenure in perpetuity and had a provision that granted the right to purchase a part of the land at a reasonable rate. Pappu Subbaiah did not evict Satyamma's father; instead, Subbaiah 'charitably' donated the land to the local devasthanam.

After her father's death, Satyamma stepped in with the consent of her sister to establish her rights. She was married to a man in Tatiparthi, five kilometres away, and the land was close to her new home. When she tried to establish her rights, her landlord took her to the civil court. If Satyamma had continued there, she would have lost. So she cleverly began parallel proceedings in the MRO's court and won her case.

Every time Satyamma came to me for help, I sent her away saying, 'You are not a labourer, you are a pattadar. You cannot be a part of our organization. Don't come to me.' Satyamma wanted land for herself and we were not yet clued into matters that affected protected tenants. She insisted: 'But they are not allowing me to cultivate my land.' It was a long time, perhaps a month or two, till I came around to her point of view. She was entirely right. She had no land, only an inheritance. For her to win her entitlement, she needed the support of the Sangam. She never lost patience despite our initial reluctance, her resolve never flagged through her years of struggle. Even after she won her land, she attended every meeting, however far away it was. She presumed that all meetings were for her. She stood in the early years in 1987 as the only woman among a crowd of men. She was often the earliest to arrive, opening up her cloth bundle which contained her meal of jowar roti and chilli powder when it was time to eat. She never complained about her difficulties, never asked for bus fare and never took anyone for granted. Consequently, she was popular among all the Sangam activists. Everyone volunteered to accompany and help her out of difficulties at any office.

Satyamma was loquacious and could talk the head off any

official. She was also inventive in getting past stern chowkidars and police sentries. The last time I talked to her was in 2002, some ten years after our previous meeting. She came with her little pouch of important papers and press clippings. There were yellowed pieces of interviews in newspapers—she had kept an article that I had written about her, there was even a photograph of her in a newspaper with the chief minister at a function. She brought her legal papers, her fifteen-year-old membership card in the Sangam, and several other memorabilia.

'Nenu putangaane mayamma sacchipoindi.' My mother died when I was born, said Satyamma matter-of-factly. 'Her sister, my aunt, took me to her house in the village of Sakannapalli near Kalwakurthy and raised me. She got me married when I was nine years old. One day, my husband sold the sheep that I had brought as dowry. My mother-in-law beat me because I was supposed to safeguard them. My husband sold them to a lambada at Kalwakurthy. The landlord of my village wrote me a note that explained how the sheep were mine and that payment should not be made to my husband for the sale. I took this to Ramachandra Reddy who was the landlord of Kalwakurthy. There were no buses in those days, we had to walk. When he read the note, the landlord refused to pay my husband. So my husband beat me. He broke my arm.' Satyamma showed me the scar when she said this.

'As the sheep had been taken away, I had to go and find them in the general herd. Yellagolla Muthyalu, the golla in charge of the sheep, asked me to identify mine. "If they are yours, you will know which ones they are," he said. I recognized all my sheep one by one and pulled them out. Then I saw that one sheep had recently delivered a kid. "Where is the baby?" I asked. Muthyalu said, "If you can find the baby, take it. If you can't find it, you are not born to a golla, you are born to a madiga." There were twelve baby sheep there. I lifted one up and it ran to its mother. That is how I retrieved my sheep.

'My father, who lived in Nazdik Singaram, had no sons when he died. So my sister and I are his heirs. When I was returning from his funeral, I came across the patwari of Nazdik Singaram, Naddi Rammulu, a mala Christian. He said, "Don't worry, I will get you your land." I wrote a petition and gave it to him and got the legal heir certificate. The patwari had inherited his matriarchal grandmother's land in Chintula, a village ten kilometres away. That is how he knew that daughters can inherit land.

'I put my nine-year-old daughter to work in Morayya Reddy patel's house in the city when he promised to get me the pahani papers. Morayya Reddy is a landlord in my village and is also a pairvikar. I had to do everything without my husband's knowledge because he would have beaten me and said, "Lanjadana, are you doing pairvi? Whore, so you are brokering at offices?"

'When the landlord Pappu Subbaiah came to know that I was getting my papers together, he sent me a notice for an injunction suit in the Ibrahimpatnam munsiff court. I engaged the lawyer Ghulam Hyder to represent me. Meanwhile, the big landlord in my village, Janga Reddy patel, got angry that I was not going through him, since he was the village elder. I was not asking him for advice. He told my husband, "Your wife is going into politics. See that she stops it." My husband beat me and dragged me to the panchayat. Then Janga Reddy told me, "Satyamma, you are roaming somewhere. Your husband wants to divorce you."

'I asked him, "Where am I roaming? You know that since

Telugu text visible on card:

ఇబ్రహింపట్నం తాలూకా
వ్యవసా...

పేరు ... ఇచ్చల్ల సత్యమ్మ
తండ్రి పేరు మునయ్యప్ప
ఊరు ... లొడిపర్తి
రిజిస్టర్ నెం ... 11

1988
199
199
199
199

Satyamma's ITVCS membership card which she brought to me along with other papers in 2002

I came to your village as a bride, I built your houses, put up the roofs, worked at your wells and fields. Slave work. I worked during weddings. When our villagers were ill in the hospital, I volunteered to nurse them. But I don't have even an acre of land. If I die, there is no land to bury my body. I will fight for my mother's land." Janga Reddy shouted, "Do you want your husband or your land?" "I don't want my husband, I want my land," I replied. I left him and went to stay in Nazdik Singaram.'

వందా :

దా	తేది	సంతకం	చందా	తేది	సంతకం
౭	21-5	10/-			

Satyamma heard of me and the Sangam in 1987 when her case was in the Ibrahimpatnam munsiff court. 'You kept sending me away,' she said. 'After Cyril Reddy heard me and read my papers, he told you to listen to me carefully.' We filed a case for restoring the PT in the MRO's office in Yacharam. Pappu Subbaiah's son-in-law Somaiah was his advocate. 'When Somaiah came to the MRO's office, he said, "Some women have such courage." When I came to know who he was, I said loudly, "After my father has died, it's as if I have no right to inherit his land. Pappu Subbaiah has only one daughter. When he dies, will she get her rights? Let me challenge her. Let Subbaiah give his property to the public. Then I too will do so." Somaiah heard this and asked me, "Who are you? Why are you talking of Pappu Subbaiah's death?"

'When I explained who I was and why I was petitioning the MRO, Somaiah told his father-in-law about the law. He refused to represent him. Subbaiah resigned and the MRO awarded me the land. But then, Subbaiah regretted his resignation and filed an appeal in the collector's court. I went to meet his son-in-law and he promised me that he would not represent his father-in-law. So Subbaiah had to ask another lawyer. He died while the case was pending and I won my case.

'Now, my husband is working the land—the husband who said he didn't want me as his wife. Those who opposed me run after me now for everything. "Satyamma can get anything done", they say.'

Satyamma faced many insults from officials and reddy advocates during the case, but never feared them. One official tried to seduce her, another advocate shouted, 'Rakshasi! I will see to it that you never get your land,' in open court, in front of a surprised joint collector. She braved curfews to attend her case and even got an official asking a bribe suspended after she appealed to the anti-corruption bureau.

Dandumalkapuram was another site of a major land struggle. The village is named after Malik Ibrahim, the Shia ruler of Golconda who visited here with his army ('dandu' in Telugu refers to an army). This is a village in Choutuppal mandal of Nalgonda district. When you drive about thirty-five kilometres out of Hyderabad towards Vijayawada on the south-east and approach Choutuppal, the land on both sides of the road is disputed property. It stretches for miles, especially to the undulating right of the road, reaching Dandumailaram. The 4,000 acres of contested land originally belonged to the nizam who gifted it to his inamdar, Raja Venkata Narasimha Rao, for his services. The title of inamdar comes along with land grants as an inam (gift). A small group of reddy landlords formed a farmers' cooperative society, the Tenants' Cooperative Farming Society, supposedly consisting of poor farmers, and managed to get the land assigned to them in 1959. They wrested total control of the land from the inamdar's sons Naganna Naidu and Venkatarayalu Naidu, who lived outside the state. The sons, for their own part, had given the land on a permanent lease to one Varakantham Gopal Reddy, who litigated with the farmers' cooperative society from 1954 to 1970. He, in turn, surrendered the land to the government after a bout of litigation that went all the way up to the Supreme Court, with many complications along the way. The henchmen of the landlords were the middle peasants who continued as sharecroppers while the landlords retained control. The dalits who sided with the inamdars worked as bonded labourers of the landlords.

Over time, with aspirations rising, leaders emerged from the non-landowning sections of the village, but these were easily co-opted by the landlords, finally raising the tally of the membership of the society to nearly three hundred in 1985. Much of the land is on hilly terrain, picturesque and uncultivated. In 1986, the society opened negotiations to sell most of it to V.G. Paneerdas and Co., a private limited company based in Madras, to build a film studio. (The VGP firm was famous for its amusement park along the beach on the outskirts of Madras established in 1975.) The sale, of course, was illegal, it being government land.

Dandumalkapuram borders Ranga Reddy district where the Sangam was active. In March 1987, the dalits of the village came to us and spoke about bonded labour. When I visited the village, they also told us about the land situation. We filed petitions for the release of bonded labourers and submitted these to the collector of the district at Nalgonda, to the sub-collector at Bhongir, and the MRO at Choutuppal. In the matter of land, we moved cautiously. This was a big village, outside the normal circuit of Ibrahimpatnam taluka villagers. Our people did not have marital relations here and did not know the people well enough. We did not attempt any proactive measures on the ground such as ploughing. What followed was as much due to the active interest of the officialdom as to our Sangam's intervention.

An energetic group of three IAS officers checkmated the landlords at every turn in 1987. Mamidipudi Nagarjuna, who was the registrar of cooperative societies, attempted to reform the landlords' cooperative by removing dead and ineligible members and enrolling new and eligible ones. When faced with stiff opposition, he simply superseded the society and took it over. Noted writer and madiga IAS officer A. Vidyasagar also came to our rescue. He has published five collections of poetry in Telugu, and is the author of a volume of short stories, *Bhadrachalam Mannem Kathalu* (Stories from Bhadrachalam, on the woes of an underdeveloped area, translated and published in English by the National Book Trust). As sub-collector at Bhongir he took steps to prevent the sale of land by putting up warning boards and taking over the land under Section 145 of the Criminal Procedure Code that empowers the RDO to take over contentious property. They were aided by the collector of Nalgonda district, P. Dayachari. All these matters went to the high court as usual. The landlords had a peculiar arrangement with their lawyer, Mahmood Ali. They did not pay him fees; instead, he got half the land. Mahmood Ali was thus enthused to file case after case in the High Court and frequently resorted to recusing himself when he found the judge to be impartial. The landlords had important political mentors—Congress ministers Jana Reddy and Vandemataram Ramachandra Rao. The latter was born Vavilala Ramachandra Rao but got the moniker Vandemataram in 1948 from Veer Savarkar when he sang the ultra-nationalist song (banned by the nizam of Hyderabad) in Osmania University and was, as a result, lathi-charged and jailed. Ramachandra Rao was also president of the Arya Samaj which was known to be a Hindu communal organization at that time. He was appointed chairman of the Official Languages Commission by Chenna Reddy.

The landlords tried to get the best portions of the land regularized privately under the Telangana Abolition of Inams Act of 1955, but we were able to stall this. As for the labourers, some of them were eventually released from their bondage a year later and some not at all officially, but all of them repudiated their debts and stopped working as farmhands. Our land struggle in Dandumalkapuram dragged on for a few more years after this.

I was now finding it increasingly difficult to represent matters to officials and often faced open opposition from them. 'Why don't you ask for a ceiling on industries?' was a frequent question. 'You are fomenting violence. The poor people are addicted to alcohol. They will end up selling the land in the end. Why do you encourage them to struggle for something they will lose anyway?'

Caste played itself out peculiarly in the villages. While the ruling caste was reddy, there were a few brahmins who also cheated on land reform and retained a couple of acres illegally. It surprised me when in a number of villages where we discovered such brahmins, people refused to touch their land. 'Papam, Bapanaina, manaku papam tagulltadi.' (We must not bother the poor brahmin; it is a sin.) It was not in fear of some divine retribution that people desisted, but a sense of pity for the brahmins who were now down and out. The brahmins in question begged the people to leave them alone or left the village in fear. They did not respond aggressively as the reddys did.

The cases of atrocities against dalits were also now being brought to the Sangam. In Cherlapatelgudem, where a small piece of government kunta shikham land (dried-up lake beds) was disputed property between the dalits and the landlord, the haystacks and huts of some dalits were burnt and they were beaten up. Cases were registered and the dalits appealed for relief for arson victims as is prescribed in government manuals. The RDO told them, 'Were any of you killed like in Karamchedu? Why do you want government money?' We took up the matter in a big way and demonstrated regularly till the RDO was transferred. In Narapally, a village largely inhabited by goundlas—toddy tappers—one of them was brutalized by the landlord in 1987. We held a public meeting in the village, got the landlord arrested, and ensured compensation.

Women in Ibrahimpatnam were slowly and surely stirring. They discovered the law and how many of these had been designed for their benefit. Freedom from bonded labour, minimum wages, government land—all these were legally their right. So, they not only fought their own battles but participated in every meeting, every rally, every event where trouble was anticipated and help was needed, with gusto and militancy. They walked in the Sangam padayatras with or without their children. The more militant ones among the women were those in their early forties, whose children had grown up and were married, and whose matriarchal status allowed them to participate in public events without the name calling that younger women could have been subjected to.

Most of them had not stepped out of their villages—natal or marital. But their participation in the struggles took them to faraway places like Karamchedu, where they went to express their solidarity, to encounters with police, and to meetings with collectors, police superintendents, chief ministers and governors.

Some villages had exceptionally militant women. The women in Nandiwanaparthy, some three kilometres west of Yacharam, on the road to Meerkhanpet, waged a different kind of battle in 1987. Subbamma, a child widow who was now in her mid-thirties, came to Hyderabad from Tenali looking for a livelihood. She married a sixty-year-old, Munugode Rangaiah, who owned twenty-five acres of land and a house in Nandiwanaparthy. She was candid. 'I married him so that I could live in comfort because he had some property.' After a few years of their marriage, he left her. She asked him to settle some property in her name, but he refused. She then filed a petition for maintenance. Rangaiah died before the court could give a judgment; rather, the court worked so slowly that Subbamma's petition became infructuous with his death. Apparently, he wanted to teach her a lesson because Subbamma, instead of falling at his feet, had gone to court. The old man refused to give her any property and 'gifted' it all to the village sarpanch, a wily brahmin called

Anantharamaiah, who then sold a part of it to others. For four years after her husband died, Subbamma lived by selling off her paltry possessions—pots, pans, wooden pillars and wooden doors. She then ended up selling boiled chana and bajjis near the toddy shop in the village. Appeals to the elders in the village, and even petitioning the court demanding her legitimate share in her husband's property, failed.

In 1987, Subbamma finally approached the dalit women, both mala and madiga, for support. The women worked out a plan of harassing and boycotting the men involved. A group of about hundred women cut down some trees on Rangaiah's land and scattered broken glass and thorns on another portion. This brought in the police. Undeterred, the women cut down some more trees in police presence the very next day. 'They were only four policemen, we were a hundred women, what could they do to us,' they said. This led the police to arrest five dalit men, the husbands of the militant women, and keep them in a lock-up for two days. The outraged women raided Anantharamaiah's fields and destroyed the jowar crop. 'We did this so that we could join our husbands in the lock-up,' said one of the leaders. The ping-pong battle between the women, the police and Anantharamaiah's followers went on for a few days till the village realized that the women would not back down. Subbamma's struggle ended with all parties sitting together in a compromise and Anantharamaiah agreeing to hand over two acres to her.

Since I had now spent so many years in the region, I knew some of the bad habits that afflicted the people. A big one was people getting into debt over a wedding in the family. Unlike in many other castes, a madiga family spends for the wedding of both the daughter and the son. It doesn't matter if you are on the groom's side or the bride's side; if there is a wedding you will have to spend a hefty sum. Prior to 1980, there was no practice of dowry; it was ola, as bride price was called, that was common. By 1985, with madiga boys in Telangana getting employed in government or quasi-government services, the practice of dowry began creeping into madiga households. Educated and employed madiga grooms watched their colleagues from other castes receiving hefty amounts of dowry and thought that they too deserved a similar price. Prosperous madiga families did not want to see their daughter toiling in the sun, with her baby laid out in an old piece of torn cloth by the side of the field. They did not want to have her walk long distances carrying water or firewood, they did not want to watch her die while delivering a baby. So they preferred to pay dowry and ensure a more comfortable life for their daughters.

Older women recalled that when they got married all they brought with them was a straw mat, two brass or earthen pots for water, and one set of clothes. By the mid-1980s, this had risen to a set of steel or aluminium vessels, a steel almirah, and clothes for not just the bridal couple, but for everyone in the family. The wedding feast for which one goat or more had to be cut was also spread over a number of days. There were complicated arrangements in which the bride was taken to the marital home, then brought back to her natal home, then again taken to the marital home and again brought back to her natal home. Each time, hordes of relatives had to be fed mutton and given alcohol.

Due to my leftwing work and a definite lack of understanding of the place of culture and ritual practices in the lives of people, I agonized over this 'wasteful' expenditure.

Why couldn't social weddings or stage marriages, as they are called, practised by the Ambedkarites and leftists in the Telugu states, be taken up here, I wondered. Such weddings were essentially public meetings: dalits had a picture of Ambedkar on the stage and leftists had those of their own icons. An elder gave a speech and the couple garlanded each other. While working in HBT, I often set up makeshift bookstalls at many such weddings, whether invited or not. Often, food was not provided; sometimes a cup of tea and a samosa sufficed. Very rarely was the mangalasutram tied in such weddings.

Many of the weddings in Ibrahimpatnam were child marriages, and I did not know what to say about that. Instead, I arm-twisted my union colleagues (they had not wanted to waste our time on weddings and suchlike) to arrange weddings where the ceremony was short, less wasteful and performed by the baindla elder. The baindlas are a sub-caste among dalits who serve both the malas and madigas as priests. They are primarily employed as agricultural labourers, like other dalit sub-castes. Officially there are sixty-two castes within the Scheduled Caste category in the two Telugu states. In Ibrahimpatnam, and across Telangana, the baindlas are linked to the madigas and are classified as their dependant sub-caste.

In the weddings the Sangam arranged, we bought a tiny piece of gold to serve as the centrepiece of the yellow thread mangalasutram. The union fed the invitees, many of whom were not relatives, but Sangam members. The villagers organized the simple wedding feast—watery dal and rice—together. On one occasion, in 1997, we invited social activists from Hyderabad to legitimize the weddings. Snehalatha Bhoopal was a delightfully feisty feminist. She was the daughter-in-law of the Sirnepalli Samsthanam (an elite Hyderabadi reddy landowning family of yore), but she and I got on well. She was a frequent visitor to Ibrahimpatnam. I also invited Malladi Subbamma, a noted writer, rationalist and women's rights campaigner. Shantha Sinha also came along. The wedding was to happen at Kappapahad. All three were horrified to find that the bridal couple were children. I was properly chastened. After this, the Sangam did not facilitate any child marriage.

18 The left, NGOism, Ambedkar

By the end of 1987, ITVCS was involved in what is, for want of a better word, called 'rural development' activities. I had not intended to involve myself in such work. Coming as I did from the ML movement, I saw agitational and 'developmental' (or constructive) activities as two separate entities. The terminology is certainly disturbing—as if there is a dichotomy between agitational and constructive work, as if agitation is destructive. As I perceived it, agitational activity was taken up by those who wanted to bring about a total change, and constructive activities by those who wished to reform and tinker with bits and pieces of the system, but did not see the immediate and vital need for a systemic overhaul.

We sometimes speak of soft and hard options. With soft options one did not build up the capability of people to confront the state; with hard options one did precisely such things. The politics of Marxism–Leninism as practised in the 1980s virtually precluded constructive activity, which was looked down upon as Gandhian work or charity. It is possible that leftists think that when people are politically empowered, they will organize their own constructive politics. A more nuanced left opposition rests on the premise that welfare programmes, particularly credit programmes, divide the poor and even create the illusion that existing systems can work and deliver the goods. This illusion was not to be promoted.

At the other end of the spectrum were NGOs who saw the situation from another angle—most of them felt that working with government institutions was impossible due to the red tape. Since foreign assistance was available liberally in the 1980s, why not make use of this for helping the poor, they argued. I was unsure where I stood in 1984 on this spectrum. I wanted to be open-minded but suspected NGOs of welfarism—the belief that social welfare depends only on individual welfare, and hence activity towards individual welfare will lead to social good.

Graduating in radical politics, I had a flair for agitational activity. As a student organizer, I went from college to college, harangued, persuaded, orated, pleaded, till we got students to raise demands, march in processions and stand up to power. In Ibrahimpatnam, till 1987, I was mostly fixated on agitational work. But when I observed life in the villages, the divide began to appear artificial. I observed the unemployment and the destitution of the people, and felt that the old dichotomies were pretty useless in understanding the ground realities. Changing agrarian relations and ensuring a minimum living wage to the poorest was not going to happen in a day. Meanwhile, how were they to eat, have a roof over their heads, educate their children and address their medical needs? How were they to protect their environment with the meagre resources they had? How were their children going to get an education and be in a position to claim their rightful entitlements if not in this generation, then at least in the next?

By then, what was called 'rural development' was already taking place in the villages. These included organizing or slotting people for activities around better farming practices, greening the habitat, programmes for skill training and better livelihood options, and help towards constructing shelters. Ignoring this was tantamount to leaving an entire political space to ruling-class politics. Unsustainable practices were being encouraged by politicians for short-term benefits. If the organization of the poor was strong in a village, surely it could have a voice in deciding the manner in which funds were levied from a village (as in, say, an alcohol cess) and then how they were put to use. It seemed incongruous to me that people had something like the Sangam to address one concern, and in other matters they had to be subservient to the ruling class and its institutions.

As things went, government programmes reduced the less privileged to the status of beggars and divided them in the clamour for a share in the welfare pie. Was it possible to organize people so that they could participate in government programmes with dignity and agency? This idea went against the grain of radical politics, where we firmly believed that development programmes co-opted the people into the ruling ideology. But welfare programmes of the government are run on people's money. Why should people not intervene positively to increase their own space and make their own decisions? Why should we have to bring in foreign money (with heavy strings attached) for welfare programmes when we have funds in our own country well within our reach? Poor people anyway were accessing government programmes through middlemen like the pairvikars. Was it not possible to mobilize people for speedy and efficient implementation around the various programmes that existed, help them get aware of their limitations and possibilities, help them unite instead of be divided?

This was linked to a perception of the constitutional and extra-constitutional framework of the state. The left was suspicious of any programme within this framework. The CPI leader Chandra Rajeswara Rao, one of the organizers of the Telangana armed peasant rebellion, made a perceptive observation while addressing a meeting of the party-led Agricultural Workers' Union in the late 1980s at Kodad in Nalgonda district. Some of us from the Sangam attended this meeting as fraternal delegates. He said, 'During the days of the Telangana armed struggle, there was a movement of the poor, but no laws favouring them. We fought for these laws. Now there are all kinds of progressive laws for the poor, but no movement of the poor.'

The left ignored the space of legal action and state institutions as an arena of struggle. Most activists were unaware that these institutions provided possibilities and scope for fruitful intervention and that a large part of people's daily lives were intricately woven into these institutions. The ration card, for example, is a vital document for rural and urban poor. Yet, the delicate mechanism by which this vital document is secured is left completely to the machinations of the pairvikar.

The People's War Group organized large-scale land takeovers in the north Telangana districts between 1985 and 1990. There were red flags all over such occupied territories and most of this land should genuinely, by law, have gone to the poor. Yet, no attempt was made to legitimize (in terms of ownership and occupancy rights) the occupation. Any suggestion to this effect was shot down as counter-revolutionary and as helping to legitimize the role of the state and state institutions. Today, most of this land has been sold by the landlords to the intermediate classes who have capital and can resist attempts by the landless poor to recapture the land. Did the PWG realistically envision a successful revolution to come after such land occupations? More importantly, can pockets of armed resistance in a country with well developed armed forces ever lead to a revolution?

The left, for its part, was adamant in its distrust of any governmental institution. For a period of time, ML activists in Andhra Pradesh even refused to defend themselves or appoint advocates in criminal cases. They boycotted the courts, remaining silent and without defence throughout their trials.

This attitude clearly indicates a preference for a certain type of agitational politics.

Exiting such a framework now felt vital to me. When activists demonstrate to the state that its own laws are being violated, it sets the stage for a winnable struggle. It produces sympathy for the struggle within diverse social groups and compels the state to respond favourably to preserve its own legitimacy. Then again, focusing on illegalities is relatively easy. In contrast, to work within the legitimate space of state institutions and still subject the legal nature of the state to a painstaking analysis is a frustrating tightrope walk.

There was the problem of balancing the survival of a movement while also coming up with winning strategies. Goals had to be set based on people's daily lives, under their own supervision. Broad mobilization and protest politics to bring about structural change could not by themselves be sufficient for those confronting both immediate threats to survival and small opportunities for betterment. It was also important to expand the spaces within the system into concrete local sites to pursue democratization. Pushing existing systems to their logical extremes was an important process in the work of conceiving new systems. How to do this, both without creating an illusion that all is well within the system, and at the same time generating a knowledge base which drives progressive politics along concrete lines, was the dilemma.

At this point of time, I had not read Ambedkar except for his *Annihilation of Caste* and his biography by Dhananjay Keer, *Dr Babasaheb Ambedkar: Life & Mission*. It took me a further decade to read about his insistence on constitutional entitlements for dalits and his disapproval of violence. When I came to Ibrahimpatnam, I naturally began working with the dalits. I did not set out to help them after reading Ambedkar. It was they who led me to him. Sometimes I feel that had the left read some Ambedkar and worked closely with dalit groups, it may have been easier for them to deal with their lack of clarity on constitutional issues.

In 1987, with the clout we had acquired through our other militant campaigns on land, wages and atrocities, it was not too difficult to take to constructive work. Between 1987 and 1994, we dealt with housing, education, loan programmes, joint forest management, health programmes and livelihood issues. I also had the distinct feeling that the district administration was encouraging us. Perhaps they felt that they could now co-opt us. We took advantage of any available space that was helpful to the poor and the dalits in development programmes. At one time, MLAs in the Ranga Reddy district development board even complained that Ibrahimpatnam and Yacharam mandals were hogging most of the district funds because ITVCS pressured officials.

The first cause we took up was the rehabilitation of bonded labourers. In 1985, every person who was freed from bondage was allocated Rs 4,000 as rehabilitation; this was usually given in kind in the form of a pair of oxen. The oxen would then be immediately bought back by the officials of the Mandal Development Office for Rs 3,000, and then recycled for the same purpose. We ensured that only land was given as rehabilitation in lieu of the money. In village after village, we identified suitable plots of land, negotiated with the landowners and mediated between them and the Scheduled Caste Corporation (which made the purchase) till the deal was done. Such land remains with the rehabilitated families even today. In Mondigourelli village, Yacharam mandal, twenty-three acres were purchased for the twenty-three released bonded labourers, mostly dalit, in 1986. As there was no money left for developing the land, we negotiated with the cooperative society department, set up a Joint Family Cooperative Society over the twenty-three acres, which enabled the families to receive considerable monies for development, digging bore wells, and setting up a dairy which runs even today.

Another scheme that was important to the people was the loan programme. The main institutions involved in this activity were the District Rural Development Agency, the Scheduled Caste Corporation and the banking institutions in the district. We refused to take part in their usual charade of rotating cattle that were produced only at the time of the loaning and then immediately disappeared. Mekala Galaiah, a telaga of Cheeded, was instrumental in organizing us to tackle such institutions. A short young man with intense, piercing eyes, he had an equally piercing voice. Since I visited Cheeded frequently, and Gungal (where I lived) was on his way out of the village, we met often. He was part of a group of agricultural labourers that rented a crane to dig wells. Digging wells was a group activity in the 1980s for contractors had not cottoned on to it yet. This group needed a loan to buy a crane so that they could save on the exorbitant rent.

Their calculations of expenditure and division of income within this group were intricate and perfect. They had options for men who needed a day or two off for personal work, they had options for illnesses; in all such cases the group could continue to be cohesive and carry on with the work. They marked their calculations on their thighs with pieces of coal. Galaiah kept telling me that we needed to concentrate more on people's actual requirements in their economic activities. He said that if their group was to go on, they needed a crane as soon as possible. Since schemes like these were not listed for sanction, we had to fight to get them on the list. Officials did not sanction a loan to a collective; they sanctioned it only to one man. We worked our way through all these wrangles. The success of the first loan helped many others to come up with inventive and creative ventures.

Another concern that people brought to our attention was that of housing. The government schemes for housing were taken up entirely by landlord contractors. Beneficiary lists were drawn up by politicians. When the TDP was in power, those who were aligned to the Congress assumed that they would not be selected, and vice versa. When we entered the field, we made up our own lists and also drew up construction plans. All our lists were made in open meetings in the dalit-wadas. Since our lists comprised the really deserving landless who were already active in our programmes, there was no pressure on us to include the undeserving. We only had to scrutinize the lists drawn up by the officials and the MLA who had signed the recommendations to point out the flaws in it. Some people on their lists already had pucca houses, some were government employees, some did not even live in the village. When we made it clear that we would expose this on a large scale, the officials and the MLA hastily agreed to our lists.

We refused to agree to the government plan of a reinforced cement concrete structure—a model comprising two tiny rooms and a bathroom. We insisted on the traditional tiled housing and a single large room (large enough to accommodate cattle and poultry during heavy rains). The district functionaries gave in to most of our demands. When the first set of fifty-two houses, built entirely by the people themselves, were completed at Yacharam in 1987, it was a beautiful sight and people came to see them from all the surrounding villages. After that, there was no stopping

312 LAND, GUNS, CASTE, WOMAN

the housing programme. The district functionaries were not unhappy; their targets were getting completed on time. With contractors, much of the work remained incomplete, bills did not get released owing to disagreements about the bribe involved, and people did not move in because the work was substandard.

Our problem was with the customary commission (another word for bribe) that the official received when bills were produced for compensations. The first time we faced it was when a mandal-level functionary did not send up the file to sanction the bill amount, and also did not ask for the commission directly because he was afraid of us. When our representative went twice and returned empty-handed, we put our heads together and thought out a strategy. Our people visited each tier of officialdom and explained that we could not give bribes because the entire accounts were read out at open village meetings. Did they want their names to be read out openly? No, of course, they didn't. We explained that each delay entailed one demonstration. Our demonstrations were feared. We did not give traditional left slogans of 'zindabad' (long live) or 'murdabad' (death on you). Our people were not communist supporters and didn't know these. They came up with their own ingenious slogans that were always hard-hitting, naming the official concerned, and making the chants as personal as possible. The women went a step further. They sang wonderful songs about the exploitation by a particular official who had robbed them of their rights. When we had a demonstration, I sat back and enjoyed the lovely songs and inventive sloganeering. The crowds of people who came out to see what was happening nodded their heads in acquiescence, and urchins took up the refrain when the official came out of his office. Officials were always shaken by what they called name-calling and told me so whenever they got the opportunity.

No bribes were given except on one occasion. Even then, when there was a cut in the bill, the entire village—men, women and children—went to the MDO's office at Ibrahimpatnam and held a meeting. Representatives of the villagers called the mandal development officer out of his office in front of everyone and explained to him which officials had cut the bill and siphoned the difference. The two minor officials returned the money immediately.

Dandumailaram Acchaiah was the leader of the released bonded labourers in Endlagudem, a tiny hamlet of Polkampalli, some ten kilometres east of Ibrahimpatnam. He cared for his flock deeply and visited our other villages regularly to take note of activities there which could benefit his own hamlet. He told us, 'The Sangam has got our bonded labourers released. If we cannot provide them with work, they could well return to bondage. We cannot get work because the labourers at Polkampalli get all the work and we live far away from other villages too.'

Of the various schemes sponsored by the government, some were implemented by the Khadi and Village Industries Commission. In 1986, I visited the KVIC for more information and they pointed to the possibility of setting up a khadi yarn spinning unit. They said they could supply cotton, but had a shortage of yarn. If we could get people to spin yarn, there would be a ready market available to them. We worked with the SC Corporation on this, and its enthusiastic executive officer, P. Ratnam, eased the way whenever other authorities like the bank and the KVIC stalled us. (I soon found out that Ratnam was an Ambedkarite when I ran into him at Ambedkarite meetings in Hyderabad.) We ran the khadi spinning unit at Endlagudem for four years. The spinning assured guaranteed work all through the year for about fifty-five women, who earned wages of fifteen to thirty rupees a day. The Bhagyanagar Khadi Samiti under the KVIC supplied the cotton, our women spun the yarn, and it was then delivered back to the source.

Acchaiah shouldered the entire responsibility for yarn and was the driving force behind the four-year miracle that the unit was. About fifty years old, he had lost most of his teeth. His speech was sometimes difficult to understand, and yet his demands were clear and insistent. He hounded the Bhagyanagar Khadi Samiti, the district administration, the KVIC and related organizations and also us, when yarn was over, when the charkhas needed repair and when payment to the women was due. He also got the SC Corporation to build a big shed as a working space for the women. The shed still stands, but is empty. The khadi operation was shut down in 1993. Personally, I found the spinning unit to be exhausting. Beginning 1987, the land struggle took up most of my time, and I never knew where I was needed for what. But Acchaiah and the spinning unit could not be let down either. May through November were extremely busy months for the union's agitational activity. We needed to rope in all hands during this period. After November, the converse was true. Naturally, constructive activity suffered. Poor Acchaiah and others like him found little help. I resented the fact that the responsibility for both agitational and constructive activity was vested in me and I was answerable to everyone for everything.

Nevertheless, people always managed to stand up and be counted when challenges or opportunities arose. When the women of Pethula learnt that the forest department was going to parcel out the use of land to people, they organized themselves into a tight group under Bacchamma and demanded that they be given the first opportunity. Bacchamma had nothing to do with bonded labourers. A mala, her husband had a minor job in the railways and their family therefore did well. She was a natural leader, who, intrigued by the movement in her village, stepped in to take an active role in the Sangam. A block of 100 acres of forest land was equally divided among the women. They were paid to dig pits, plant trees under usufructuary right and water them. They were also allowed to use all the produce from this area. The result was so good that the forest department took up this scheme for women elsewhere in the state.

The poor had many ailments. The older men and women complained of knee pain inevitably and many women were bent double after decades of transplanting paddy or weeding. Their diet was poor, no doubt due to poverty, but the situation could still be improved with all the produce that was available in the region. Papaya trees were plentiful but the people did not eat the papaya fruit. Drumstick trees were all over but the leaves were not used. The sorrel leaf, locally known as gongura, was used only for a spicy chutney but not in curries. The younger generation was gradually getting averse to the only source of protein they had—beef—due to the stigma attached to it by the savarnas. In the 1980s, there were still berries and wild fruits like the sitaphal which people could access, but this was sharply reducing with the clearance of jungles and the cutting down of trees growing in farms to aid better crop produce. Added to this, N.T. Rama Rao's scheme for rice costing two rupees a kilogram was introduced in October 1983. While this certainly averted starvation and gave food security to the impoverished, it ended up changing the diet of most people in Telangana. Prior to this, the staple was jowar and other millets like bajra, ragi, foxtail millet and little millet. Millet is a whole grain that has protein, antioxidants and nutrients, and unlike rice, is not polished white. Millet also has a lower glycemic index when compared to rice. That is, it causes a slower rise of our blood sugar levels than does rice. Foods with a high glycemic index like rice are quickly digested and absorbed, causing a rapid rise in blood sugar. Now, with a whole population preferring cheap white rice, diets worsened, and in the 1990s, diabetes was on the rise. Rice had always been a privileged food and its ready availability led to people depending on this as their primary calorie source.

There were public health centres in Yacharam and Ibrahimpatnam, but the doctors, when they attended at all, were uninspired tired beings who doled out tablets to keep the sick at bay—red for fevers and white for everything else. Pregnant women, for anything more complicated than a normal delivery, had to go to the Osmania General Hospital in Hyderabad.

Dr Vasudevan Kidambi, an old friend, was an institution in Marredpally in the 1980s. During our college days, he and I were part of a group, the Science Club. He was a gifted, public-spirited general physician. I asked Vasudevan to help us. From 1987 to 1994, he and Dr V. Arumugam (a trained acupuncturist) ran a makeshift weekend clinic in Ibrahimpatnam. They drove down from Hyderabad on a scooter every weekend, and camped at our office or any available space. They examined patients, distributed medicines that could be organized free of cost, and suggested possible treatments. Vasu's treatment regimen was unique. In his Marredpally clinic, he was famous for bluntly telling obese patients who came to him to cut down food and reduce weight. In Ibrahimpatnam, many people came with complaints of constipation and Vasu regularly doled out paddy husk to them. This was recalled with much amusement by villagers who were used to tablets and injections for every ailment. He treated infections, the common knee and back aches, children's fevers and other common illnesses. He arranged a heart operation for Kusuma Reddy, a woman from Pulimamidi, who, forty years later, is still alive and recalls his work. Vasu helped organize several other health initiatives. In 1988, we tied up with the Bowenpally National Institute for the Mentally Handicapped which sent its volunteer-experts to identify children suffering from mental and physical disabilities. They ran training programmes and arranged bus passes for the parents to take the children to NIMH for further training and follow-ups. Vasu also organized special camps with senior doctors. In 1988, I was delighted to find my old friend Sarojini Reddy—the gynaecologist who had kept me grounded in the post-Emergency Delhi phase—among other doctors at a camp in Yacharam.

The same year, I happened to meet B. Venkatesh of Action on Disability and Development India in Penukonda of Anantapur district. He and his team worked to organise the disabled people of Anantapur district by forming sangams or Disabled Persons Organizations. These organizations worked like self-help groups and advocated for the rights and inclusion of disabled persons in their villages. I was impressed with the energy of the organization. Their first demand was that the word 'handicapped' be dropped from our vocabulary. At that time, the concerned department in the government was called the Andhra Pradesh Handicapped Persons Welfare Cooperative Finance Corporation. This corporation certified the disabled, enabling them to get free passes for public transport and preference in some government schemes. Hence the term handicapped was popularly used everywhere, including among our people. ADD insisted repeatedly and on every possible platform that disabled people not be called handicapped.

Venkatesh himself is visually challenged and extremely tenacious. In my discussions with him, he asked me why the Sangam could not work with the disabled. 'Why don't you start with disabled children?' he asked. 'This way, we can get everyone—the able-bodied and the differently abled to work together.' I told him that we did not have many disabled children in our area. He asked us to do a survey. We quickly surveyed over 10,000 households in the villages where we had a presence. The results were mind-boggling and showed how ignorant I was. Over 10 per cent of the children had a disability of some kind—partial or total blindness, deafness, motor disability, or inability to speak. These children had been out of sight and invisible to us all this while. We invited ADD to work with us in Ibrahimpatnam, and help us set up correctional programmes for the children and the adults. In the course of this work, Venkatesh along with his team member, Isaac Newton, visited our villages several times between 1988 and 1999.

Kunti Ramulu of Hasmatpura, the man with the Jaipur Foot, became the Sangam person in charge of work with the disabled. With ADD's help, we began an organization of the disabled which soon became completely autonomous— Ibrahimpatnam Taluka Vikulangula Sangam. If ITVCS was a militant organization, this was even more so. The Vikulangula Sangam organized themselves for loans, schemes for the disabled from the government, and against discrimination. They demanded our help whenever necessary. Ramulu now began to devote himself entirely to this work. Their tenacity and will to fight inspired us.

19 An attempt on my life in Dandumalkapuram

Early in 1988, before the onset of summer, the ferment over land threatened to overwhelm us and strain our scarce resources and volunteers. Added to the three major land struggles in Jabbargudem, Pulimamidi and Meerkhanpet, the one in Dandumalkapuram in Choutuppal mandal also threatened to blow up. People were restive, eager to move and claim their rights, and leaders had sprung up everywhere.

In Pulimamidi, we were able to cultivate the land because the villagers were totally united and the landlords couldn't sway the loyalties of even one among their numbers. But despite our efforts we could not get our names in the cultivators' column of the pahanis. The revenue officials refused to budge. Scores of police cases were filed against us and people had to make the rounds of courts and jails continuously. The circle inspector of Pahadisharif, Ashokvardhan Reddy, was asked to keep tabs on me and I received a call from him every day. Frustrated by the lack of results, I even suggested to the villagers once that we place bombs all around the gadi and destroy it. Fortunately, no one took me up on the suggestion.

The Sangam continued to concentrate on Jabbargudem. Every time a decision was made in our favour, the landlords appealed to the higher court and obtained a stay. My old comrade, Indra Reddy, was the district minister and along with him, Manchireddy Kishan Reddy was able to organize at least four MLAs to meet and pressure the district officials against even the smallest decisions that were favourable to the poor. Kishan Reddy's father, Bhoopal Reddy, continued to terrorize the villagers. Several of our people were beaten up whenever they were caught alone. The Manchireddy land adjoined the disputed land, and Bhoopal Reddy and his men were always on the lookout for unsuspecting villagers. Shankaraiah too was beaten up like this. The police were always on their side and continued to file cases and arrest our people. The Sangam organized several demonstrations, one even at the state assembly, in August 1988, under the leadership of the AP Dalit Mahasabha and Bojja Tharakam. While a small delegation went inside to give a representation to the Speaker, Chandra Rajeswara Rao of the CPI and Nayani Narasimha Reddy (MLA, Janata Party, and trade unionist) addressed us outside as we were not allowed inside.

Somehow we survived, though I often thought that it could be one more case, one more attack, and we would be finished. How long were we going to mobilize support from outside? We were to soon discover that our strength was the villagers themselves—village after village began rising up to question their landlords. Choudaripally was one such place where the biggest landlord, Ananth Reddy, was forced to lead the negotiations to broker peace. He was a politician and understood that this stand-off between reddys and madigas would only damage the reddys.

In 1988, the madigas of Choudaripally approached us with the story of how Ananth Reddy had usurped large tracts of land in their village. Choudaripally was barely a kilometre from Yacharam, but the madigas of this village had stayed away from us for four years. Their relatives in other villages told us that the Choudaripally madigas were loyal to Ananth Reddy who served as Ibrahimpatnam MLA from 1972 to 1978. He had over 280 acres of land, five wells and a few vineyards. He had many houses and businesses in the city, and his eldest son was in the US, with the other three also well settled. He was not a native of Choudaripally. While young, he was adopted by a landlord in the village from a poor family elsewhere. He became a prominent leader in the Congress, and was twice the panchayat samiti president before being elected as an MLA. When the proposal for night schools came up in Ibrahimpatnam taluka during Ananth Reddy's tenure as panchayat samiti president, he refused to allow one in his village, saying, 'Who will look after our herds if the madiga children are educated. Today, they want to go to school, tomorrow, they will ask for land.'

When the 1973 Land Ceiling Act was passed, he supported it in the assembly, but ensured that his own land was unaffected. Seventy-three acres were transferred to a relative and to his biological father living far away. He fabricated twelve years of revenue records by getting the patwari's son a government job in return. His own two minor sons were declared as majors, and with benami transfers of seventy-three more acres, he was able to retain all his land.

But the benami transfers were not accepted by the land ceiling authority. After years of litigation, twelve of his many acres were judged to be above the ceiling and he resentfully gave six acres of rocky terrain and another six of infertile land to his farmhands. After this order was passed, he had forty-five acres of his own land sold back to him.

When we were told the whole story, ITVCS dug out Ananth Reddy's records and found out that every bit of what the madigas said was true. By now, our strategies were set. Once the revenue and ceiling records proved that there was fraud, petitions were given to all the revenue authorities concerned and the villagers commenced operations that signified control of the land. This process began faster in Choudaripally as the villagers had seen and heard of what had happened in the struggles in other villages from their relatives.

But there was no ploughing and planting crops since most of it was orchard land. People began guarding the fruit trees and clearing weeds, signifying passage of control to them. The police were unable to rein them in despite arresting a few villagers.

In 1988, the villagers surrounded Ananth Reddy's house for three days. The dharna was an epic one. The locals had stayed in his iron-fisted control for too long and now the dam had burst. The women sang songs recreating his family's past cruelty, from his parents to him, the story of his childhood, his growth into a full-fledged landlord, his criminal activities and worst of all, the bad luck of his wife who had to put up with him for so long. The verbal abuse was unremitting and terrifying. Ananth Reddy stopped all agricultural operations and fled to the city.

At the same time in villages elsewhere, police repression was increasing severely—they refused us permission to hold meetings, refused to accept petitions, beat our people up when they went to the police station to give a petition, always ensured that a non-bailable section was added to FIRs to prevent easy bails. I was also out on bail in several cases and had to attend court hearings frequently. Revenue authorities, from the mandal level up to the commissioner of land revenue, were not so intractable against us as were the police. I always wondered at the startling difference.

I slowly discovered that the primary burden of administrative ethos and procedure, of general, civil and criminal laws, of judicial pronouncements and practices, of all these mighty institutions, was the maintenance and safeguarding of existing property relations. More than 33 per cent of the operative sections of the IPC relate to offences against property rights—the IPC lists 112 offences against property. If we add up offences against public order listed in the CrPC, the figure is 134. Thus, a police officer in rural areas can round up sharecroppers or agricultural labourers who seek to assert their right to minimum wages, security of tenure or surplus land under any of these provisions of the CrPC or IPC. While asserting his right to minimum wages, a dalit may commit an offence against the public order. While the administration is prompt in registering and investigating the latter case, it is unable to move fast to enforce minimum wages.

Our Sangam then became a crucial vehicle through which the poor could navigate a system that was heavily weighted against them. Right in Yacharam, we found twenty acres of government land occupied by landlords. The leaders of the struggle who organized activities to retrieve this did not take an inch of the land. Instead, the poor communities of the village (madiga, mangali, chakali) sat together and came up with a list of the poorest among them who needed the land most. Pattas were issued according to this list. When it was discovered that Krishna Reddy had encroached on two acres for his cattle sheds, we freed this up, and the local revenue administration, which till then had rented offices in the house of Malla Reddy, built buildings for all its offices there. A tamarind copse was identified to be on government land. The reddys who had been enjoying this for generations were summarily ejected and the poor took the fruit.

These land struggles changed my focus entirely and offered new lessons. Wage struggles, even after they were successful, meant the landlords continued to hold the reins of power. The labourer remained a supplicant. The landlords can turn punitive and refuse to give you work. When land is liberated, the person becomes relatively self-sufficient. It portends wealth and well-being. If dalits—who for centuries have been slaves and bonded labourers—came to own and till their own land, however modest, they would not have to stretch their hands before the bloodsucking doras. The wresting of the monopoly of a few over the land breaks the very spine of systemic exploitation. The political mobilization that comes with land struggles cannot be compared to anything else. The saying goes, 'All a person needs is six feet of land to be buried in.' Yet people are willing to die for land. Fighting for wages was one thing; land was something else entirely. It is the key for any work in the countryside.

Perennial and silent processes shape the struggle for land. Ten guntas (one-fourth of an acre) are earned through the grinding labour of one's children, another ten from a dowry that has made another family destitute. A landless labourer may do years of unpaid work for the patwari or village revenue officer in the hope of the allotment of a small patch of government land in his name. A landless labourer may remain a landlord's strongman all his life, invoking the strong displeasure of his community, in the hope that his master may favour him with a piece of land surrendered under the ceiling surplus legislation. A landless labourer may marry a woman whose family has land and no male heir, and shift his residence permanently. A widow with children to raise may choose to have a relationship with the landlord, displeasing her caste panchayat, so that her son has some land when he comes of age.

The kind of mass mobilization that ITCVS anchored made it possible for individual struggles to cohere and have a larger meaning. Usually, villagers know only their relatives in other villages. Discussions are carried on in this closed context. The Sangam created a political space and a forum for discussion for the poor of the area, a space which exists even today. Villagers often met other villagers from as far as twenty-five kilometres away. This brought richness into the texture of their daily lives and struggles.

The lives of landless dalits were transformed by these struggles. One can argue that land alone cannot make a difference in the lives of poor dalits. Yet, for a whole people to rise in one generation and make substantial improvements in their lives, land is crucial. Education and employment can make more of a difference in the lives of the younger generation. But the struggle for ownership of land, a valuable asset, affects the lives of adults who consider themselves beyond the pale of education and employment.

Due to our efforts, more than fifteen hundred bonded labourers were officially released and rehabilitated, another 1,420 released unofficially and their debts repudiated. Agricultural wages rose from a range of eight annas to two rupees to a range of four to five rupees for women; from a range of six to seven rupees to twelve to fifteen rupees for men; monthly wages for farmhands rose from sixty to eighty rupees to Rs 180–300. Over two lakh rupees were settled by landlords as back wages to agricultural labourers and Rs 66,000 settled in workmen's compensation cases for injuries. We freed some 14,000 acres from the control of landlords in the mandals of Ibrahimpatnam, Yacharam, Kandukur, Maheswaram, Hayathnagar and Choutuppal, and helped the village poor to cultivate these. Most of these plots have either pattas or cultivator status recorded today. The price of an acre of land in Ibrahimpatnam varies from Rs 80 lakh to Rs 5 crore now, which means, by current estimates, the Sangam transferred assets worth between Rs 11,200 crore and Rs 70,000 crore from the landed gentry to the landless poor in land alone.

In addition to this, over a hundred acres of good land

was purchased for the rehabilitation of bonded labourers, apart from repudiation of debts and the rise in wages. During our activities, we did not beat or hurt anyone physically and tried to follow constitutional means all through. We also intervened in development programmes of the government and organized the poor to bypass middlemen and bribes, and access the agricultural labourers' pension, programmes of the District Rural Development Agency and the SC Corporation. We helped set up a cooperative khadi spinning unit, organized social forestry programmes, and helped construct locally designed housing colonies without contractors. One of our biggest contributions was to get hundreds of out-of-school children into government hostels and schooling programmes, and to actively run a health programme for the poor. We created a political space and a forum for discussion for the poor of the area which exists even today. Most important of all, the sense of self-respect and entitlement the dalits in the area recorded with the growth of our union was immeasurable.

I was now meeting people who were in some positions of authority for help. I frequented the offices of the CPI and the CPI(M) as they still had MLAs to raise questions in the assembly. Suravaram Sudhakar Reddy had been in the CPI's national council and worked in various capacities for the party's state unit. He always gave me a patient hearing, and CPI MLAs frequently issued statements and raised questions in support of ITVCS. At this time, the CPI(M) was in an alliance with the ruling TDP and gave us the cold shoulder. The reddys dominated other parties in Telangana. The BJP had only a small presence in Andhra Pradesh in 1988 and its leader, Kishan Reddy, is from Thimmapur, barely a kilometre from Jabbargudem. (At the time of writing, Kishan Reddy is the Union minister for culture, tourism and development of north-eastern region.)

In 1988, I went to Delhi twice and made our case with several authorities. I met the secretaries of the departments of home, social welfare and labour. I went to Dr B.D. Sharma, commissioner, Scheduled Castes and Scheduled Tribes (later to be called commissioner, National Commission for Scheduled Castes and Scheduled Tribes). I met Ela Bhatt, founder of the Self-Employed Women's Association, a trade union representing self-employed female textile workers. She was an MP in the Rajya Sabha and chairperson of the National Commission on Self-Employed Women. The secretaries to the Union government told me that law and order and land were state subjects, they could do nothing.

B.D. Sharma and Ela Bhatt were responsive and gave me long, patient hearings. Ela Bhatt was gentle and warm and offered to let me stay at her place whenever I was in Delhi. (Subsequently, she invited me to several meetings, none of which I could attend; nevertheless, she continued to keep in touch.) Sharma was known to be responsive to activists working in tribal areas and as an IAS officer in Bastar, then in Madhya Pradesh, he had strictly enforced laws in favour of tribals. He was instrumental in bringing the Fifth Schedule of the Constitution back on the national agenda as a vital instrument for the survival of tribal people. He was responsible for the formulation of tribal policies, particularly what is known as the 'sub-plan' strategy. His instructions were: 'If rules come in the way of stopping exploitation, break them.' HBT had also translated one of his books into Telugu, *Bailadilla Aduvullo Dagapadina Chellellu*, published in English as *Forced Marriages in Bailadilla*. He took me home and grilled me for a whole day on our work in Ibrahimpatnam. We then kept in touch, especially when he came to Andhra Pradesh and I travelled with him on some of his official visits to the Scheduled Areas in 1990–92.

In 1988, Ela Bhatt came with members of the National Commission on Self-Employed Women, which included the journalist Mrinal Pande, to Maheswaram where they sat all afternoon with the women and recorded the testimonies of those who were assaulted by the police. Nothing changed, but we, both the Sangam cadres and the people, were heartened to see the support extended to us.

It was a time of contradictory experiences for me— shuttling between the authorities in Hyderabad and Delhi, while the landlords in the village continued sabre-rattling. At this time, Dandumalkapuram caught me unawares.

Most of the landlords stayed in the city, so I had not foreseen a big threat. In April 1988, late in the morning, we were sitting in a meeting in the madiga-wada when groups of men—local landlords and their gangs—came menacingly towards us, shouting that I should either pay back the debts owed to them by the bonded labourers released under my leadership or send them back to work. The situation turned ugly in a few minutes. The madigas took me a little distance away from the mob, pushed me into a tiled house, locked the house from outside and told the mob that I had left.

Evidently, the mob discovered where I was because soon, there were two people climbing on to the roof, removing the tiles and the rest screaming outside the house. The madiga men had run away. It was a strange situation. Time stood still, and I had no one to support me, but I remember not being afraid. The situation was raw, unmediated. It was totally up to me whether I would live or die with dignity. I looked around the room, found an axe and sat with it, promising myself that if I had to die, I would take someone with me. I shouted this to the men sitting on the roof, removing the tiles. I don't know what their response was, I was focused on keeping myself calm and alert. I had come in a van from Hyderabad and the driver Mallesh had meanwhile rushed to the police station in Choutuppal. From the police station, he drove to Hyderabad to inform Cyril. In about half an hour the sub-inspector of police, who had hurried here on being informed by Mallesh, reached the village while the tile removal was well under way. There was a commotion, the people on the roof stopped their work, and the sub-inspector opened the door to let me out.

He abused me and blamed me for the attack. 'What else will people do if you take away their jeetas and their land?' he asked. He called me a Naxalite, and told me that I had to leave the village, that he would not be responsible for my safety. 'Why did you come,' I asked him, 'if you cannot escort me safely out of the village?' 'I came to ensure that you are not killed, but you should learn your lesson not to go around villages like this and disturb law and order.' He left soon after and I began walking to the road, the women of our union weeping alongside me. The village's madiga men had run away, knowing that they would be attacked if they came to my defence; they were unprepared to face attack. I soon began to run, and the same mob of angry men followed behind gesticulating and shouting abusive curses. I ran faster and faster, leaving the madiga women behind. By the time I neared the highway—the Vijayawada–Hyderabad main road barely half a kilometre away—the mob was close behind. This is how I remember the day. I thought I would be killed, but perhaps the attackers were bent only on teaching me a lesson and frightening me. Couldn't they have thrown stones at me, injured and stopped me? I stopped a bemused moped rider, hopped on the pillion, and told him to turn back towards Hyderabad. 'If you don't take me that way, I will tell the mob that you work with me.' The poor man turned towards

Hyderabad and we went a few miles before the van with Cyril in it rushed towards us. This was how I escaped from the village.

A few days later, a fact-finding committee with the economist and professor D. Narasimha Reddy, academic and civil rights activist Kancha Ilaiah, Shantha Sinha, lawyer G. Manohar and others went to the village and presented their findings on the attack on me at a press conference. When B.D. Sharma visited Dandumalkapuram in July 1988, I did not accompany him. I never visited the village again. I felt unsafe and unsure. Our local union men had fled when I was attacked and this bothered me.

I continued to push the paperwork and attend to the court cases. The high court had granted stays on all the proceedings, which naturally favoured the landlords. The proactive officials were transferred, the landlords were trying to split the peasants by promising membership to cooperative societies to their leaders. I couldn't see a way out of this in the face of the disunity among the agricultural labourers. There was a long lull.

What happened next had nothing to do with the Sangam. In 1993 after I had left the scene, the PWG stepped into Dandumalkapuram. They must have had sleeper cells here among the youth, and within a record time of three months, they had united the labourers and small peasants. This was at a time in Andhra Pradesh when the PWG resorted to kidnapping important politicians to force the government to release its cadres in jails. Almost the whole of Telangana was under the influence of the PWG at this time. Their activists moved around in armed squads, created deliberate terror in villages, and few villagers had the gumption to stand up to them. The PWG's armed squad forced the landlords at gunpoint to withdraw their appeals in the high court and to hand over the government-issued pattas to the poor. They even killed a madiga labourer who had functioned as the eyes and ears of the landlords in the village. This was in consonance with their policy to kill informers and create 'revolutionary terror'. The villagers of Dandumalkapuram were now free of the domination of the landlords, who had fled the village, but lived in fear of the police who refused to allow them to cultivate their own lands. It remained a pyrrhic victory.

I had been in regular touch with B.D. Sharma. On my asking, two months after this incident, Sharma visited Jabbargudem, Pulimamidi and Dandumalkapuram in June 1988. After he left, we had a small meeting in Eliminedu where we discussed what to do about the disputed land in Jabbargudem. Activists from several villages had gathered. The Jabbargudem villagers had ploughed and sown jowar and the landlords had then brought about two hundred men from the city to keep guard while his tractors ploughed over our seedlings. The landlords' men were planting castor. We sat late into the night and when I urged that we get our ploughs and replant jowar, everybody shot down the idea. The landlords and their men had guns, and nobody wanted to get killed. Everyone was despondent. At midnight I announced that I was going to the fields anyway. I was tired of sitting there, and if anyone was brave enough, they could follow me. I got up and walked out.

Everyone followed me. It was then that I became part of their decision making—I must have been able to judge their mood and how they would react. We cleared the castor crop at 2 a.m. It was cold—July is often colder than the winter because the rains have cooled the land and the gusty winds are chilly. At dawn, we had completed most of the work.

With the rising sun came the landlords with their guns, jeeps, cars and men. We heard the sound of six shots being fired. But for our large numbers, the people would have fled. People told me to hunker down among the shrubs because I would be targeted. I remember that no one was afraid for themselves, they only worried about me. It was a moment of total freedom—I was flying like a bird in the open skies, yet totally protected by the love of my people. I had no need to look out for myself, everyone was watching my back. It was a beautiful moment—tense, so tense. The two sides faced each other for what felt like an eternity. We could clearly make out the men and their rifles a little over a hundred yards in front of us in the foggy morning mist. Then the cars and jeeps and men slowly turned away.

We returned to the village, forty-two pairs of cattle pulling their ploughs, and there was Bojja Tharakam, come from Hyderabad to greet us, the most wonderful sight in my life. For the first time in a life shorn of aesthetics, I could appreciate the sight of cattle-drawn ploughs making their way along the horizon, during sunrise.

We had to pay a price though. The Manchireddys were able to get a blockbuster mandamus—a judicial writ issued as a command ordering a person to perform a public or statutory duty. The Jabbargudem villagers were picked up at night, taken to Pahadishareef police station far away and sent to remand. We got them out on bail only later in the week. Cyril and I were picked up from our Chikkadpally home the same night. The police headed by the circle inspector of Pahadishareef came knocking at our door at around midnight on a Friday. This is a usual practice so that the victims cannot approach the court for bail over the weekend. They planned to keep us in custody all through the weekend. We were kept all night at the Rajendranagar police station more than fifty kilometres away from the city, and the next afternoon, taken to the magistrate's house in Hyderabad. The magistrate was writing the remand to jail us when I asked him to allow me to make one phone call to our lawyer Padmanabha Reddy. His eyebrows rose at the name—Padmanabha Reddy's name was legend. I made the call. Thankfully, Padmanabha Reddy was there to receive it and he sent his son Praveen Kumar (a judge in the Andhra Pradesh High Court at the time of writing) over to the magistrate's house. We were released on bail.

Anurag Sharma was the superintendent of police at Ranga Reddy at the time. He had married his batchmate Mamta who hailed from a reddy family near Hayathnagar close to Ibrahimpatnam. The reddys of Ibrahimpatnam hailed the couple, proclaiming that their son-in-law was now the SP. After we were released, we brought out a leaflet, saying the reddys of Ibrahimpatnam are declaring that their son-in-law as SP shall solve their burning problem. Anurag Sharma was upset with this pamphlet. He sent word through the collector that I should meet him. I refused. I was angry at being picked up in the dead of night like a criminal. When I finally met him, he insisted that he was not responsible for my arrest and had not reacted because his father-in-law was a reddy. Instead, it was because of the court mandamus and because four Ranga Reddy district MLAs had walked into his office to insist on my arrest.

We had yet another land case against the Manchireddy family in Jabbargudem in the same year. This had to do with their illegal possession of eighteen acres of government land in the village, which was adjacent to the already disputed land we were fighting for. They had this land assigned to three benamis (minor government officials), then got a court decree of purchase. As government land in Andhra Pradesh cannot be sold or purchased, we took this up with representations. The revenue department officials, from the MRO to the collector, refused to act. We went to the high court and the collector was directed to take action.

The Manchireddy family grew even more aggressive. K.G. Kannabiran, a senior lawyer and human rights activist and co-founder of People's Union for Civil Liberties, was also the lawyer for a cigarette company. Knowing that Kannabiran worked with activists, the Muslim owner of the company told him that the goondas who sometimes worked for him had told him of an unusual supari—for a young woman who organized the poor in Ibrahimpatnam. We received word from Kannabiran that a supari of one lakh rupees was out on me from the Manchireddy family.

I had to be careful now. I left home and stayed with the banker and Cheyutha co-founder Diwakar Reddy for a while. At this time, the Salaha office was on the ground floor and the HBT office on the first floor, where we also had a room to ourselves. Since both the HBT and Salaha offices were open to the public, we decided to shift our home and rent a room nearby. Almost no one knew about our new accommodation. Our neighbours near the offices were told about the threat and any new person found loitering in the street was questioned. Cyril began monitoring my every movement and was meticulous in the arrangements for my security. I now had a driver and a van owned by Salaha to travel in, and the driver was to strictly follow Cyril's instructions. I was to always move in a group of trusted villagers. I was to always sleep in the interior of a madiga hamlet, never elsewhere. I was never to go anywhere except in the company of our own people.

The whole arrangement was really irksome and I felt

like I had no freedom of movement. If I ever ignored the arrangements, I got a dressing-down from Cyril. Once, particularly vexed, he told me, 'This is how we lost George. He was foolish like you.' I tried to be careful after that because he had never ever spoken of his brother and I had upset him greatly.

Trying to find a way out of the labyrinth that I was trapped in, I went to the superintendent of police, Anurag Sharma. His advice was to get good locks for the doors. I toyed with the idea of getting a gun licence but knew that I was not going to be able to get trained and was more likely to shoot myself. While in the Naxalite movement, I had not been involved in any militia training.

20 Tackling rudeness with rudeness

Thanks to all of Manchireddy family's machinations, our villagers did not dare to enter the small piece of eighteen-acre property that had been formally seized by the MRO by October 1988. The landlord's family continued to have control over it. Shankaraiah, the Sangam president, has an interesting account of how we broke this in a daring move. Many years later, in 2021, in his interview with me, Jhumur Lahiri and Sashi Kumar, he reminisced, 'The MRO was due to come for an inspection before he took over the land. The Manchireddys had raised castor on the land and it was important that the crop not be recorded in their name. Gita had given Pandi Maisaiah and three other people fifteen days to destroy the crop. When he didn't complete the job, she brought bangles and put these on him in a meeting inside our office in Ibrahimpatnam. Then she asked me, Shankaraiah, you are not wishy-washy—you either do things or you don't. Will you do this?

'I agreed. But I was really scared. I thought that I should not take people from either Eliminedu or Jabbargudem with me. The Manchireddys would call the police after the event, who would beat up the poor people and make them spill the beans. I was scared but keen to do the job. I hated the Manchireddys. They were so cruel to poor people. Earlier, I had gone to Jabbargudem with the village map to show the people the outlines of the land. While I was returning on the road to Eliminedu, a jeep with Prabhakar Reddy and Dayanand Reddy, sons of Bhoopal Reddy, stopped me on my moped. I knew that some villager of Jabbargudem had informed them. Kunti Ramulu was riding pillion and as soon as he saw them, he said, "Sir, I have nothing to do with this, I am a lame man." They caught me, tore the map into pieces, abused me foully, and beat me up. Their slaps rang in my ears for days after that.

'I planned to take seventy-five people from the Yacharam villages because I knew these villagers well and because the area is far away from the Jabbargudem land. I also recruited strapping young men from Mondigourelli, Maal, Yacharam and Nandiwanaparthy, called them separately and told them that they needed to reach our Yacharam office at 8 p.m. after eating dinner as we were to go to Hyderabad for a meeting which Gita had arranged. I arranged for a van (the driver slept near our office and we were friendly with all the workmen in the area) to take us to Kuppalagadda, though I did not tell him exactly where we were going. If he had known it was to do with the Manchireddy family, he may not have come.

'It was only after everybody got into the van that I told them where we were going. Some people were scared but they could not escape now. Bandi Sriramulu, the mala who contested for the Ibrahimpatnam Mandal Parishad Territorial Constituency, was also there. We did not know the way to Kuppalagadda. When we reached Madapur, we got down, sent the van back, and asked a trusted union member there for the way. He directed us to the fields. We picked up sticks from the stream (then dry) which flowed between Madapur and the Jabbargudem fields, and in half an hour, we destroyed the ripening castor crop, striking it with sticks. Bhoopal Reddy had some six motors for his wells. We threw some of these inside the wells, and we took some home with us. Our people also picked up sheep and goats from their corrals near the well to take home and some others tapped the eeta (palm) for kallu.

'After this we went our separate ways back to our villages

using the small pathways, and not the roads. I reached Yacharam at around four in the morning and then came to meet Gita in Hyderabad that evening. The stress of the whole event made me fall ill and she took me to a doctor. I stayed for two whole days with her, going to the cinema and eating nice food—simply relaxing and escaping the tension of the past two days.

'A case was filed against 130 madigas of Eliminedu and Jabbargudem and some of them were taken to the police station and beaten up. Since they knew nothing, the police got no information and eventually gave up the case.'

Despite the earnestness with which the Sangam took up the issue, and despite Shankaraiah's concern, nothing moved forward though the illegal possession of the land by the Manchireddys had been summarily dismissed. A writ petition filed by the landlords (and their benamis) was rejected and a further writ appeal, that was to come in February 1996, was also dismissed. This land remains in Manchireddy control even today. In 1995, after I had withdrawn from the area, the landlords moved forward to have the villagers arrested and beaten up for entering the land. The then collector Pushpa Subramaniam wrote to the superintendent of police, Narsaiah, stating that the police had no locus standi to book any case against the villagers in matters concerning government land. She contended that if any action had to be taken, it was to be by the MRO concerned. The superintendent of police ignored her instructions. The collector then booked a contempt of court case against Kishan Reddy and his men. Interestingly, the file containing the case is now missing. By the late 1990s—the time of the IT boom and Hyderabad becoming a neoliberal investments hub—Ranga Reddy district had become too important for politicians to ignore. It contained invaluable land—lucrative gold mines for them in the coming decades.

Back in 1988, I had my own personal upheavals, which I had to juggle with the intense land struggles I was already involved in. Cyril fell seriously ill with jaundice in 1988, almost going into a hepatic coma, and had to take bed rest for a year. I had to return home every day, and could no longer have extended stays in the villages. I cooked early in the morning and left for Ibrahimpatnam in the Salaha van. The villagers sent a young girl to help with housework. For the first time, I had help at home and I remember both the fifteen-year-old yerukala girl, Ailamma, and Cyril, anxiously waiting for me on the steps outside till I returned late at night. The Eliminedu struggle was going on, and I found it so difficult to manage all of this at the same time. I cannot imagine now what Cyril was going through—on his own, seriously ill.

One night as I was setting out for Hyderabad after a long meeting in Eliminedu, we were told that an ambush was planned for me at Cherlapatelgudem on the road from Eliminedu to Ibrahimpatnam. We left in a grand convoy: one lorry loaded with people was the pilot, followed by the van in which I was travelling, and behind us another lorry with people forming the tail. The convoy stopped at all the dangerous points, looked for people behind the bushes by the road, and escorted me safely out of Ibrahimpatnam. Now travelling was also a threat to my safety. On another occasion, we were told that a group was waiting past the Ibrahimpatnam tank to stop my vehicle and attack me on my way to Hyderabad. This was at the village of Sheriguda where the upa-sarpanch Narasimha Reddy had occupied ten acres of prime government land. He had got certificates issued in the names of his sister and a benamidar. He was also the local TDP strongman. The Sangam had taken up the case, and the MRO had issued notices to the benamidars. There was no other way to go to Hyderabad and I couldn't leave Cyril alone for the night. At that time, the circle inspector in Ibrahimpatnam was Bhadra Reddy. When I explained my problem, he got into a jeep, asked another to drive behind him and escorted me to the road to Hyderabad. We saw the gang waiting at Sheriguda take off as soon as they saw police jeeps approaching with horns blaring.

We managed for a couple of months like this. The same year, I stayed for a long time in Hyderabad, for a good few months, without going out on ITVCS work, when Cyril's condition deteriorated. When we realized that it was going to be a long recovery, we decided to move him to his brother's home in Chandigarh. I left him there and returned to Hyderabad. I can't even remember how 1988 passed.

The year also saw a significant rise in the number of smaller land cases, mainly related to tenancy. These were individual cases, that is, a single person stood to benefit if we helped them. Initially, I did not view these cases as important but slowly realized that the fighters were tenacious. They displayed single-minded determination and courage and their struggles energized all the village poor. We supported them all the way.

We were now fighting cases in all kinds of courts—labour courts, revenue courts, judicial/civil courts and criminal courts. We found that the revenue courts and the judicial courts both heard cases of land disputes, and possessed similar juridical powers, with overlapping areas of jurisdiction. A case which could be heard in a revenue court (without court fees, without even an advocate and with far less intimidation) could also be heard in a civil court. These could include cases of protected tenancy and government-assigned land. While the civil court granted an injunction to the petitioner (prohibiting them from encroaching or changing the status quo), the revenue court had a similar power—it could enforce Section 144, restricting unlawful assembly.

I found enormous differences between the civil and revenue courts. The civil court was invested with much pomp. The judge was seated higher than others on an imperial chair, a balustrade separating his area from the laity like a fence. There was the overdressed attender ready to push you if you stood where you were not supposed to, and scold you if you crossed your ankles. Then, there were the advocates, literally black crows waiting to feast on poor litigants. Having given their vakalat to an advocate, the poor were entirely at his mercy. The advocate could make or mar the case. He could obfuscate the arguments, dodge questions, not produce vital documents, not attend hearings, not inform the clients about the dates, even withdraw cases without the permission of his client, and often, sell his client off to the opponent for a price.

There was little of this in the revenue court. Best of all, you were allowed to appear without an advocate. The timings of the revenue court were also decent—the court sat for a few hours on particular days starting from 11 a.m., whereas the civil courts go on all day long and you have to wait till evening to find that your case was not even called. In the revenue court, you could go to the clerk directly, ask about your file, your date, and access the necessary documents. This clerk was also the one people approached for unrelated needs such as the ration card, caste certificates and other such documents. In the civil courts, you could do this only through your advocate. The attenders did not allow you access into the office.

The presiding officers of the revenue courts are the MRO, the RDO and the collector, all of whom have visited villages, met poor people many times, and whom the poor have often approached with petitions outside the court. This familiarity helped the poor enormously. They felt comfortable talking to a revenue court judge.

Many of the gains made by the landless poor in revenue courts were later lost in the civil courts. The land reform statutes enacted by state governments clearly state that civil courts have no jurisdiction over government land and tenancy matters. Yet civil courts (like the police, who have no jurisdiction in these matters either) entertain these concerns, and more often than not, it is the landlord who wins the suit. He can afford a more competent advocate, his advocate belongs to his caste, he has access to land records over the years to press his claim, he can buy over witnesses, such as the sarpanches, sub-inspectors and patwaris to testify on his behalf, he can induce the government pleader and revenue officials to absent themselves during the proceedings. Meanwhile, advocates leech the poor systematically, the poor have no control whatsoever over his conduct during crucial moments in the case and no recourse to a second opinion.

We gained immensely because of the support from Salaha and its lawyers. Cyril being a lawyer himself meant that every case I brought to him benefited from his careful investigation and thought. He explored loopholes in the law to ensure that the poor could get justice. It was because of this support that I could engage with law with a relative lack of bitterness and resentment, given that the poor always had the short end of the stick. Salaha lawyers G. Manohar and Arjun Reddy made themselves available to come anywhere at short notice. C.V. Mohan Reddy, who was with Salaha and also a top lawyer, looked after most of our civil cases in the high court.

Despite such a support system, there were things I did

that I haven't shared even with Cyril. When our cases were in the court, I often suffered from anxiety, wondering about the outcome. The law allows only a narrow interpretation of the issue. The sufferings of the poor, in the context of the enormous disparity of resources and social capital in their confrontations with the landlords, are not taken into account. Very often, the facts of the case as presented in court are prejudicial to the poor. Many of them have unwittingly signed on a blank paper in the past, and they lose their cases in a lower court based on such 'evidence', since they are judged ex parte.

Fearing such an outcome, in one case I mustered the courage and went to the house of a high court judge. I met his personal secretary, gave my name and details, and why I needed to meet the judge, a reddy but a liberal by reputation. When I met him, I poured my heart out and told him the story of the Jabbargudem land struggle, none of which would appear in the arguments before him in court. He gave me a patient hearing for maybe over an hour and I left. We won the case. I dared not tell anyone about this, though there was no question of contempt of court as I was not the petitioner in the case. Still, my advocates would have thought it unethical. I didn't. Judges met rich landlords and their relatives at parties, at their houses, in weddings and other functions. Landlords always had their ear. I thought my move somewhat squared the circle of disparity and I never spoke anything but the whole truth as I knew it. After this, I continued this unorthodox petitioning whenever I could. It always yielded results.

By this time, the paying members of the Sangam were over six thousand, though many thousand more claimed to be part of it. No doubt they were, but they were not card-holding and dues-paying members. We were nine full-timers though some among us doubled up in looking after the NFE schools too. One of the important jobs of the Sangam activists was to accompany people to the offices and ensure that they were given a fair hearing and that the paperwork moved forward. All of us visited the government offices. The RDOs and higher officials had their offices in Hyderabad and we were never sure when they would be in. I therefore met them alone, most often late in the evening. I had a lot to learn when I began accompanying people to the offices. It was not so difficult with the MROs and RDOs because they were impolite to poor people to begin with and this led me to get aggressive with them. Besides, they were often overawed by me. Where the collectors and higher officers were concerned, I was taken in by their replies in the early days. They almost always treated the poor people politely, offering them chairs and sometimes tea. In their replies to our petitions too, they promised to do something, and when we returned the second time, they usually gave believable excuses.

I then returned home to have Cyril analyse the conversations keenly and point out where I was defeated by smooth talk. He was able to understand how the collector evaded the point, avoided his constitutional responsibility as district magistrate in implementing the law, and gave excuses of political interference (which was not our concern). The officers almost always cited the local MLA's objection as a concern. Cyril took up each of their arguments point by point and explained how the officer was trying to evade his responsibilities. After this brainstorming, it was easy to go the next time and not get caught out. I knew what questions to raise and how not to get sidetracked by the wily answers the officials gave. I was more worried about getting a talking-to from Cyril than of appearing impolite to the collector. Slowly, I lost my fear of being rude. I got so good at this that I later became known for my blunt talk. I learnt not to be ashamed to ask embarrassing questions, not to be ashamed to point out glaring errors, not to worry about offending 'important' people, and never to be afraid to say things that had to be said. What I did not learn was when to keep quiet.

In general, there was an inverse relationship between an official's place in the hierarchy and their friendliness with the poor. The village patwari in the 1980s was a key figure in the village, next only to the dora. Most patwaris were reddys and they were powerful. The collector was transferable, but not the patwari (this system of land management and revenue collection was introduced by Sher Shah Suri just before the Mughal era and cemented by Akbar in the sixteenth-century Mughal period). Often, the patwari could get the collector transferred due to his long association with the district minister. After NTR abolished the hereditary posts, the patwaris became relatively tame. The mandal-level staff however, even if some did not belong to the dominant caste in the rural areas, were subservient to them and unwilling to help a poor labourer and risk antagonizing the powerful.

As one went up the hierarchy, the distance from the village landlord became greater and less direct. There were more chances of finding an official from the marginalized communities willing to help. The new recruits to the IAS were idealistic at the start of their careers and often helpful. Many of the silent movements for land have been initiated by the quick response of such sub-collectors. Much of Tandur subdivision, about 150 kilometres west of Ibrahimpatnam, went through a silent upheaval in the late 1970s when M.V.P.C. Sastry, as sub-collector, took up the protected tenants' register and restored their lost landholdings to poor tenants. It is another matter that many such reinstated tenants lost possession of their land after Sastry was transferred, when the landlords went to the civil courts and the government did not defend the tenants. The agency areas (scheduled areas where adivasis live in large numbers) in Telangana had their golden period in the 1970s when young officials posted to the Integrated Tribal Development Agency took up verification of ownership of adivasi lands and were able to eject settlers and reinstate many adivasi families on their ancestral lands.

I met several officers in the course of my work. Those who were close to S.R. Sankaran were open and willing to help. Others were different. There was a commissioner of land reform whom I had gone to meet on an issue—I don't recall his name now. He was interested in me as a person, not in the problem I had gone to him with. He asked me several questions about myself, some of which I answered, but found disconcerting because they were personal. After some time, he picked up the phone, spoke to someone and said, 'Mana pilla. Aama pani chesipettu.' (She is our girl, get her work done.) All he had understood was that I was born a brahmin and wanted to help me.

There were other kinds of IAS officers. Ranga Reddy district attracted some of the worst because of its importance— the rich landlords of the region lived in Hyderabad in close contact with politicians and were able to get their cronies posted here. Soon, the district became even more important because of the value of its real estate to politicians and realtors. Satish Chandra, the collector who helmed Ranga Reddy district from 1993 to 1995, was one of the worst. He spoke politically correct language but was a master in the art of doing nothing. A. Ramalakshman, the collector before Satish Chandra, was a mala who did not do anything either, but also wanted us to not criticize him and instead, excuse him, because he was a mala. Satyaprasad Tucker was a no nonsense collector between 1988 and 1990 who did what was in his power. He was not particularly favourable to the poor, but when violations in the law were pointed out, he did not care how powerful the violators were. He went by the book and did what a district magistrate ought to do.

We found that most non-local officers were more inclined to favour the poor. Trainee IAS officers posted as assistant collectors or in an equivalent post were both supportive and cooperative. Though they had no inherent powers, they borrowed the files that we needed, and allowed me to read them in their office or even take them home to be returned the next day. When court orders were to be written, we often got to write them so that they were watertight and withstood judicial scrutiny. I took the file home in the evening, Cyril sat up at night, writing the order and I returned the file with the carefully prepared order the next morning. I had a capacious bag which could hide all the files.

The judicial bar, on the other hand, was almost entirely reddy. All the advocates were linked either directly or through marriage with the prominent reddy landlords we were fighting. Any aggrieved small peasant fighting a landlord had to go to great lengths to import a non-reddy advocate to argue his case. We could never find a single advocate in the munsiff or district courts even to file a bail petition for our people. Poor people fighting the powerful have languished in jail for untold years, so when we offered free and reliable help through Salaha, it was as if a dam had burst and they surged forward to fight for themselves without reserve.

Our only problem was that we had no one at the Ibrahimpatnam court, this being full of reddys—the only exception was Ghulam Hyder. Hyder got most of our cases and though he didn't cheat us, he was lackadaisical. Even if bail was granted, he was unable to get the bail order out by evening, and the prisoner would have to spend one more night in jail. Hyder also worried about his close association with us and often requested me not to meet him at his office but telephone him instead. He had to survive in a system full of reddys, the poor man. Consequently, the Salaha lawyers Kondaveeti Arjun Reddy or Nallapu Prahlad had to come to the Ibrahimpatnam court frequently.

Conditions were similar at the Ranga Reddy district court. Naturally, there was no question of trusting any of the countless reddy lawyers there either. It is surprising how at the high court, we had a plethora of gifted and supportive reddy lawyers, the most gifted of them being C.V. Mohan Reddy. Then there was C. Padmanabha Reddy who looked after my criminal cases. I have not met a kinder or more efficient man. He got every criminal case against me quashed with ease. It became a matter of routine for me to appear at his office in the morning with an FIR. He would study it and tell me calmly that he would call me when the case was listed. This call would come one morning, when I least expected it. He would tell me that the case was listed, and that I need not bother appearing. By this time, I would have forgotten about the case, having placed it in his hands. I would go to his office in the evening and collect my quash order. He often asked if I needed money. I loved him.

We also had a problem with sureties to be produced in the courts for bail. The ownership papers of land, housing and other properties have to be attested by the sarpanch. Since the sarpanch was almost always a reddy and often someone with whom we had a direct clash of interests, we could never get sureties from the village in which the police had booked the case. We learned to ask people from other villages to offer surety for people whom they had never seen before. Turning our weakness into a source of strength helped build a strong sense of solidarity among our people.

21 A murder in the family

The year 1989 was surreal. The work that the Sangam had done over the past few years was inspiring a host of villages to take up the fight for land. Many villages on the way from Hyderabad to Ibrahimpatnam, in the peri-urban category, were now coming to us with their papers. Then there were people from villages like Kalwakurthy, which was nearly three hundred kilometres away from where we were. The Sangam was drowning in a sea of papers, hopes and demands. But not all villages near our main centres of Ibrahimpatnam, Yacharam and Kandukur were with us.

It was difficult to understand why villagers near Pulimamidi or Jabbargudem stayed away from us when villagers from farther away pursued us with dedication. Thimmapur is the village to which Jabbargudem is attached. The minister for tourism in the Modi cabinet at the time of writing, G. Kishan Reddy, is from there. The madigas of this village never joined the Sangam though we held meetings and cultural programmes there. Kodlapadkhal near Pulimamidi is a major village with a substantial madiga population. Chandraiah, a madiga from this village who later became the sarpanch, attended our meetings and was friendly with us. We conducted a padayatra through this village, but there was no unit of the Sangam there. Our members constantly told their relatives in other villages about our activities. I think people in all villages hated the scourge of bonded labour, low wages and untouchability, but it required one of their own persons to go beyond this hatred and think of organizing against it. Till this one person kindled the fire in his belly and mobilized his community, people hesitated to step out of line.

Our usual protest tactics included hunger strikes, relay hunger strikes, food strikes (where our people brought pots and pans and cooked in the open) in front of MRO offices and police stations. We also had rallies and demonstrations. These were easier to set up at the mandal headquarters but when we had to organize them before the RDO's office or the collectorate at Hyderabad, it was difficult. Police permission for a meeting or rally in Hyderabad city was mandatory, but this was never granted to us whenever we decided to protest before an office. Getting permission to protest anywhere was a process fraught with red tape. We had to be stealthy, slowly gathering one by one and then suddenly coming together as a group as in a flash strike. Slowly, the police began tightening up and they often imposed Section 144—a law abused at this level to stymie any political action or protest—at the mandal headquarters where earlier protests could be held freely and did not require permission.

By 1989, Cyril had recovered from hepatitis and was back in Hyderabad. He was helping out with Hyderabad Book Trust and had started work on something of momentous importance—*Nalupu*—the first Telugu dalit little magazine. Started as a fortnightly, its masthead bore the credo: 'prajala paksha patrika', meaning a magazine biased towards people, and in effect it was driven by the people. It was considered a 'dalit magazine' because it focused on dalit issues. The first issue of *Nalupu* was published by HBT in April 1989 to mark Ambedkar Jayanti. When I had time, I helped sell HBT books and *Nalupu* wherever I went. *Nalupu* was the brainchild of Bojja Tharakam and Cyril; they worked closely on cases of atrocities on dalits and on fact-finding missions where an atrocity took place. They began preparatory work for the magazine some months earlier. Subeditors were employed, stories were collected, and after a few rounds of editing, the magazine was launched. They thought up the name *Nalupu*, which means black and blackness, as a challenge to society's base colourism. *Nalupu* declared proudly that black was beautiful. 'We want to examine people's issues from all angles, contexts and backgrounds. We want to help people to be able to understand their problems and find a solution …. This is the inaugural edition, so we are talking about ourselves. After this, you will talk about us,' the first editorial proclaimed.

Nalupu invited people in the two Telugu states to send reportage, articles and photographs on the struggles in their areas. Tharakam was the editor. The others on the editorial board were writer and activist Kancha Ilaiah, journalist R. Akhileshwari, her husband and professor at Osmania University P.L. Visweswara Rao, K. Balagopal from the human rights movements, Cyril and D. Narasimha Reddy, economics professor at the University of Hyderabad. The first subeditors were Gudipati Venkat (who later founded the magazine and publishing house *Palapitta*) and S. Jaya (who went on to become Anveshi coordinator.)

I continued to be the managing trustee of HBT from 1980 but this involved mostly signing cheques. It was only when I had time off from my Ibrahimpatnam work that I took up marketing of *Nalupu* and HBT books. I also wrote regularly for *Nalupu*. All through my Ibrahimpatnam work, I kept in touch with the goings-on at *Nalupu*, writing for it, selling it wherever I went, and getting people to subscribe.

Nalupu was a fortnightly save on the rare occasion when it was bundled into a monthly special. It was initially priced at three rupees and later at five; our double issue for the Babasaheb Ambedkar's birth centenary and Mahatma Phule's death centenary in April 1991 (featured pp. 354–7) was priced at six rupees. The initial print run was 3,000 copies and the number often went up to 5,000. Some of Kancha Ilaiah's earliest writings were featured in this magazine. These formed the basis for his seminal work, *Why I Am Not a Hindu*. Some of Tharakam's most important essays (later to be anthologized into books by HBT in 2018 and 2019 after his death) were first published in *Nalupu*. Tharakam also wrote the editorial page for every issue. Hundreds of people from all over the state contributed reports and articles—more than half the magazine was written by guest contributors. The entire Mandal Commission report was translated and published as a special issue in 1991 and was a bestseller. It was reprinted three or four times.

Nalupu explicitly proclaimed that all those who were being subjected to exploitation and violence, all those who faced discrimination and inequality, were the subjects of the magazine. The editorial body consisted of those active in and thinking about the myriad of progressive movements unfolding at that time. The magazine voiced the concerns of all the identity movements that were coming into their own, and played an extraordinary part in nurturing these for five years.

The *Nalupu* work kept Cyril on his toes. He commissioned articles and chased writers and translators, oversaw the magazine's small body of reporters and ensured that the deadline set by the postal department, which gave concessional posting, was always met. The reporters and the marketing executive were paid employees. While there were subscriptions and a few advertisements, *Nalupu* was mostly subsidized by HBT. Cyril supervised the marketing of the magazine and made sure that it reached all parts of Andhra Pradesh, despite the rampant police repression. Marketing *Nalupu* was tough work and for some time Sudershan Reddy

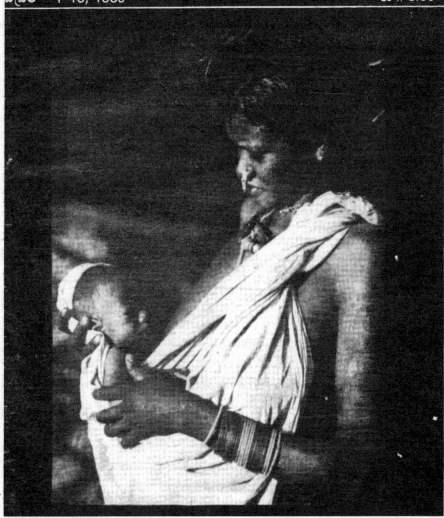

నలుపు

ప్రజల పక్ష పత్రిక

ఏప్రిల్ 1-15, 1989   రూ‖ 3.00

The inaugural and the second issue of Nalupu, *April 1989, above and right; p. 356–7, the Ambedkar centenary special issue of April 1991 that coincided with Phule's hundredth death anniversary, and the June 1992 cover focused on Punjab*

నలుపు

ప్రజల పక్ష పత్రిక

ఏప్రిల్ 16-30, 1989   రూ॥ 3.00

and separatism following the abduction and murder of M.L. Manchanda, director of the All India Radio station in Patiala, who was abducted by members of the Babbar Khalsa and beheaded on 27 May that year.

ఏప్రిల్ 1991   వెల రూ. 6-00

నలుపు
ప్రజల పక్ష పత్రిక

డా.అంబేద్కర్ శత జయంతి
మహాత్మాపులే శత వర్ధంతి

ప్రత్యేక సంచిక

'స్ఫూర్తి' వాదనలో మూర్తిభవించిన బ్రాహ్మణిజం

నలుపు
ప్రజల పక్ష పత్రిక

జూన్ 16–30, 1992

వెల: 4–00

పంజాబ్ భాషా సమస్య
మనచందా హత్య

was our point man. We did not send freshly printed copies to the regular bookshops. Instead, we targeted newspaper and magazine sellers at the bus stands and railway stations all over the state, particularly in the Telangana region.

At that time, the activities of the PWG and other ML groups were on the upturn, and the police were looking for any opportunity to lock people up. In their raids on the different ML dens, they had recovered copies of *Nalupu*. We regularly caught wind of a newsagent being arrested for selling the magazine in different parts of Telangana and one of us had to rush to the police station and explain why this was not the publication of a banned outfit and that the arrested person was allowed to sell it. In 1989, we organized a series of open theoretical lectures for the Sangam members in Ibrahimpatnam. One such was organized over three days at the SC community hall in Eliminedu where we had G. Haragopal of the University of Hyderabad, well-known writer and civil rights activist K. Balagopal and Chandra Rajeswar Rao of the CPI as speakers. Rajeswar Rao spoke of the administrative and revenue system in Telangana, the various revenue records and how one could use these. Haragopal spoke of basic human rights while Balagopal spoke on the rights of arrested people. Tharakam was a regular at these smaller meets which were to continue later at different places.

Meanwhile, Jabbargudem remained a bubbling cauldron of uncertainty. It was a peculiar situation—on one hand, the revenue authorities had declared the disputed land as government land; and on the other, there was a permanent injunction obtained by the Manchireddys against the elders of the village in 1975. We circumvented this by removing these elders from the list of eligible assignees. Still, aided by the police, the Manchireddy landlords terrorized the villagers. The revenue authorities did not take any action against the people, but the police consistently sided with the landlords.

In April 1989, I was walking with the madigas of Eliminedu and Jabbargudem on a cart track that ran along the land in question at around noon. The Sangam's Pandi Maisaiah and Masku Abbaiah were with me then; the rest were local villagers. It was a routine visit and we were tracing the survey stones for our petitions. Suddenly, Bhoopal Reddy, with his sons, nephews and henchmen, descended on us in tractors towing trailers. We were under attack. As soon as we saw them approaching, our people dispersed, seeking safety. I was pulled away by Yacharam Anjaiah of Jabbargudem and hidden in a well nearby. I could hear the attackers outside asking for my whereabouts. Anjaiah did not allow me to even sneak a peek, and only let me come out after they had left. I was told that they hurled Juttu Narsaiah to the ground, placed sticks above and below his body, and pressed them together, asking him where I was. Dandu Mallaiah and Thotla Ramaiah, both madigas, were also beaten up but not as badly. Narsaiah died that evening in the government hospital at Ibrahimpatnam. The three who were most affected by the attack—Juttu Narsaiah, Dandu Mallaiah and Thotla Ramaiah—were from Eliminedu. None of them was young; Narsaiah was about fifty years old.

After the attackers left, I headed back to Jabbargudem. I did not know about what had happened to Narsaiah and left for Hyderabad to lodge a complaint with the superintendent of police, Anurag Sharma, because we were sure that the local police would not act. At the office of the superintendent of police, I gave a complaint which was the basis of the FIR filed. By that time, the head constable of Pahadisharif had

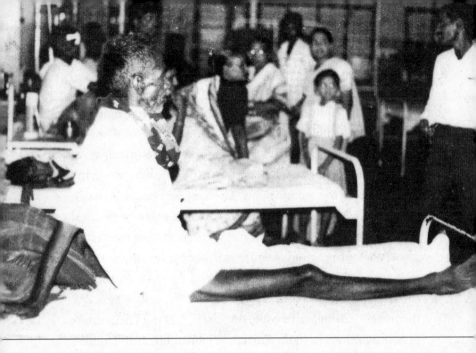

Dandu Mallaiah after the Eliminedu attack, in hospital

come to meet the SP with the news that Narsaiah had died at the Ibrahimpatnam hospital late in the evening. I immediately rushed back. Ravinder Reddy, then a budding young photographer, took pictures of Narsaiah's body and of the other injured persons—there was no photographer for the post-mortem, so he stepped in.

Juttu Narsaiah had died because he refused to tell the landlords where I was. No one stated the obvious—if only he had pleaded with the landlords, or just pointed them in the vague direction of where I was, or even mentioned the name of the Jabbargudem people who had taken me, he would not have been tortured. The madigas took it for granted that this was what he should have done anyway. But I knew that this was not what always happened—one often gave in to such unforeseen pressures, unable to take the pain and torment. Usually the first instinct is to look out for oneself. Juttu

Narsaiah had done none of this; he supported the movement and saved my life at the cost of his own. When I was with the ML movement, we often rehearsed scenes of possible torture and interrogation at the hands of the police. And here was Narsaiah, with no such preparation, tortured and killed not by the police but by the landlords. I had never imagined that a peaceful movement such as ours would result in anyone's murder. Where do we go from here? I was in shock.

Then the funeral rituals happened. Narsaiah was buried the next morning after his post-mortem, and we sat in the village, dazed, for the next two days. The police came and took statements from everybody. They arrested thirteen of the fifteen people named in the FIR; Bhoopal Reddy and his nephew Ramnath Reddy absconded. The sitting Ibrahimpatnam MLA, K. Satyanarayana of the TDP, and the district minister Surender Reddy, did not visit the place, enquire about the incident or even make a statement condemning it: the perfunctory things that most politicians tend to do. Nine days after the incident, Surender Reddy, however, visited Ibrahimpatnam to enquire about the losses farmers had suffered due to a hailstorm. By his side was Raghunandan Reddy, brother of Bhoopal Reddy. Villagers from Eliminedu came to the meeting and asked the minister how he would render justice to them when the killers were all around him.

We went through the motions and had a fact-finding committee enquire into the death. Several organizations gave press statements condemning the murder, and newspapers and magazines reported the event. When Bhoopal Reddy's lawyer applied for anticipatory bail in the district court in May 1989, about 150 landlords from Ibrahimpatnam attended in a show of solidarity. We had the government appoint us a special public prosecutor—Bonala Krishna Rao—who was suggested to us by a friend. We were to soon discover that he was the same lawyer who had defended Raghunandan Reddy in the spectacular rape case in the 1950s. Bhoopal Reddy surrendered in court after three months in July 1989 and was sent to jail for a brief period.

Back then, I had vented my concerns and frustration in a long 'Letter to the Editor' published in the *Economic & Political Weekly* (27 May 1989). It ended like this: 'When Naxalites kill landlords, there is immense police repression. People are herded into camps, tortured for weeks and even shot. Why is it that when landlords kill poor labourers, politicians still hobnob with them, attend meetings with them, and the criminals are able to abscond with impunity? Their family members are not picked up and tortured to reveal the whereabouts of the absconders. Their houses are not raided, their guns are not seized. While we are certainly not calling on the police to do such things, we wish to point out the double standards operating. In such circumstances, what is the future of activists like me who are operating within the constitutional framework? Should I stop my work, should I carry guns, should I build up a private army?'

Narsaiah's murder was one dark extreme of the landlords' machinations. More often they try subtle methods of sowing discord. This results in a fracture among people who should by all counts stand united. Activists know about, but often ignore, the internal dissensions which are the constant accompanying chorus of land struggles. Is it because we do not want to disturb the grand narrative? This despite the fact that far more time is spent in patching up quarrels and settling panchayats among people than on anything else. What I learned from Jabbargudem is that unity is the lifeblood of a struggle.

There was one complex quarrel that I recall as being particularly satisfying since we were able to put an end to the factional infighting within the village. Despite being a small hamlet, Jabbargudem was famous in the entire taluka for its intra-people feuds. Half the village did not talk to the other half. The madigas constituted one half and the rest were the telagas, gollas and a sprinkling of reddys.

The most bitter enmity here was between Yacharam Yellaiah, a madiga, and the rest of the village. There are two pieces of land involved in this story. The bigger dispute was over a plot of 150 acres which all the villagers, including the madigas, cultivated, and a smaller one was over a separate three acres which only the madigas cultivated. Back in 1950, there were only twelve households in the village—seven madiga, three golla and two telaga. These twelve families cut down and cleared shrubs on some government land and cultivated it collectively. They dug a well with their bare hands, since they had no proper shovels and implements, and raised paddy crops.

At this time, Yacharam Yellaiah's family supplied all the bonded labourers to the Manchireddy family. Bhoopal Reddy then happened to offer a patta for three acres of land which was made out only to Yacharam Yellaiah. The land had been cleared by all the madigas together and should have been, by rights, commonly owned. Bhoopal Reddy's move was to ensure Yellaiah's continued loyalty and also to introduce a fissure among the madigas. Naturally, the other madigas got involved. At this time, the other families already had pattas for three acres on another piece of land, so the elders collectively decided that one-and-a-half acres of the wetland that Yellaiah had just acquired would be retained by the latter, and the remaining one-and-a-half acres would be given to the other eleven families. This arrangement was premised only on the sanctity of the word or 'maata'—as is common in Telangana even today. Even in the 1980s, when I roamed the villages, maata was commonly accepted. If someone did not stand by his word, he was considered a man of poor character. So the twelve families peacefully cultivated the three acres for a decade. By 1986, the twelve households of 1950 had grown to seventy-five.

The bigger question of the Manchireddy claim on the 150 acres of government land was directly linked to the contentious three acres. After the joint collector of Ranga Reddy district rejected Bhoopal Reddy's claims in 1967, Yellaiah was summoned by the landlord, and told that the deed for the three-acre land was his alone and that only he should cultivate it. This, despite his caste elders deciding that he should cultivate only half of it. Advocate Manchireddy Venkatram Reddy, who was Bhoopal Reddy's brother, filed a court case on behalf of Yellaiah to evict the other eleven shareholders.

The bigger land struggle was now shelved and the madiga families spent two fruitless years, quarrelling among themselves, beating each other up and spending time in police lock-ups. At the end of the two years, four families left the village in disgust and settled in neighbouring villages where the long arm of the Manchireddy family could not reach them. The remaining eight families sat down in a three-day village panchayat and resolved to resume cultivation on the old basis. Yellaiah was asked to pay a fine for having broken the peace. Three more families sold their shares to Yellaiah after this panchayat in 1972.

Meanwhile, Yellaiah dug a well on his own land, not far

from the common land. When the old community well dried up, Yellaiah refused to pitch in to repair it. The other group went ahead and deepened the well. Yellaiah was refused access, according to established community practice. This outraged Yellaiah. Now the feud was again at a fever pitch.

When ITVCS entered the scene in 1986, and encouraged the villagers to cultivate the disputed 150 acres that had until now remained under Manchireddys' control, the landlords stepped up their efforts to sow discord once more. In 1987, Yacharam Mallaiah, a madiga, was called over by one of the Manchireddy brothers and told that a bairupula boy was regularly 'meeting' his daughter in a nearby field. The bairupula community is not commonly found in Ibrahimpatnam, but the little hamlet of Jabbargudem had one joint family. Bairupulas are traditionally dramatic artists and perform epic plays all over Telangana. They use leather puppets (tholu bommalu) in their plays. In the 1980s, they were facing a crisis of sorts. With cinemas ruling the roost, their plays were not drawing any crowds. They had no land or property to speak of. Being a nomadic community, their children were not educated and they were unfamiliar with agricultural work. The bairupula household in Jabbargudem, which consisted of two adult brothers, their parents and their children, worked as agricultural labourers. Most of them, children included, begged food from house to house in the day. They also reared pigs to provide for their daughters' dowries.

The Manchireddy brother gave some liquor to Mallaiah to distribute among his kin and off they went, to get after the lone bairupula family in the village. The latter promptly decamped, and in the space of a single hour, their tiled house was dismantled by the angry mob. I was nearby in Cherlapatelgudem at the time, and when the bairupulas came to know of this, they approached me, desperate for help. I visited the village the next morning. By then, the heady effect of liquor had died down. Had the bairupula youth actually had sex with the madiga girl? Who had seen them? Where? Had her parents questioned the girl? After some discreet investigations, the villagers found that no incident of the sort had occurred. They inferred that the girl's virginity was intact. Mallaiah sorrowfully owned up that it was a Manchireddy who was his informant. A panchayat ensued and the two groups, the madigas and the lone bairupula family, agreed to patch up.

Meanwhile, the police arrived. Clearly, they had been informed by the landlords to book a case against the madigas for dismantling the bairupula house. It was now the madigas who trembled. When villagers told them that there was no incident, the police pointed to the stripped-down house and said that they had to register a case. Bairupula Jammaiah then stepped forward to say that he and his family had brought down their own house. The police left quietly. Within a week, the madigas had rebuilt the damaged house. The unity of the people had suffered, but was still intact.

When the Manchireddy family failed to break the village with the fake news of the seduction of a madiga girl, they summoned Yellaiah again and urged him to revive the quarrel over the three acres. Manchireddy Venkatram Reddy again filed a case for perpetual injunction in the local court against the others. Yellaiah's long boycott by the entire village community now began. He was not allowed to till the part of the 150-acre government land that had been recovered earlier; his motors disappeared mysteriously, and he was harassed in a number of ways. When we tried to get the two groups to sit in a panchayat, both refused to listen. We were anxious because the smaller dispute threatened the bigger one with the landlords. We also discovered that the villagers fought Yellaiah with much more gusto than they did the landlords.

In 1989, the matter took another turn with Juttu Narsaiah's death. With this, the tables turned. For the first time, the administration was neutralized and the police stopped attacking the villagers. The landlords were hounded out of Eliminedu, their motors disappeared, their haystacks were burnt, and their caste arrogance threatened. At this juncture, Yellaiah realized that his alliance with the landlords did not make sense. While the village of twelve households had now grown to seventy-five, his branch had only grown from one to five. This was not enough to confront the rest of the village.

He approached us in some desperation. The other group, the majority, was hardly in a mood to listen. They wished to bring Yellaiah totally down to his knees. Finally, in 1990 to resolve the dispute once and for all, we mobilized villagers from elsewhere and seized the cattle of the bigger group. This was how we forced them to sit down to talk. Elders from many surrounding villages came to settle the dispute. They explained that the landlords were the enemies, not Yellaiah, who was ready to talk. After a few nerve-wracking days of discussions where almost the entire village was present, the glimmer of a compromise emerged. It was decided that Yellaiah would get back his shares of the smaller and larger pieces of land, and he would also be paid Rs 2,000 towards the cost of his lost motors.

The compromise now had to be implemented legally in the court. This was not easy. Our idea was to file it in court as part of the pending legal dispute so that the compromise was legalized. On the decided dates, neither party appeared and this went on for some time with repeated adjournments. The

court decided the suit ex parte and Yellaiah found himself
again to be the owner of the entire three acres. Prodded by
us, he moved the appellate court to get the favourable decision
quashed. Never before in the history of any court had the
beneficiary of a court decision moved a higher court to have
a decision favourable to him overturned. Such resolutions of
conflicts, though minor, were our greatest victories.

22 Swaying the vote in elections

In November 1989 came the assembly and parliamentary elections. This was important for us. If the police were to be reined in, the local MLA and MP had to be defanged—they were the ones who were in the pockets of local landlords and got the police to act. If they were to be cut to size, we had to participate in the polls and ensure that someone or some group that did not hurt us was elected. So we did it, if only just to prevent our struggle from being annihilated.

When I first came to Ibrahimpatnam in 1984, the Congress had just returned to power at the centre with a resounding majority, but the Telugu Desam Party under NTR won in the state with K. Satyanarayana winning in Ibrahimpatnam. M. Raghuma Reddy of the TDP was the parliamentary victor from Nalgonda. In 1989, however, the NTR regime was suffering a strong wave of anti-incumbency in the state due to his unpopular measures, the rise of his sons-in-law Chandrababu Naidu and Daggubati Venkateswara Rao, his pro-kamma bias in important appointments, along with the prevalent corruption in the TDP cabinet.

NTR's imposition of prohibition had led to both dissatisfaction among people and huge loss of revenue to the state government resulting in a drastic cut in welfare measures; the Karamchedu massacre alienated the dalit voters; and the killing of the Congress MLA Vangaveeti Mohana Ranga Rao by a TDP kamma caste leader in Vijayawada alienated the large kapu community in the coastal area. The TDP also suffered a major internal crisis at this time when some of its most prominent leaders—K. Jana Reddy and K.E. Krishnamurthy—broke away and formed their own faction, Telugu Nadu.

Elections have always been a tricky issue for those of us who emerged from the radical left. The Sangam and its members had no experience of participating in elections except for the earlier debacle in 1987. As for myself, I had always been told, by the leaders of the Naxalite party I was in, that electoral politics was a farce, and what I experienced merely confirmed this. I had never entered a polling booth and have never voted in all my half-century of the right to franchise. Even when the Emergency was lifted in 1977 and Cyril went to vote against Indira Gandhi's Congress, I refused to vote. A.K. Roy, whom we admired quite a bit, had been an MP for two terms from 1977 to 1984 and then again for a third term from 1989 to 1991, but people like him were few and far between. The goodness of a few did not affect a rigged system.

Our previous involvement had confirmed that participating in elections meant the involvement of an established mainstream political party and deep pockets. Yet, with elected members totally at the beck and call of the big landlords, pressuring the police to foist cases on us, forcing the revenue administration to drag their feet on important cases, it left us with no breathing space—we couldn't just leave this whole field free for the ruling classes to take advantage of. We needed an MLA and MP who would at least remain neutral, even if they did not support us. There were no expectations of radical change that could result from the elections.

People voted together, as a block—they could think that one party was better if in power at the Centre, and then turn around and vote for a completely different one in the assembly elections. Opinions of caste elders and the money that came from parties concretized the decisions. We knew that we had to invest heavily in training our people for what was coming, so we decided to put all our energies in making someone lose.

This way, we contended that we could never win but certainly get some real villains off our backs. The parties which stood in the elections had to be mindful of us, and think twice before harming our people in the intervening period.

For the 1989 assembly elections, the Ibrahimpatnam seat had been conceded by the TDP to its ally, the CPI(M). There was no doubt that a Congress win in the region would be very disadvantageous to our work. So we stood behind the CPI(M) and supported its candidate Kondigari Ramulu. The party may not support us in the future—they had not in the past—but they would not actively harm us. Besides, there had never been a CPI(M) MLA from the area until then.

After we had decided that we would support the CPI(M) candidate and the parliamentary candidate, Dharma Biksham of the CPI, we conveyed our decision to both parties. We said that we would canvass separately but work to get our constituency to support them. The CPI(M) and its candidate Kondigari Ramulu did not approach us for help. They were still wary of us. Dharma Biksham went a step further. He didn't want to be seen in public with me. He told me candidly that he would lose the reddy votes. Piquantly, we were campaigning for candidates who did not want us by their side.

We actively began campaigning for two parties in October 1989. The CPI(M) had tied up with the TDP and our land struggle was against Kishan Reddy who was the TDP's district president. There was an election meeting in Ibrahimpatnam with the minister, MLA and others attending, and I was asked to speak by the CPI(M). I expressed my apprehension of appearing in public with the TDP. They asked me how ITVCS members would know of our support to their party if I did not speak.

I attended, but I spoke openly about my difficulty in

appearing on stage with the political party of our greatest enemy. I asked why this political party wanted to ally with us when their representatives—and I named Kishan Reddy— saw the landless poor as their greatest enemy. It was a great public rebuff to the dreaded landlord.

ITVCS and I devoted an entire month to campaigning. Our single point in the campaign was not the policies or the work of the CPI(M). We simply said that they would not harass us like the Congress did. We campaigned only among the madigas and the BCs, walking from village to village, and sometimes driving in the Salaha van, which Cyril was brave enough to lend us. Some friends, including N. Prahlad of Salaha, came campaigning on their two-wheelers. Food was never a problem because the villagers fed us everywhere. We also had many bodies on the line, since plenty of men and women came forward, giving us all their time and effort. Other than fuel for the van, we had no huge expenditure. Booth and polling agents also sprang up miraculously from educated BC youth and we made many friends at this time. They saw us as putting up a spirited fight against the arrogant reddy landlords and pitched in. Some of them had experience in polling too. I lost my voice towards the end of the month. Doctors said this was due to overuse and I simply had to rest the vocal cords, communicating only through notes for a period of time.

In the end, Kondigari Ramulu of the CPI(M) defeated A.G. Krishna of the Congress by over four thousand votes. The Congress was defeated for the first time from that area by a party of the left. In fact, Ramulu went on to win in 1994 as well. Of course, the CPI(M) would like to think that they won on the strength of their policies and work, but I do know that we swung a whole lot of traditional madiga votes which would have gone to the Congress. All the elders among the madigas had never voted for anyone other than Indiramma. They told us so in no uncertain terms. 'You are pulling us away from Indiramma's party. We do not trust the communists. We are doing so only because we trust you. Don't let us down.' We succeeded in swinging this entire bloc, which, according to our calculations, amounted to 28,000 votes. When the Congress under Chenna Reddy returned to power in the state in 1989, winning 181 of the 287 assembly seats it contested, Ibrahimpatnam went against the tide. Chakilam Srinivas Rao of the Congress won the Nalgonda MP seat defeating CPI's Dharma Biksham, and was to give us much heartburn in the years to come. Yet to have an MLA who did not continually plot against us was a great relief.

Chenna Reddy became the new chief minister and this brought the Pulimamidi issue to the fore. While the police could come down harder on us, it also meant that this was an embarrassing issue for the father-in-law of the village. The villagers had stood strong and united, were cultivating the land and reaping the harvest. While Chenna Reddy becoming chief minister worried me, it did not faze the villagers. They felt that they were in control of their village and only this mattered to them. They had defeated the tyrannical landlord Ramachandra Reddy, and according to them, it was this man who led Chenna Reddy by the nose after taking his daughter into his family. Pulimamidi now needed every available avenue of help. I met leading politicians of all the parties on this matter. The CPI had always been cooperative, and its leader Suravaram Sudhakar Reddy was always helpful.

With some hesitation, I also met Vidyasagar Rao, the BJP MLA of Metpally from 1985 to 1998, to ask for his help. In the early 1970s, Vidyasagar Rao was a leader of the ABVP in

Osmania University, and Cyril and his brother George were their keen opponents. Cyril and Mahipal Reddy, a comrade in college, had beaten up Vidyasagar Rao in the Old MLAs' quarters on one occasion. If he knew that I was Cyril's wife, he did not show it. He also visited Pulimamidi. I called upon P. Venugopal Reddy, a pracharak of the RSS. He edited their magazine *Jagruti* and headed their farmers' wing. I was told he was a good man and worked in villages. I met him a few times and was astonished to find that I rather liked him. He was a bachelor living rather austerely. I found him simple and direct and willing to support ITVCS.

From the Congress, I met MLA V.H. Hanumantha Rao, MP Chokka Rao and Kodanda Reddy, all of whom were willing to support us since they disliked Chenna Reddy, but none of them did so openly. The CPI(M) had six MLAs and the CPI eight, and I met all of them. The CPI(M) considered Ibrahimpatnam important because it had given the party one of its six seats, so P. Madhu, a member of its state secretariat, was assigned the job of coordinating with me. I also met Vidyadhar Rao and Devender Goud, both MLAs of the TDP, but Madhu insisted that we meet Chandrababu Naidu, the powerful son-in-law of N.T. Rama Rao.

My meeting with Naidu in early 1990 was a short one. After CPI(M)'s point man Madhu introduced me, I briefly described our predicament to him. Naidu was already familiar with all our work and the hurdles we faced. He asked, 'What are you doing about money? You need money to mobilize for the issue.' I saw red and said that we were managing very well, thank you. Naidu replied, 'Your struggle is important only as long as Chenna Reddy remains chief minister. Once he goes, no one will care. You need a lot of money to mobilize in the short period you have. I can arrange that for you.'

This made me angry and I insisted that I had not come for money, I was asking for their party's support. Madhu intervened to say, 'He is offering money with good intentions. There is nothing wrong in taking money from him.' I said that we didn't need money and we left immediately.

23 The voice of Gaddar

By January 1990, we had scaled up our NFE programme to a hundred schools after Uppula Lingaiah joined the programme as project officer. He was young, had completed his teacher training course after postgraduation and was interested in working in villages. Both teachers and supervisors worked enthusiastically and our village unions zealously oversaw the entire process. Since most of the schools were in hamlets and lambada thandas where there was no school, the teacher-volunteer cycled or walked down from the nearest village.

It was a grand sight to witness the monthly meetings where a hundred teachers and their six supervisors discussed issues with great energy late into the evening. It was a pleasure for me to sit in the back row and listen when they spoke to our teachers about pedagogy. Some of the teachers even doubled up as supervisors in the Sangam and were regular in union activities. They saved up money from their training budget and for two glorious years the group could afford summer excursions as a treat. It was not so grand to see the pitifully poor schools functioning in the evening under a petromax lamp with thin underweight children scrabbling in the semi-dark with their slates and chalks. These NFE schools now served as a regular conduit to transition students into bridge schools and later to regular schools, and some even further to the different kinds of social welfare hostels functioning in Telangana.

Work in the mandal development offices to access entitlements for the poor such as housing, loans and training programme for the youth under different government schemes, went on apace. It was a strange, contradictory time: the MDOs invited ITVCS full-timers to their meetings and reviews, but the police hunted us. Not only did we have to fight hundreds of criminal cases on our people, but we also had to deal with civil litigation in the scores of land cases that were being filed. Our lawyers argued in the munsiff court, in the district sessions court, the district metropolitan court and in the high court. The Pulimamidi and Kappad cases went as high up as the Supreme Court. At that time, we had Supreme Court advocates Rajeev Dhawan and Gopal Subramaniam arguing our cases pro bono. We won the Kappad case and Pulimamidi was a partial victory.

I was stretched thin, travelling through Ranga Reddy and Mahabubnagar districts. I had to be careful now as I moved around the villages and towns that had police stations—I never knew when I would be arrested. In 1990, I went to the Kalwakurthy court to secure the release of agricultural labourers arrested on charges of boycotting farming work. I met the advocate to arrange for bail. While leaving his room, I was accosted by a constable who told me that the circle inspector wanted to see me. Those fateful words! They never tell you that you are being arrested. It is always that the sub-inspector wants to see you, the CI wants to see you, or the DSP wants to see you.

At the police station, the CI told me that I was being arrested for inciting labourers to get minimum wages: that was the actual content of the FIR filed. It was 4.45 p.m., the court was about to close for the day, I wouldn't get bail till the next day, and would be taken to the smelly police station to stay overnight. I sat down and wept. It was so sudden—it was a stressful time and I had been running around all day. I had an important meeting at Jabbargudem the next day and people were to come there from all over Ibrahimpatnam taluka. The CI was so taken aback at my tears that he offered

NFE teachers from Ibrahimpatnam pose by the Dowleswaram bridge in Rajahmundry while on an excursion

me a glass of water and said, 'Madam, please drink water.' Somehow, I managed bail when the court was about to close. An unknown lawyer came forward to argue bail. He later told me that he sympathized with our movement. In about a month, the case was quashed in the high court as the FIR was based on flimsy charges.

The same year, I met the superintendent of police, Mahabubnagar district, A. Shiv Shankar, because the agricultural labourers in Talakondapalli had been arrested. After all, the SP claimed, inciting strikes of agricultural labourers was an offence under the IPC. He said that the IPC was his *Bhagavad Gita* and if anyone committed an offence under this code—drafted by the British in 1860—he would 'flay' that person. Bonded labour and minimum wages were not under his purview, and he was not bothered if the laws on these issues were flouted.

If the Mahabubnagar police were brutal, the Ranga Reddy district police were even worse. CI Muralidhar Rao was posted in Ibrahimpatnam under the express directions, I am told, of the then MP Chakilam Srinivasa Rao of the Congress, to wipe us out of existence. While controlling the two police stations of Ibrahimpatnam and Yacharam, he lost no opportunity, however small, to give us trouble and beat our people up. Tatiparthi in Yacharam mandal had a land struggle involving 105 acres in the village. There was a skirmish between the madigas and the henchmen of the landlords, and the police slapped attempt to murder cases against our people. This meant that securing bail for them would be extremely difficult. The landlords' henchmen faced only minor charges. We decided to demonstrate in front of the Yacharam police station in July 1990 and some three hundred Sangam members gathered with black flags. The sub-inspector called for the Central Reserve Police Force that was stationed in Tadipatri, and ordered a lathi charge on us. He justified it to the press claiming that a policeman was injured in stone throwing by the Sangam members. I was later told that the women in the demonstration had come prepared with chilli powder (this was Tatiparthi Satyamma's idea) and that one woman had actually flung it at the policemen, precipitating the lathi charge.

However, the poor SI could not admit to being threatened by some chilli powder thrown by a woman, hence his story of stone throwing. As people fled, the CRPF chased them into tea shops and hotels without letting up. Bystanders and clients at hotels were also beaten up. They chased us to our office in the village in Yacharam and beat us there too. They abused the madigas dreadfully. The SI went around with a revolver, threatening to open fire. That evening, Madhukar Reddy, a local TDP leader, was picked up and brutalized badly at the police station. The SI had a grudge against him and this was the best time to settle scores. The charge against Madhukar Reddy was that he was helping us, though this was not true.

Our organization was strong in Yacharam, and the next day we announced a boycott of the police. Madiga Kongara Maisaiah went around Yacharam with his dappu, proclaiming, 'No house owner should give his place on rent to a policeman, hotels and tea shops should not supply them anything, no milk, groceries or vegetables should be sold to policemen, their houses should not be swept.' This threat forced the higher officials to signal peace and we had some respite.

In 1990, the trial of those accused in the Jabbargudem murder of Juttu Narsaiah by the Manchireddy family and their henchmen began. On the first day of the trial, a dazzling array of landlords arrived. All of them, along with their uncles, brothers, fathers-in-law, were present. Our witnesses literally collapsed at the sight, their legs buckling under the collective strength of the reddys.

We decided to retaliate. The next day, we had over two hundred of our people fill the court and the benches. It was not a big room and the reddys could either stand next to our people or stay outside in the corridors. Of course, they would not stand next to the madigas and remaining in the corridor was of no use. They never came again in such numbers after this. We continued to mobilize villagers in large numbers for the trial so that the witnesses stood strong and spoke the truth.

Bhoopal Reddy had a paralytic stroke soon after attending one of the trial court sessions and died in 1990. His brother Ramachandra Reddy or Ramulu patel as the locals called him, died even before the trial began. Some people said that god had punished them; others reckoned that I had performed black magic on the killers. I am sure that the determined presence of the villagers in large numbers during the trial not just unnerved them, but turned their whole world topsy-turvy.

We had to plan on how we would face the trial, and help our ten-odd witnesses to stay strong and speak without fear. We hosted camps at my house in Chikkadpalli which also served as the HBT office where the witnesses were told how they would be grilled by the opposing advocate. It was a small room and was packed. We held mock trials with our advocates helping out with the questioning. Despite this, when we faced the court as witnesses, we did not do well. Even I was taken aback by the aggressive cross-questioning. The defence lawyer was bent on establishing that I was a Naxalite, that I had a bias against the reddys as established in the various articles I had written, particularly on the Karamchedu massacre. He referred to my surname which is 'Ramaswamy' and not 'Reddy' (like Cyril's) and concluded that I was not married but living in sin with several partners.

I frequently lost my temper and had to be told by the court to simply answer the questions and not say anything else. The questions for their part were just innuendoes and even if I answered in the negative, the cruel insinuation remained. We could only say 'yes' or 'no'. I must have been a bad witness indeed. It all seemed like such a charade. When the Manchireddys were acquitted of murder, it was a big blow to me. I was shaken for several weeks—justice did not prevail even if one worked hard. Every time we had gone to a criminal court with a private complaint against powerful people, we had failed. We had wasted so many days in court, prepared exhaustive case histories, recorded witnesses' testimonies, yet we failed in case after case. After the Jabbargudem trial, I always advised poor people, who came to me for help in their search for justice, to be proactive. 'I can get you bail and help you evade punishment even if you commit murder, but if you seek justice from the criminal system in India, you will fail. Don't get stuck in court,' I said.

The Pulimamidi villagers were also facing a difficult time. We asked B.D. Sharma, then commissioner of Scheduled Castes and Scheduled Tribes with the Union government, to visit the village a second time. He had earlier visited in June 1988. This time, he walked through the fields, with the people showing him the land they were cultivating. In attendance were the RDO, MRO and other subordinate staff. 'Whose names have been entered in the cultivators' column?' he asked the revenue inspector. 'No one,' replied the man nervously. 'Give me the pahanis,' Sharma demanded. When the revenue inspector gave him the big book, he sat down, entered the names of all the people, signed it with a flourish and had his stamp affixed. 'This is what we do in jamabandi,' he said jocularly. Jamabandi is the annual programme when senior revenue officials verify the revenue records personally. 'We visit the villages and actually verify the different columns.' This is how the names of the people of Pulimamidi were entered in the pahanis.

The next day, I was told, a furious Samarasimha Reddy, who was the state revenue minister, summoned the joint collector, Chitra Ramachandran, to his chambers and upbraided her for this breach of protocol. 'How could someone other than the concerned officer rewrite the pahanis?' he asked. It was a fair question, no doubt, but the deed was done, to the loss of the landlords for all time to come.

In his 'Twenty-ninth Report (of 1987–90) of the

Commissioner for Scheduled Castes and Scheduled Tribes' which came out in June 1990, Sharma wrote about Pulimamidi, 'About two hours drive from Hyderabad, the capital of Andhra Pradesh, is the village 'Pulimamidi' in Kandukur Mandal. The feudal stranglehold in this village after independence has become extremely strong through open misuse of law. The ordinary cultivators, most of them belonging to the Scheduled Castes, are the sufferers. But they are no longer helpless. They are fighting for their rights. It is said that the story of this village is not exceptional. The situation of this village is just illustrative of the situation in the Telangana region of Andhra Pradesh.'

Sharma reflected on how the situation in a village in Bihar and in Pulimamidi portended a larger reality: 'The issues in the struggles of Sole in Bihar and Pulimamidi in Andhra Pradesh appear to be very simple but they raise some vital basic questions. Firstly, should this reality, that a person is actually cultivating a field, be put on record in government paper or not? The reality on the ground has got to be reflected somewhere or the other. If this is not allowed in our system there is only one conclusion—that the system has allowed an easy device for ignoring the valid rights of the poor. This process may be legal, but it can neither be said to be just nor it is in consonance with the spirit of our Constitution. The dissonance between law, justice and Constitution is clear in this situation …. The question which has been raised by the cultivators in these villages does not relate only to one village. It is a question for the entire country. In reality the very right to life of all those who earn their living through cultivating the land throughout the country is directly linked with this question. Today the number of such cultivators who have no right over land is maximum and most of them are members of the Scheduled Castes. Some of them are also members of the Scheduled Tribes. It is the struggle of life of these people which is most difficult and the right to life of theirs, the most crucial.'

❱

On 14 April 1990, we set up a grand bronze statue of Ambedkar at Yacharam. The local Ambedkar Yuvajana Sangam had mooted the idea in the run-up to his birth centenary year. Till then, there had been no statue of Ambedkar in any of the five mandals of Ibrahimpatnam, Yacharam, Kandukur, Maheswaram and Manchal. An Ambedkar statue is an extremely important symbol. In our case it announced that the age of the landlord was over and the dalit-bahujans had arrived. We raised money from the sarpanches of Yacharam mandal and nearby mandals. Even the NFE teachers donated part of their salary. The statue cost upwards of Rs 50,000, a huge sum back then, but my colleagues in the Sangam were insistent that it should compare well with the iconic Ambedkar statue in Hyderabad's Tank Bund.

The nine-foot statue arrived from Hyderabad. Dalit electricians from Yacharam requisitioned a chain block hoister. The pedestal was quickly raised and the statue was put up in no time. The meeting to inaugurate the statue was attended by CPI's Dharma Biksham, former Nalgonda MP; Veeranna, PDSU leader and later CPI(ML) organizer; Dr Cheruku Sudhakar, CPI(ML) organizer and now Inti Party leader; and the well-known movie actor Nagabhushanam. We had a three-day cultural programme to celebrate the event.

Later that month, the Sangam organized an Ambedkar padayatra in Maheswaram mandal. Around seventy people participated, including our Sangam's drama troupe. Lingaiah and Shankaraiah first toured Maheswaram on a scooter to plan the route. When they reached Subhanpur, the village of erstwhile Maheswaram panchayat samiti president and strongman Gopal Reddy (his son Ram Reddy is an advocate in the Ibrahimpatnam bar), they found separate glasses for dalits in a tea shop. They broke these glasses and then continued on with their work. The planned padayatra started from Ghatpally in the southern extremity of Maheswaram mandal. We had baindlas playing the jamidike (a one-sided drum, open on the other side and manipulated by a string fastened to a wooden baton) from Nallavelli, malas from Ayyavarigudem doing the kolattam (a rhythmic dance with sticks), madigas from Mondigourelli doing the yakshaganam or bhagavatham (musical theatre) led by Kattela Narasimha pantulu, and we had Ramulu from Akulamailaram doing the Beerappa kathalu (ballads in praise of pastoral heroes) with his dhol (drum).

We reached Ghatpally at 9 a.m. and finished with the staging of the drama and the meeting by 11 a.m. We were hungry. Many people from the village attended the meeting and then we pleaded with them, 'We have come to your village. Feed us whatever you can and in whatever manner. You can take one person home or more if you can manage.' All of us were fed lovingly. We did this in every village. In some villages, they had already prepared food, since they knew we were coming. For the fifteen days of our tour, we were fed wherever we went.

We also organized a padayatra in the adjoining Kandukur mandal. While in Pulimamidi we received a warm welcome and plenty of food, we met a hostile reception in Gudur, where the reddys glowered at us from their balconies, while our people were performing in the village centre. It was tense, and as our local unit was a small one, we left the village in haste.

NFE teachers take out a procession to help raise awareness

We raised funds for these programmes in different ways. In one instance, eleven people cycled to Hyderabad, one of them in the traditional gochi (the dhoti tied between the legs above the knee). Mora Narasimha, Pandi Maisaiah, Ravula Ramaiah and others were part of this team. They met government officials and well-wishers, explained about the work of the Sangam and its programmes, and asked for money. They even met police officials (Bhadra Reddy and the notorious K. Rajaiah, assistant superintendent of police at Saroornagar), doctors and reporters. They kept at it for seven days and raised Rs 20,000.

The same month, I participated in the 1990 Chittoor Ambedkar Padayatra organized by the Ambedkar Centenary Celebration Committee of Chittoor district in the Rayalaseema region. The padayatra conducted an elaborate door-to-door survey of 249 villages to assess the prevalence of untouchability. Many of the participants of the yatra were from the dominant castes. Gorrepati Narendranath (who died in 2009), a human rights activist and organic farmer of Chittoor district and author of *Dilemmas in Agriculture*, participated alongwith C.K. Narayan Reddy. I think the participation of people from the dominant castes happened because after Karamchedu, savarnas became aware of how deeply caste affected existential aspects of life.

By then, the dalits had become active in mobilizing people for the cause. Bojja Tharakam was at the helm of the Dalit Mahasabha. He had wide-ranging contacts with a cross section of people and followed an inclusive policy. The Chittoor Ambedkar Padayatra was the precursor of the 1991 state padayatra in the Ambedkar birth centenary year. It resulted in widespread mobilization of dalits against untouchability, on their entitlements concerning wages and land, and a strong feeling among dalits that they too are citizens of India and would fight to assert this right. At once, it was a wake-up call for the dominant castes that these concerns could not be subverted or set aside any longer. Those among them who agreed with the dalit agenda of the abolition of caste were invited to join.

On 22 May 1990, the Sangam invited Gaddar, who was at that time with the People's War Group, for a programme at Eliminedu, on the first death anniversary of Juttu Narsaiah. We had announced that Gaddar will be in attendance but not on behalf of Jana Natya Mandali, the party organization that he headed. This was to draw a line between him and the PWG. We did not want to associate with an ML group, and invite further police repression and the ire of those who saw them as violent. Gaddar indeed was Jana Natya Mandali's founder and also associated with the PWG, but he transcended these associations. He was a people's poet, and a charismatic leader who had inspired an entire generation.

We faced some resistance from his party when we invited him. Maybe his association with us was not to the liking of the PWG, or maybe they were concerned about his safety, even though he was participating in a host of programmes all across the state. Initially, they did not give him permission to participate in our meeting, so there was a lot of toing and froing from our end. Gaddar finally came dressed in trousers and shirt, and not in his trademark lungi, gongadi and anklets. He sang but just one or two songs. This was the only meeting in Ibrahimpatnam where I spoke on Gaddar's insistence. I said that the Sangam had been formed to fight in a constitutional manner, in a peaceful manner, but now that we were faced with violence everywhere, we would leave and request the PWG to take over the area and solve the people's issues. Two madigas from Eliminedu, Thotla Mallaiah and Jangaiah, spoke, as did Bandi Sriramulu and Giramoni Ramulu from Gungal.

Gaddar issued a warning from the stage. He asked me to move around in the villages alone and without fear for the next fifteen days, and dared the landlords to lay a finger on me. The meeting had some two thousand people attending, but the entire place was ringed with about a thousand policemen. Did they think that we were going to attack the reddys of Eliminedu? The SP of Ranga Reddy district, Kamal Kumar, and ASP K. Rajaiah, were also present. Several people who were not ITVCS members or supporters also attended, owing to Gaddar's personal popularity. I was not surprised when reddy landlords of other villages came with baskets of fruits for Gaddar.

On 16 August 1990, the Sangam took out a big procession

of two thousand people from Nizam College in the heart of Hyderabad city to Raj Bhavan to give a representation to Governor Krishan Kant. We would not meet anyone in the Congress government because it was headed by Chief Minister Chenna Reddy, the cause of all our troubles. The governor, whose liberal reputation preceded him, was a better focal point for our struggles. Krishan Kant, a scientist by training and a socialist by choice, was always interested in the issues raised by ITVCS during his stay in Andhra Pradesh (1989–97), though he could not influence the administration to even transfer a sub-inspector.

In the procession, our people, both men and women, sang wonderful songs. Professor Chekoori Rama Rao, who worked as editor at Hyderabad Book Trust in its early years, was a literary critic, an eclectic scholar, and a valued friend. I recounted one of these songs to him, asking him why this was not considered great literature. He said that he would like to visit the villages and came with me to Pulimamidi where we sat all evening and most of the night listening to their songs. He published an article, 'Jana padam lo Janapadam' (People's poetry in people's steps) in *Andhra Jyoti* on 7 October 1990. This was at a time when the origin of literature from balladry and orality was not yet recognized.

By this time, we had a skilled troupe which performed street plays without any props, mics or costumes. They were trained by Purnachandra Rao of Hyderabad who worked with an NGO, the Rural Development Advisory Services, and trained villagers in street plays. The troupe even performed in Hyderabad to raise money on one occasion. Different people here specialized in different skills: someone was great at dancing with sticks, one specialized in skits, one sang burrakathas and another oggukathas ... each was able to perform individually and also in a group. In 1991, there was a cultural festival held by a consortium of NGOs and people's organizations in Srikalahasti, in which all our trained artistes participated. Cultural troupes from across Andhra Pradesh gathered at this grand event, but I still best liked our women who improvised their songs on the spot and sang clearly and beautifully.

24 The surrender of mighty landlords

Close to sixty-five villages, spread over the seven mandals of Ibrahimpatnam, Yacharam, Kandukur, Maheswaram, Manchal, Hayathnagar and Choutuppal, participated in land struggles led by ITVCS. At the height of the movement in 1990, over fourteen thousand acres of land under various categories (government, tenancy, temple and ceiling-surplus lands) were cultivated by the landless poor. A large portion of this land has remained with the people and their possession has acquired legitimacy through official relinquishment by landlords, through patta certificates to the landless or by recording of the names of the landless poor as cultivators, giving them security of tenure.

Land struggles transformed the Sangam into a militant union. We formed strong electoral blocs to force the defeats of unsuitable anti-poor candidates in the panchayat, assembly and parliamentary elections. The union confronted the district administration on tough decisions, it enforced a stiff boycott of landlords to break their resolve and mobilized agricultural labourers from surrounding villages rapidly to support any given village in difficult times. We were now able to match landlords in garnering support from outside the village. The violence instigated by landlords and the police was manageable at this stage for two reasons. One, the movement was peaceful and largely composed of women, who came up with innovative strategies to counter the landlords. Two, the proximity of PWG squads in neighbouring districts troubled both the landlords and the police.

We had now created a political space for discussion among the poor in the area. Whenever a madiga met another madiga of a different village, they struck up a connection beyond caste and family. Madiga also met kurma and golla met chakali, and the same equation worked. In *Annihilation of Caste*, Babasaheb Ambedkar says that the very idea of caste is an obstacle to an 'associated mode of living' based on 'fellow feeling'. He speaks of how fraternity can come only from 'social endosmosis', and how equality is impossible without fraternity. Ambedkar calls democracy a 'mode of associated living, of conjoint communicated experience'. It was this feeling of fraternity and solidarity that made equality a real and habitable experience among a people who had not read Ambedkar and had known him only as an icon and an inspiration, including me. Hindsight can give you a history (like this one), but nothing can match the high of experiencing equality in the present of its unfolding.

Usually, people only know their relatives in other villages, but in all of Ibrahimpatnam people were now recognizing each other as political allies, and discourse was generated in this fashion with or without us. Madigas were getting elected as upa-sarpanches (deputy panchayat chief) and ward members on the basis of their own strength, and not as the stooges of some reddy. The Sangam brought key welfare institutions to the area. We helped bring a labour office to Ibrahimpatnam, and instituted labour inspections in the shops of the area. People became familiar with the Scheduled Caste Corporation, the DRDA, the KVIC, the disabled welfare corporation, the zilla parishad, the survey and settlement office, the directorate of school education, the social welfare residential schools society, the director general of police office, the women's protection cell, the Victoria Hospital for leprosy patients, the Sarojini Devi Eye Hospital—all located at the district headquarters or in Hyderabad, all now used by disadvantaged villagers without fear.

Women leaders were emerging in every village. They had become confident, participated in every activity, and mobilized fearlessly. Most of them became leaders of self-help groups which were formed by later governments. Earlier, if we had to resolve a panchayat, we required numbers. Now, even if one or two Sangam activists sat in a panchayat, it could be resolved.

Struggles around land remained a constant. Near Ibrahimpatnam, and not too far away from Jabbargudem, was Kappapahad—a hillock to the east of the village was shaped like a koppu, hair wound in the decorative knot. A section of the BCs of the village was loyal to the CPI(M). This had prevented the villagers from coming to us earlier. The tension within the village remained after our arrival in 1990. We felt that no decisive step could be taken because one section always had to validate any activity with their party, making the open village meetings pointless. The CPI(M) was uncomfortable with any person or group that was not in their exclusive domain.

B. Sudershan Reddy was the sarpanch and patwari of the village. He had several properties, including a rice mill in Hyderabad. He had also concealed close to a hundred acres of land from the Land Ceiling Act which was passed in 1973. He forged papers to show sales under Section 50B of the Act to his father-in-law and his two maternal uncles, and then this very land was sold back to his son Jayabharat Reddy. Their work was careless, and one glimpse at the records revealed the fraud. Sudershan Reddy's father had already declared the extent of their landownership during the older Ceiling Act of 1961, but Sudershan Reddy's forgeries were claiming that their land had been sold off (to his father-in-law and uncles) as far back as 1959.

We began petitioning the collector in 1989, but disunity among the villagers marred the proceedings. Every time they tried to plough the land, cases were filed against them and they could not unite even on the question of bail and sureties. In 1991, the joint collector cancelled Sudershan Reddy's validation certificates issued in 1972 under Section 50B, and ordered necessary action by the land ceiling authorities. The reddy then appealed to the high court but lost his case in 1997. By the time the land was ready to be assigned to the poor, a new law was enacted by the state government prohibiting assignment of lands within thirty kilometres of Hyderabad. Sudershan Reddy lost the land but the people did not get it either, thanks to CPI(M)'s tactics.

One of the more tragic land disputes we were involved in, happened in Ajillapuram. This was far away from Ibrahimpatnam, fifty-one kilometres by road, and we had not worked in the area at all. The nearest point where we had a union was in Talakondapalli, which was still forty kilometres away. All our expansion had happened because of close relatives residing in the soon-to-join village who would take responsibility, or because of places where there was frequent exchange of labour and trade between villages. But Ajillapuram stood out.

Ajillapuram, Iruven and Chedurvalli are three villages in the erstwhile Kalwakurthy taluka of Mahabubnagar district. Most of the land in these three villages is owned by a single family—the Kundaram Reddys. Originally, there were three Kundaram men: Pedda Lakshma Reddy, Chinna Lakshma Reddy and Seetha Reddy. Their sway was undisputed, all the agricultural labourers were bonded to them, and all the peasants their tenants.

In the late 1940s, the Telangana peasant movement swept through the area. It is no coincidence that Vinoba Bhave started his bhudan movement after the Telangana peasant movement. He was propped up by the ruling class to counter this movement. He started the movement in 1951 in Pochampalli, an hour away from Ibrahimpatnam, and declared that he would attempt to persuade wealthy landowners to voluntarily give a percentage of their land to landless people. That he failed to do so is another matter. The institution he founded, that was also given statutory authority, was the Andhra Pradesh Bhudan Yagna Board. According to the law enacted for bhudan lands (Act 13 of 1965), every donation of land made should be filed with the tahsildar, in the form of a relinquishment. After the expiry of two months, and after due notice to all parties, the tahsildar can accept the donation and then assign it to the landless poor.

Vinoba Bhave visited Ajillapuram in 1951 along with Bhudan Yagna Board officials. Raghuma Reddy, the eldest surviving son and his relatives donated a thousand acres and signed all the relevant documents in front of Bhave. The BYB officials present in 1951 recall that Raghuma Reddy was dead drunk early in the day. One of the dalit elders in the village, Salvadi Salaiah, said, 'None of us asked when we would get the land. We were too afraid. Can a madiga ask a question of the dora?' Twenty years passed before people began murmuring.

On 14 June 1971, forty-five certificates were issued to the landless poor, mainly dalits. The patwari collected twenty-five rupees for every certificate that sanctioned two acres of land. Meanwhile, the doras filed objections before the BYB, an organization which had dawdled for twenty years after Raghuma Reddy donated the land in the presence of Vinoba Bhave, and which now, within the day, wrote to the tahsildar staying the pattas. (When I went to the BYB office in 1988, I could find no record of the earlier relinquishment—it was missing. However, the donation was recorded in the general register which, unfortunately for them, could not be destroyed.)

In 1971, the people refused to wait any longer and directly entered the land, clearing it of shrubs. They were arrested by the police, beaten up, and sent to jail. They ended up paying a fine of twenty-five rupees per person, a hefty sum. By 1971, Raghuma Reddy, Murali Reddy and Bucchi Reddy had passed away, but the wily Mohan Reddy, the local heir, single-handedly managed to tackle the entire village. As early as 1988, six of the Reddy children were working abroad; the rest had good jobs in Hyderabad and other metropolitan cities in India.

Mohan Reddy evicted even the other cultivators from land nearby. Madiga Peddachandraiah, a protected tenant, was evicted. Mohan Reddy brought liquor in barrels to the village. He got the villagers drunk and about a hundred of them, most of them dalits, gathered to pull out the budding castor crop of Peddachandraiah. The landlord's men were paid grains as wages so that they would feel no compunctions in harming their own brethren. Salaiah was one of these men. He recalled, 'I was a kavalkar (village servant). They told me I'd be stripped of my kavaltanam (payment for service to the village) if I didn't join the others. When I saw liquor being brought in drums on bullock carts, I thought that my people would be killed. After all, Peddachandraiah is my brother. But what could I, a single man, do? Sarpanch Lakshmikant Reddy said, "pallu pallu kottandi" (beat them black and blue). Peddachandraiah's father was beaten up badly. Their huts were burnt and all their ploughs and implements were seized. This was how brother was pitted against brother.'

Krishnaiah recalls the second skirmish in 1976. 'We again asked them for the land. They promised us ten acres. Our then sarpanch Neela Yadaiah brought the Bhudan Board officials in a jeep to the village to carry out the compromise. We were to give up our claims and certificates for ten acres. We were ready for this. But when the bhudan officials came to the village, none of the reddys was there. They were not prepared to give up even this. The sarpanch had fled in fear, the reddys had told him that they would kill him. The bhudan officials sat in the gram panchayat office for two hours and went away. These officials were not willing to implement the original certificates, but were willing to help out in a compromise for a mere ten acres.'

Every year, when they attempted to cultivate the land, hundreds of them were arrested and thrown into distant jails. In 1985, after PWG cadres visited the area, people from five villages—Duggyala, Iruven, Anthareddygudem, Jalalkhanpalli and Ajillapuram—went to clear the land once again. They sowed twenty-four acres with castor. Three days later, the circle inspector of Kalwakurthy came in a jeep. 'Why are you sowing the land?' he asked. 'Vinoba Bhave gave it to us,' they replied. That very midnight police vans came to the village. They kicked open the doors of their huts and pulled everyone out, men and women. Eighty-nine people, including five women, were kept in a lock-up for three days and were brutally beaten up. 'Sons of prostitutes, how dare you cultivate the landlords' land?' they said. Many of the madigas had head injuries and many bones were broken. Three of them, Gorantla Pentaiah, Gorantla Mutthamma and Maisaiah died within a month of the beatings.

The villagers were produced before a magistrate who did not ask them how they were injured and why the blood still flowed from their broken bodies. Fifty-five people were booked in two cases and taken to Mahabubnagar jail where they spent a week. The reddys themselves arranged bail, possibly because they wanted to keep the line of communication between themselves and the people open. Since then, they had been roaming the courts, almost once every month. 'Pegu leni vaallam'—we are so poor we have no intestines—they said. 'We have sold our cattle, our wives' mangalasutrams, we ply rickshaws in the city, all this just to pay the bus fare to go to court and to pay the advocates.'

I met the Ajillapuram villagers sometime in 1987 when they first attended our Ibrahimpatnam meetings. In late 1989, they came to Hyderabad to meet me. Not having the money for bus fare—Ajillapuram is eighty-five kilometres from Hyderabad— they set out with jowar rotis and pickle, and walked the whole distance. It took them a little over two days, they said. So a visit to my house in Chikkadpalli meant a week for them. I went through all the records possible—at the Bhudan Board behind Gandhi Bhavan in Hyderabad where the entire file was mysteriously missing; at the additional RDO (land ceiling) office in Mahabubnagar to find out whether the landlords had declared any land from this acreage; at the RDO's office in Kalwakurthy and the MRO's office in Iruven. I drew a blank everywhere. It was totally frustrating and I had no answer for the people who visited me repeatedly in vain.

At that time, there was only one man from the landlords' family living in the village. Everyone else had migrated, many to the US and many in highly placed jobs elsewhere. How could such people, who neither needed the land nor lived by it, deny it to the poor? When it looked like all doors were closed to the poor, I finally told them that they should kill this man and I would defend them. It was easier to get acquitted in a murder case than to get justice, I told them. If you don't want to do it yourself, call the PWG, I said, though you might get into more of a mess that way. I sat up many nights, fantasizing how I myself could kill this man and free the villagers from his clutches. But reality was different.

Sometime in 1994, I came to know that they had indeed approached the People's War Group. I don't know what happened to the landlord or if anyone was murdered. Many of these villagers were stuck in serious cases in jail for their involvement in PWG activities. I continue to be aggrieved by what happened in Ajillapuram—brave villagers fighting such a long battle and still not achieving what they had set out to do. Perhaps, they were early for their times, but their struggle surely was not wasted. I like to think that they won the other bigger battle in perseverance, grit and courage and raised their children to be fighters and another generation of militants has been spawned.

In 1990, when the Pulimamidi struggle was embarrassing the Congress government, we had an offer of compromise from Shashidhar and Ravinder Reddy, sons of Chenna Reddy. The mediators were Kodanda Reddy, Congress MLA (a native of Yacharam), and Peddireddy Chengal Reddy (chief adviser, Consortium of Indian Farmers Associations and son of Peddireddy Thimmareddy, the late Congress leader and influential minister from Chittoor district), both of whom were known to me. There were a number of meetings between them, Cyril, Salaiah, Mangali Ramulu and myself, in our office in Hyderabad.

At the same time, I had been meeting leaders of all political parties and they were keen to have an all-party meeting at Pulimamidi to nail Chief Minister Chenna Reddy. ITVCS called for this all party meeting on 22 April in Pulimamidi. This was called off at the eleventh hour as the mediators hastened us to a meeting at the CM's house. Cyril, C.K. Narayan Reddy and I went to Tarnaka where the CM lived, where we met Shashidhar Reddy and his brother. Mangali Ramulu and Salaiah waited at our office. We had a long discussion where an agreement was reached to surrender all benami lands and withdraw all cases in the high court. It was decided that about 684 acres would be distributed right away. I wept when we reached the settlement. I wept because our long and difficult struggle had to be called off and the tedious job of explaining and working out the settlement taken up instead. It was easier to fight than to settle, after all.

The all-party meeting was called off but the TDP and CPI(M) went ahead, with TDP chief Chandrababu Naidu, former minister and former royal Ashok Gajapathi Raju (also of the TDP), the senior communist leader B.N. Reddi, and MLA Kondigari Ramulu from the CPI(M), speaking. I did not attend but several of our people went as spectators.

The actual settlement, wherein 684 acres would be relinquished, was postponed again and again. It soon became clear that the talks had failed. They were held either only to prevent the all-party meeting from being held or it was possible that one of the stakeholders had refused to play ball. Much later, after I had withdrawn from the area, the landlords reneged and sold some of the land to a few Rayalaseema reddys in the early years of the twenty-first century after buying over some important villagers. However, the reddys did not get control of the land, and the people retained it. Some of them made deals with the reddys and received the sale amounts as compensation.

The tide was turning now. Our willingness to negotiate with the Pulimamidi mediators was noted by others, and Kodanda Reddy, the Congress MLA, took a keen interest in mediating between ITVCS and the Ibrahimpatnam landlords. Besides, the threat of the PWG was not far away in Rachakonda, and all this could have pushed the landlords to compromise. The sarpanch of Choudaripally, Mohan Reddy, came forward to give up nine acres of valuable roadside land. He did not want to face the situation that landlord Ananth Reddy had—when the villagers led by dalit women laid a siege on his home for three days in 1988 and he was forced to flee to the city.

Soon after came Krishna Reddy of Madapur. He was known to be friendly with the madigas of his village. When we discovered twenty-six acres of benami land with him, the landless went en masse to talk to him and brought him to our office to negotiate. 'We listen to her,' they said. 'Now you do the same.' Radhakishan Reddy of Pethula, whose son was an Indian Police Service officer, also came forward to surrender land. A literal flood of landlords descended on our Chikkadpalli home. Very often, they were accompanied by the madigas of their village, whom they had approached first. Now, whenever I returned home, I was careful not to drop in at the office downstairs where people waited. If there was some landlord waiting, I consulted with the villagers before deciding whether or not to meet him.

The negotiations were long and protracted, but did not fail. The landlords had already been defeated before they walked into our Chikkadpalli office and we only had to be careful not to bring them to breaking point. Ananth Reddy was one of the last to announce that he too would surrender the land— he owned some 280 acres—to the village poor. We were also careful in formalizing the surrenders and the distribution to the poor. For the land to be formally transferred to people, the landlords had to first relinquish it to the government, after which it was allotted to people. Transferring land directly to the poor involved a high registration cost which no one was prepared to bear. We wanted a formal transfer because we had seen how the land distributed by the Naxalites was reclaimed and repossessed later by the landlords.

All of this culminated in a grand celebration of our

success—or the shutting down of the Ibrahimpatnam land struggle, in hindsight—in the governor's programme on 15 February 1991. Governor Krishan Kant liked meeting social activists and discussing current affairs with them. I had met him several times and he followed the Sangam's activities with great interest. When the landlords began negotiating with us and settling the disputes, he suggested to me that the government could organize a formal patta distribution. The planning of the programme saw its ups and downs with Ananth Reddy wanting the land to be distributed to his hired hands, while we insisted that selection should be entirely based on genuine eligibility. We won after I threatened that we would scuttle the programme. A heated discussion between the governor and me took place in the Raj Bhavan where his private secretary was shocked that I 'spoke to the governor so harshly'. The programme was held with great fanfare and the governor handed over patta certificates to the women of the family, with leaders of all political parties in attendance. There was Chandrababu Naidu from the TDP, MLA Chandra Rajeswar Rao from the CPI, MLA B. Venkateswara Rao from the CPI(M), and the state Congress president V. Hanumantha Rao. At that time, the Ibrahimpatnam struggle was widely touted by the media as a breakthrough for peaceful action and an alternative to the Naxalite path of the gun. This was embarrassing because I felt that our work was still at an experimental stage, and was backgrounded by the PWG threat that the landlords faced.

❧

The year 1991 was Ambedkar's birth centenary. It was a celebratory programme and the Sangam took enthusiastic part in the various rallies, cycle yatras and padayatras. At the state level, the 1991 yatra brought together the state

Cyril taking part in the Ambedkar cycle yatra, 1991

Ambedkar Yuvajana Sangam, the AP Vyavasaya Karmika Samakhya, Nehru Yuvak Kendra and the Dalit Mahasabha. There was a central coordinating committee and Paul Diwakar, P. Chennaiah (now in the National Alliance of People's Movements) and Cyril were members among others. There were many more collaborators, particularly the Ambedkar Yuvajana Sangams that functioned independently in the villages of Andhra Pradesh. Five yatras took off: from Srikakulam, Krishna, Chittoor, Anantapur, Nellore and Adilabad to converge at Hyderabad. Cyril was part of this rally from Srikakulam. The framed photograph of a beaming forty-three-year-old Cyril riding a cycle on that yatra hangs on a wall in our house—defining him and his life and our happiest time together. On 19 February 1991, the Ambedkar cycle yatra was welcomed in Pulimamidi. Some 212 yatris travelled 750 kilometres from Anantapur to Hyderabad, and at their penultimate stop in Pulimamidi, they ate lunch, conducted a meeting and held cultural programmes.

The Sangam organized another padayatra of its own in April 1991. We set out from the Marrigudem and Chintapalli mandals, fifty-two people in all, seventeen of us women, including me. I was the only one who was not from the villages. Most of the padayatris were dalits, cattle grazers, agricultural labourers, night school teachers and one Christian novitiate. Though Chintapalli and Marrigudem are adjacent to our Yacharam mandal, these were new areas on our radar and we were taking Ambedkar's message to them in the centenary year. Would the people hear us? Would we get food to eat? Would we get a place to sleep at night? Would the landlords attack us? We were preceded by our anti-landlord reputation that could worry dalits. This was a padayatra in the peak of summer and the weaker among us could get sunstroke. Such thoughts beset me.

When we reached Umanthalapalli on the border of Mahabubnagar district, all the houses were locked. The agricultural labourers had gone for work. We asked one lady we saw for drinking water. She showed us to a bore well and said, 'Drink water there.' She must have wondered which caste we belonged to. Another old lady brought a pot of water and a pitcher. We sang songs on Ambedkar and went through the village, the local children following us. Adults watched from afar. 'Who are you? From where have you come?' they asked. We went to the centre of the village and enacted a skit that our troupe had prepared. They danced to the kolattam. Slowly some two hundred people gathered. Our skit was about the exploitation of labourers by landlords and their unity and determination. The older people started nodding their heads. After the performance and meeting, we asked the onlookers, 'Can you give us food? One person per home will be fine. We are hungry.' They said, 'No, we are cooking together.' They took us to their huts. They told us about an incident when two of their youths were not allowed by the dominant castes to participate in the village drama. They asked us to tell this to everyone in the other villages.

We moved on to Mallareddypet by evening and madiga youth came with dappus to greet us outside the village. They escorted us into the village, our eardrums on the verge of bursting with the sound of their drums. They told us that the government land was occupied by landlords, that the Naxalites had raised wages and lowered rates of saara, country liquor. Every village had tales of atrocities and oppression, migration, bonded labour, low wages. Fluorosis was rampant. We passed through Chintapalli, Krishnampalle, Kurmapalle, Thiragalapalle, Vottipalli, Battalapalli and Polepalli, visiting two or three villages in one day.

Polepalli was the village of the late Alwal Reddy. People still shivered on hearing his name that brought memories of bonded labourers bent with rocks on their backs, newly-wed brides taken to his house for the first night, beatings with iron chains and such. Indira Gandhi had visited the village once and Alwal Reddy was by her side. His son was now the sarpanch and drove down to the village once a week from Hyderabad to supervise his holdings. The people not only filled our stomachs with food, they filled our hearts with love. Word of our padayatra had travelled ahead and we were welcomed in every village with dalits leading us on with dappus.

Peedita vargalaku nayakudu ammo
Nagadharilo Babasaheb Ambedkar amarudu aye ammo
Maarindannavuro, ekkada marindi be
Eppudu marindi be, Maarindanadaniki siggetla ledu be

A translation of the spirit of this song:

He's the liberator of the oppressed
He is immortal, he's blue-dressed
Here comes Babasaheb, your time's up
You say things have changed—
what has changed, you bastard?
Have you no shame saying this
while remaining the master?

When we returned to Ibrahimpatnam fifteen days later, sunburnt, callused and sore-limbed, we found that the police noose around us in Ibrahimpatnam had tightened. The new leader of the landlords was the former Congress MP, Chakilam Srinivas Rao, a strongman of the adjoining Nalgonda region who boasted that he had successfully exterminated communists from his area. He had officers of his choice posted in our area. The district superintendent of police was V. Bhaskar Reddi, the additional superintendent posted at Saroornagar was K. Rajaiah, and the circle inspector of Ibrahimpatnam, Muralidhar Rao. Rao was one of the three policemen who had shot Ghulam Rasool, journalist and stringer in the newspaper *Udayam*, in cold blood, in December 1991. Rasool was suspected to be a Naxalite sympathizer. Muralidhar Rao was circle inspector of the Vanasthalipuram police station at the time. We got the worst possible treatment from them and could not even get appointments to submit petitions.

On 27 April 1991, Chakilam Srinivas Rao led a rally to the Raj Bhavan to highlight what he perceived as 'oppression by Gita Ramaswamy'. He claimed that I was threatening landowners and instigating people to steal land. I was taking a commission from the relief and rehabilitation amounts given to bonded labourers. I was collecting four to five hundred rupees per person, promising them land. I was instigating people to burn the motors of those who complained to the police. I had travelled on a cycle through Ibrahimpatnam earlier and was now moving about in a jeep, he said.

I ignored this. On 1 May 1991, we took out a May Day procession from our office. Circle Inspector Muralidhar Rao was particularly vicious with us on the day. Our procession was on one side of the road and the CPI(M)'s on the other side. The CI led a lathi charge on us, scattering our procession and injuring many people. Tipparthi Pochamma of Choudaripally, who was eight-months pregnant, not only fractured her hand, but fell down and lost her baby. Several agricultural labourers had injured limbs. The CI himself led the lathi charge. He saw me but did not hit me. He said, 'The next time I see you in a dharna, I will strip you and beat you up.' I pleaded with Ramakrishna Reddy of the CPI(M) as they passed by us, raising slogans, 'May Day Zindabad', 'Workers of the World Unite', and so on. I asked, 'Of what use are your slogans of workers' unity when you pass by silently when we are being beaten?' He and the other CPI(M) people did not even look at us. The police also raided our office, demolished the shamiana tent we had pitched on the road, and took away all our papers and files. The district superintendent of police V. Bhaskara Reddi claimed that prohibitory orders were in force and hence the lathi charge. He refused to reply to the question how these prohibitory orders did not affect the CPI(M) procession.

At a meeting on Buddha Purnima, on 13 May 1991, we announced a boycott of the ensuing parliamentary elections, protesting against the extreme police brutality in Ibrahimpatnam. We were after CI Muralidhar Rao's blood. We followed his every move. When he called the local dommari caste women (dommaris were the traditional sex workers in this part of Telangana) to the police station, we put out a pamphlet of how he was forcing prostitutes to service him free of charge. When he asked contractors supplying sand and cement and bricks to send materials to Vanasthalipuram where he was building a house, we exposed this too. Everybody knew that no police officer ever paid for anything and the contractors often complained loudly. We added to the noise. We insisted that he should not be transferred, because he will then trouble poor people elsewhere. We asked for his suspension. Higher police officials, even of the rank of DIG, confessed to us that they could do nothing in the matter. 'Approach the politicians,' they said, 'the CI has their ear.' Even Governor Krishan Kant expressed his inability to do anything.

▶

At about this time I had a personal downswing. N. Prahlad was a junior lawyer working with Salaha. He had worked actively and vigorously with ITVCS for a year, even campaigning along with us in the elections. In 1991, he was confronted by Salaha for having taken money from landless labourers in their cases although he was a paid employee of Salaha. It was expected that he would leave and practise law on his own. Angry, he turned on me—without cause, I thought. He gave an interview to an *Udayam* reporter (a leading Telugu daily at that time) and also had a pamphlet printed. The gist of his arguments was: I took money from landlords to settle cases and led labourers to fight aimlessly and without any chance of success so that I could make a profit. And that I had sexual relations with officers like S.R. Sankaran and B.D. Sharma, and this was the reason why officials cooperated with me.

I was shocked by all this rubbish that was circulated widely by the landlords. I was miserable and stayed back in Hyderabad. I stopped going to the villages. It felt pointless now. Out of nothing people could lash out at me and make me suffer. Cyril and my friends repeatedly told me that nobody believed the allegations, I should ignore them and go ahead with my life. But I couldn't. The villagers visited me and tried to persuade me to forget it. When I refused, batches of people gheraoed Prahlad in his house in Bagh Amberpet for three to four days and demanded an explanation but he denied everything.

Within a week, I went to Padmanabha Reddy and asked him to represent me in a defamation case, both civil and criminal. He promptly sent a legal notice to both Prahlad and the newspaper. *Udayam* immediately published a retraction and an apology. I filed a civil case in the city civil courts with Suryanarayana as my lawyer and a private criminal case in the Ibrahimpatnam court. Everyone, including Cyril, advised me strongly against filing the cases and said that I would continue to suffer. Prahlad's accusations carried no weight, they said. The cases dragged on, but I did not let go.

In 1991, soon after it became clear that I was not going to take Prahlad's accusations lying down, Prabhakar, one of the leaders from the PWG, called on me at home. He introduced himself one morning at the entrance of our house and said that he had come because Prahlad had asked him to mediate. Prahlad was close to the Maoists at one point of time. I said to him, 'So you have come to threaten me and use strong-arm tactics? You think that I will get frightened?' I was aggressive but I had met my match in the soft-spoken Prabhakar who was gentle and calm. He charmed me with his reply: 'Sister, why should you think that? I have come to meet having heard so much about you.' After that, he became a regular visitor to our home. I ended up liking and respecting him. He ate with us, helped us cook, and washed up. We had long arguments about the PWG and its use of violence. Through Prabhakar, we met other PWG cadres and had long discussions with them. I found them intelligent and warm, caring and respectful. I could talk freely to them and rail at the PWG's violence against the poor and its neglect of the caste question. I would prepare issues for them and pile on criticisms but they never lost their cool. I always wondered how the party could be so pig-headed but its activists so admirable. None of them, Prabhakar included, ever raised the Prahlad issue again, and we continued to be friends.

Prahlad was represented by V. Pattabhi in the criminal case. I remember writing a long recriminatory letter to Pattabhi and calling him on the phone, chastising him for taking up the case. He was shocked. Prahlad approached the top civil rights lawyer K.G. Kannabiran for a stay in the high court. I did not speak to Kannabiran because of the 1985 incident where his wife had attacked Cyril ostensibly for my sake. In the high court, the judge told me, 'I plead with you with folded hands to accept Prahlad's apology. Kannabiran, his lawyer, is also willing to apologize on his behalf.' The legal fraternity was closing ranks behind one of its own. I refused initially, but when Padmanabha Reddy also urged me to accept the apology, I wept for a long time in open court, but acceded. Lawyers close in on their own.

Prahlad also apologized in the civil court and I accepted this with a donation from him (in the form of damages) to Manohar's organization Swayam Krishi. The ordeal ended somewhere in 1994. I had advised villagers never to approach the courts as plaintiffs. They had far greater chances of success as defendants, I had said. I did not follow my own advice. The desire for justice often overshadows good sense.

In 1991, I participated actively in a study on land reform with the National Institute of Rural Development where we mapped problematic land issues in thirty-three mandals of Andhra Pradesh. The project was an outcome of a close collaboration with Dr T. Haque, an agricultural economist working at the NIRD who would go on to serve the International Labour Organization, the Food and Agricultural Organization and the World Bank. Over the years, he had been organizing several workshops on land reforms and I was a regular panelist. This was an area that greatly interested him. Our problem was always that we rarely got access to land records. An NIRD project was a wonderful way to access them. I suggested this to Dr Haque, and we began our work in 1991.

I headed the project and roped in a number of other organizations including a fraternity of nuns from the Congregation of Sisters of St Ann (established in Secunderabad in 1871). The study conducted a survey (both pahani records and actual possession) of government land, ceiling-

412 LAND, GUNS, CASTE, WOMAN

surplus land and protected tenancy land. Several groups and NGOs joined—Prajwala headed by Paul Diwakar from Chittoor; the Young India Project by Narendar Bedi from Anantapur; Youth for Action headed by E. Venkatramanayya from Mahabubnagar; Peoples' Action for Rural Awakening or PARA headed by Rev. Thomas Pallithanam of the Salesians of Don Bosco from Ravulapalem; an independent group headed by P.S. Ajay Kumar from Paderu; a group of nuns from the Kodad branch of the Sisters of St Anne, Bangalore. Cheyutha, and not ITVCS, took up several mandals in Ranga Reddy district. We felt that if the Sangam approached revenue officers for records, we would not be given access. However, Sangam activists played an important role in training all the people involved, since they were already well versed in the laws and rules governing revenue land. A number of workshops were conducted in all the selected mandals as well. Shankaraiah went as far as Paderu, 700 kilometres away, to train activists there.

The study revealed an astonishing amount of acreage available under the various categories of plain government land, encroached government land, government land assigned to ineligible beneficiaries, protected tenant land, ceiling-surplus land, and inam, kunta shikham and temple lands illegally occupied by landlords.

The Sangam expanded its operations to other mandals after the NIRD study. With the information procured from the study, we launched struggles in Doma, Kulkacherla, Pargi and Vikarabad. These mandals lay some hundred kilometres west of Hyderabad. Our activists visited villages in these areas, held meetings, and carefully discussed the results of the survey to encourage landless poor to talk about their problems.

25 To love and to be loved

I was deeply affected by the Karamchedu massacre in 1985 and the discussions it sparked, particularly because of my close relationship with the madigas of Ibrahimpatnam. This led me to view problems and events the way dalits did and caused a serious discordance in my life and some kind of a break with the friends I had earlier. I began feeling odd, a stranger, an outsider, to my old world. The Mandal Commission report in 1990 sharpened this even further. I suddenly discovered that some of my friends actually opposed reservations. The arguments, even quarrels, were sharp, over lunch or dinner, at casual meetings, and even at work. The world for me was now split into three—dalits, dominant caste people who supported them, and dominant caste people who did not. There was also a large indeterminate category (rapidly growing in number today) who took the stand of what is now politically correct—who supported reservations and entitlements for dalits, but did nothing in their own lives to associate with and learn from them.

I did not come to appreciate the dalit struggle by reading Ambedkar. While I did read his biography and some texts by him and Phule, that we published in the early years of HBT, I did not fully appreciate them. Ambedkar, for me, was one among the many leaders, and I was not fond of leaders at the time. The leaders I had known had feet of clay and I refused to engage with them. Working with people was the only road to change, I felt. When I worked among the agricultural poor in Ibrahimpatnam, there was not much awareness about Ambedkar among the dalit youth there either. I stayed with the madigas and worked with them, but only because they were the poorest of the poor. Opposition from the CPI(M) to my work further crystallized my understanding. They criticised me for staying and holding meetings in the dalit-wadas. 'Hold it in the main village,' they would say. If I did, it was clear that the dalits would not attend or would be prevented, directly or indirectly, from attending. One then had to choose. The choice was ours, mine, to make. Discussions with dalit movement activists helped, and as important was learning from the dalits in the villages. Yet, what sustained me was the extraordinariness of the madigas.

It was not as if I took to life in the village and among the madigas without effort. In time, I found that I had an entire community to love, and be loved by in return, for the first time in my life. It was not as if the balmiki community in Ghaziabad did not love me. But this was home to me. This was a part of Telangana whose culture I had imbibed, whose history I knew, whose geography I loved—home to me and to many of my friends. For a community that has seen so much suffering, deprivation, exploitation, that has seen its children die due to a lack of food or medical care, that has seen its daughters and wives raped because the landlords wanted to exercise power, that saw its people growing old at the early age of forty due to malnutrition, routine heavy work and lack of medical attention, the madigas were sensitive and forgiving. They love life, they love people—you needed to help them to the space they were entitled to and they loved you.

They dripped talent. Rhythm, melody, drama, you name it, they had it. The dappu—they beat it to signify celebration, a wedding, a death—a different beat for every occasion. It sent shivers down my spine. Boys as young as seven led the procession with wizened old men as old as seventy-seven alongside them. There was no art in which they did not excel if they put their minds to it. Dancing with sticks or with lazeems or with the dappu itself, weaving intricate songs which unfolded like majestic tapestries, honey-tongued or acerbic, whichever they chose. When they had to argue with officials, or were overwhelmingly argumentative among themselves, I loved to watch them, and be with them, the men and women.

Madiga women were more independent than the other women I knew. No doubt, many madiga men beat their wives but the wife did not take this lying down. She did not beat him back but she came out to the street cursing him in earthy farmyard language. If he raised his hand on more than one occasion, the madigas from her natal village descended in tractor-loads for a panchayat which could last days. They did not leave until the issue was settled to their satisfaction, and if they were losing work over it, the madiga caste panchayat of this village had to host them with food and liquor.

The madigas did pressure me in sexist ways—have a child, they often said; dress like Indira Gandhi did, they insisted. There was Mantri Ramulu, a madiga leader from Manchal who tried hard to get me to cover my head with the sari pallu just like Indira Gandhi; he wanted me to speak in English (as she did) instead of Telugu. People were shocked to know that after so many years of marriage, Cyril and I had no children. As happens in India, I was the recipient of much unsolicited advice. People would place a baby in my lap and say, 'Let your womb fill!' Some others, equally well-meaning, suggested that I get a second wife for Cyril so that we could have a child, never comprehending my insistence that we did not want children. Yet, it was something I could deal with and still be myself.

The madigas always told me to shut up at meetings. This happened often during langa panchayats (caste panchayats adjudicating sexual matters) and other caste panchayats.

These often went on for two or three days, breaking up in the evening so everyone could drink. Both men and women drank, though of course, men drank much more. I once had a sip and never touched it again. Sometimes the langa panchayats struck me as unjust. The whole set-up was a grave injustice to the woman concerned. I often got angry and protested. Somebody close by would tell me to shut up or the meeting would ignore me totally. But they welcomed my presence. I protested against different standards of sexual behaviour for men and women. Often, an older woman drew me aside, counselled me to be patient and reassured me that there would be no miscarriage of justice. The elders would search for a formula to accommodate all aggrieved parties.

While my position was examining the right and wrong of it, the people knew that they had to live together and looked for a solution acceptable to all. At these moments, I always thought back to my party past and the vanguardism we exhibited then We tend to think of what is right and what is wrong. People, on the other hand, think in terms of what is doable. I feel the need to draw a balance between the two. We cannot overlook right and wrong, justice and injustice, when we look forward to a society that is equal, just and humane. Just by ensuring what is doable will not bring about change. Likewise, working without observing what is doable leads to vanguardism. People's notion of justice is always about bringing a compromise between two parties, working for days, mulling the matter over and over again publicly, and never to be judgemental.

I often suggested beating up landlords. I suggested burning their haystacks, cutting their phone connections, throwing their motors into wells and several such minor violent acts. This was not simply due to my Naxalite background. I was horrified at the violence landlords inflicted constantly on the labourers and I could think of no other reaction. People never agreed. I assured them that I would get them out of jail, but they would still not agree. Gradually, I came to understand that my urge for violence came from a reaction to what I perceived as irremediable grave injustice without actually considering alternatives. People *made* alternatives, they *created* alternatives, they had patience.

When conflicts arose with someone outside the community, what was it that they looked to me to do? I could bring to the questions a certain kind of judgement about how the police would react, how the administration may view it, what help we could expect from the courts and the media— this was what I brought to their decision-making process.

I remember one of our earliest skirmishes with the police when Shankaraiah was attacked by a constable. He was quite upset. I had nothing to say. Perhaps my old fear of the police resurfaced. This was how policemen behaved. Who could change them? The group of villagers sitting together that day decided otherwise. We all went to the police station some twenty kilometres away and agitated. We shouted slogans, called out the name of the offender. The sub-inspector came out, called the offender and had him apologize to Shankaraiah. I will never forget what a lesson I was taught that day. We were never to feel guilty or ashamed for being victims, we had to fight back. If we feared mere mortals like the police, our days were numbered.

Presenting the achievements of the Sangam through its prolonged engagement with state institutions does not imply that the strategies followed here can substitute for broad political action. That ITVCS's work literally ended in 1993 points to the limited goals set by it and its inability to take up further transformative action.

At the time of the governor's programme in 1991, there was a lot of talk in the media about the 'peaceful path of land reform'. This was contrasted with the Naxalite path of armed revolution. Looking back at the movement, it seems that there indeed is a counterpoint to the ML path of the gun. Is this counterpoint the Ambedkarite path of the Constitution? Is the Ambedkarite path one of pushing the legal space available to its utmost extent, exploring judicial spaces and media pressure to their fullest? Ambedkar and Ambedkarites never had the support of mainstream judicial spaces and the media; these were always controlled by the dominant castes. But if they could garner this support, wasn't it a way worth exploring? Which leads us to the question, what was the place for ML politics in my time?

In the mid-1980s when I became active in the villages, the dalit voice had begun to rise. Karamchedu had demarcated the lines. No one, henceforth, could ignore caste and untouchability. I think that all factions of the ML made a critical mistake in not listening to these voices in time. It is true that Kondapalli Seetharamaiah's bold and aggressive moves in leading his party, the PWG, helped it gain traction. The jail escape, the kidnapping of mainstream politicians, captured public attention. But when smaller village-level politicians were kidnapped and sometimes ransomed or killed, when petty informers had their elbows and knees broken so that they had to crawl around in the villages, when leading cadres decamped with huge amounts, when deals were struck with contractors and politicians for both money and votes, when party militants were used to settle village-level internecine fights, when one ML faction killed members of another and vice versa, people began to get disgusted with ML politics.

More seriously, the ML had no response to the dalit demand for constitutionality and stretching the rule of law. What is life like after the revolution? They could not say. They addressed caste and feminist questions obliquely, but never directly. Both the feminist movement of the 1980s and the dalit upsurge of the 1990s went almost unobserved by them. One of their fundamental problems was their lack of transparency. They never admitted to a mistake, they never admitted to a public debate. People were tired of parties that continually asked people to unite but broke into several factions themselves, all of which had similar aims and manifestoes but which would not even allow their mass organizations to unite on a common issue.

The question of violence, both as strategy and tactics, has never been sufficiently debated in the two Telugu states, except on moralistic grounds. The villagers have no say in questioning the theoretical basis of ML violence. Most of the times, even the different factions appear not too bothered about how Marxism–Leninism justifies their acts. If violence is a part of strategy, as some ML groups continue to profess, where does it lead the group? Even if violence does lead the group to power, what values does the new power ecosystem uphold? Is change brought about in the final devolution of power or is it in the everydayness of events that make up the big picture?

If violence is a part of tactics, as some other ML groups state, how meaningful is it when the Indian state is at its most powerful, what has been the cost to the Indian people vis-à-vis the gains achieved, how have various splinter groups degenerated into extortion machines?

Yet violence cannot be rejected outright unless a counter-

argument and counter-strategy is built. An easy dismissal
of violence ignores the complexities which movements for
change have to deal with. Emmeline Pankhurst famously said,
'… a broken pane of glass is the most valuable argument in
modern politics.' Respect for life has to be coterminous with
diversity in tactics. Can we always have peace and justice? To
insist on peace with an absolute rejection of violence could
mean surrendering our right to change an unjust social order.

As activists, if we want to persuade people to change their
views and attitudes, we don't need to deal with the state. We
can work in civil society. Feminists, LGBT activists and dalits
do so. But if our goal is to change the fundamental balance of
forces in politics, that means grabbing the state by the collar.
We wanted to do both, and failed. We knew we could not
form our own party. The political system is stacked against
big change. What we could do was try to convince existing
major parties to advance our agendas of support to agricultural
labourers, dalits and women. In exchange, we offered votes.
So we were deeply shackled by the failure to bring forth a
larger project for ourselves.

The communist parties had the ability to set sights beyond
the horizon, to imagine what long-term change looks like.
That is what gave them clout in the 1940s. They wanted to
transform India. Yet the question of how to marry a vision
of a world transformed with the practical exigencies of a
nasty political system is very hard. We saw in the communist
movement that as its leaders aged, they became part of the new
establishment, and there was no actual organized movement
they could muster after that. There was no real, ongoing
presence to push against the state. The young activists of the
1940s became the liberal hawks of the 1970s. The CPI ended
up fully supporting the Emergency in 1975.

▶

I was burnt out by 1992. I had hoped that the NIRD survey would explore ways of taking the path of a constitutional remedy to other areas. Apart from meeting NGOs, conducting training sessions and visiting their areas, I also met several ML groups, and held meetings at their villages to explore this. I came away disappointed. The ML groups were not interested in this painstaking way of fighting battles; planting red flags was so much easier. NGOs did not want to take up anything that involved the police. Petitioning was so much easier for them. The NIRD survey covering thirty-three mandals had revealed that land recovery movements by the poor could be taken up all over the two Telugu states. But I had no energy left to take up the battle from scratch all over again.

The Sangam too had not produced any cadre that was willing to leave their villages and work elsewhere. Most of the Sangam cadre were grounded agricultural labourers and small peasants. Maybe it was their responsibilities at home that kept them from taking the work further. Or maybe their politicization was not sufficient enough for them to do it. Or maybe I had not mentored them sufficiently. Perhaps, this is both the good and bad that comes of the proletariat being the politburo, the vanguard—the collapsing of these distinctions and categories. Theory was what evolved from actual groundwork and legwork of non-violent struggle, as a synthesized hindsight, not by clinging to labels and isms, and even guns, in a doctrinaire fashion. It was such a vicious cycle—only the ML produced dedicated cadre who could take up programmes elsewhere; but the ML ideology would not entertain stretching the limit of constitutional remedies.

In Ibrahimpatnam and its surrounding areas, there did

not appear to be much work left for me unless I changed course and reinvented myself. How was it possible to reinvent oneself in one small area? The people in Ibrahimpatnam had overthrown the reddy raj, yet they were still small peasants and agricultural labourers with small holdings. Farming as an occupation could not sustain the majority of people here. Setting up more industries that plunder our natural resources and actively accelerate the pace of environmental devastation did not look like the answer in the long run. People had a marginal say in governance but if this needed to change, it needed a revolution of a different kind. An ML-led revolution was not the answer, but no one else had programmes either, except for minor tweaks in the system. The dalit identitarians I met then focused programmatically and largely on education and jobs through reservation in the cities, and not on livelihoods in the rural areas. (The focus in Telangana has now shifted to the latter under the Dalit Bandhu programme.) The struggles now were too big for me to be a part of. Rational solutions and programmes eluded me. As I reflected more and heard the voices of activists, it occurred to me that the major question in the future was sustainable development. How was one to move ahead on this when this was a global issue and even nation states were incapable of handling it? Besides, while the poor suffered the most due to the ravaging of resources, they were the ones with the least fallback to sustain a fight.

By this time, the familiar halo around my head was developing. Personal publicity was getting more and more difficult to avoid. I couldn't duck enough when photographs were being taken; reporters thought that a young woman made good copy. Ramoji Rao, head of the Eenadu group of companies, called me to his office to ask if his company could make a film on me. He even showed me a poster he had made.

I was puritanical and horrified that a people's struggle could be sidelined to boost the image of a savarna from outside. I was being invited to consultations, to various government meetings on land reforms and labour. I was getting invitations to address IAS probationers at the Lal Bahadur Shastri National Academy of Administration at Mussoorie and senior police officers at the National Police Academy at Hyderabad; to speak at various seminars at the National Institute of Rural Development at Hyderabad and the Indian Institute of Management at Ahmedabad. I accepted some of these because I thought I would meet younger students and give them insights they may not get elsewhere. The Government of India selected me as their official delegate to a UNDP exchange programme in Thailand. I declined. I was accumulating too much respectability. I refused most of these invitations.

In Ibrahimpatnam and surrounding areas, no longer was I given jowar roti and pickle. People killed their chickens for me and vied to give me food. Wherever I went, I was mobbed and I was getting tired. People had so many problems—the aged wanted their pensions, their cataract operations, they wanted their children to look after them, they wanted a little toddy, some beedis; youths wanted jobs, girls wanted sewing machines, women had demands for their families. And there were always disputes to settle—brother fought brother, husband beat wife, extramarital relationships constantly created disputes, a new land survey threw up huge problems, and fights resulting from election battles spilled over elsewhere. I was tired. I didn't want to lead. I wanted to run away.

I remember the day clearly. It was towards the end of December 1992. I dropped by for lunch at a flat in Banjara Hills that was home to my friend and her family. I arrived late, maybe at two in the afternoon. It was a bright and sunny day.

When I opened the front door and blinked into the relative
darkness of the room, a bit of sunlight caught my eye. A one-
year-old infant was playing near the door, a pretty baby with
curly hair and bright eyes. She was startled when she saw me
and bounded across the room faster than a bolt, to take shelter
behind her mother. My heart wrenched—a strong wrench.
My villagers loved me, worshipped me. My friends loved me,
so did my husband. But no one loved me and needed me so
absolutely as that baby needed her mother at that moment.
I wanted that love, that need. From that moment, my life
changed. I wanted a child. I must have a baby.

Years of logical thinking that a child would play havoc
with my life went overboard. Or it could just be that the
biological clock ticking away in my genes gave me a shock.
The desire to have a child caught hold of me. Within the year,
I had Leila.

Postscript

When Leila was born in 1993 after a difficult gestation, I
could not go on working. I was sent word through a reliable
source that the baby would be kidnapped. At this time, the
madigas from Ibrahimpatnam came to me with the offer, 'We
will raise your baby; we will guard her like the eyelid guards
the eye. Continue your work with us.' Even my own mother
and sisters could not make me this offer. But I disappointed
my people. I left.

Today, the villages in erstwhile Ibrahimpatnam taluka have
changed beyond measure. There is no 'nee kaallu mokkutha,
banchana dora'—'I'll fall at your feet, my lord, my master'—
any longer. When villagers have work with the MLA or MP,

they call on the MPP member. If he cannot get the higher up to do the requisite signing (that is all they are asked to do), he is likely to be confined to a room in the village till he puts sufficient pressure on the Zilla Parishad member who again impresses on the MLA or MP that this is serious work. This is how they get work done. The rope is now getting pulled tightly from below.

Villagers are rarely at a loss about the laws or the rules around the laws. They know precisely what they want. Our leaders are important people in the village today. They are in different parties, some even in the BJP, to counter the CPI(M) mafia. Where they do not have a place yet is in the big contracts that are cornered by the MLA—these are not the local laying of roads or works done under the National Rural Employment Guarantee Act that are already with the local people's representatives. Two persons from the BC community are even successful realtors. What they cannot access are the fat contracts like those for laying electric cable, and similar big jobs.

Weddings today are no longer pacchipulusu or tamarind onion soup affairs with rows of people squatting on the ground. Now, these take place in function halls with a buffet of mutton biryani, chicken curry, palak paneer, vegetable pulao (for the vegetarians), sambar, a fried vegetable, curd and of course, the standard ice cream and gulab jamun. I watch the children of people, who once had no food to eat for two days, throw away mountains of uneaten food on their plastic coated paper plates. It is no longer the baindla officiating at madiga weddings; the pot-bellied brahmin with his sacred thread and sonorous voice has made his entry.

When I interviewed my fellow Sangam workers while working on the final draft of this book, I was shocked to find that they had felt abandoned when I left work. 'We had succeeded in most of our land struggles, we had expanded elsewhere successfully, our education programme was spread over five mandals and we were invited to other districts too, we had successfully broken the reddy rule over the taluka. If we had continued for another five years, we would have been an independent bloc, the most powerful political entity in the taluka. We saw that it is possible for independent entities to wield local power; Kanshi Ram had risen from BAMCEF to become the most important politician of the decade. In Ibrahimpatnam, most of the dalits and BCs supported us, and even the poorer reddys were rallying under our banner. When you stopped work, we did not understand why you gave it up just when we were succeeding. We were in a state of shock for close to six months and the villagers were most upset. Where do we go from here, we wondered, with some desperation. It took us some time to get back on our feet again.'

I understand now that we had different goalposts. They were locals, they and the community would have become politically powerful and this would have reflected in their economic and social standing. But I had seen power corrupting elsewhere and I feared this more than anything. I did not see the possibility of a shift to other goalposts and reinventing the Sangam. I was deeply flawed.

Years went by. Sometime in 2012 or 2013, the villagers of Meerkhanpet came in a lorry to our house in Manikonda. Leila was home from Delhi for the vacation. ITVCS had helped the people of Meerkhanpet get 200 acres of illegally hoarded land from their landlord. The villagers had come to tell us that they had been able to sell their land to a public sector enterprise, the Power Grid Corporation of India, for a good sum and that they had now purchased land in Kalwakurthy where prices were much lower. They crowded into our living room, draped us in shawls and sat for some time, thanking us. After they left, my daughter called out to me, 'Amma, do you know what they gave me?' 'What?' I asked.

'An envelope with a cheque made in my name.'

'That's okay. You can keep it.'

'Do you know the figure?'

'Five thousand?'

'Three lakh.'

I ran behind them and caught up with their lorry. 'You can't do this,' I said. 'I did not work with you for payment, I am glad that you have got some money, but I do not want money from you. You must not give me money.' There was a lot of back and forth. They said, 'We didn't give you money. We respect your sentiments. We gave it to your daughter, for her education—she is our daughter too.' Finally, they said, 'Okay, we will take it back, but remember that you have now put us in a great deal of trouble. We sat for many days to divide the money equitably among ourselves. All of us wanted to chip in for you. Now, we will quarrel about how to divide the money you have returned. You will be the cause of our quarrels.'

I gave in. My daughter deposited the cheque in her account.

For all my principled arguing, I felt tremendously warm inside. After all this time, after a quarter of a century, there was still so much love. Only love.

Acronyms guide

ADD	Action on Disability and Development India
AP	Andhra Pradesh
APRCP	Andhra Pradesh Revolutionary Communist Party
ASP	Assistant Superintendent of Police
BAMCEF	All-India Backward and Minority Communities Employees Federation
BC	Backward Caste, Backward Class
BJP	Bharatiya Janata Party
BSP	Bahujan Samaj Party
BYB	Bhudan Yagna Board
CBSE	Central Board of Secondary Education
CI	Circle Inspector
CIT	Corporation Technical Institute
CK	C.K. Narayan Reddy
CM	Chief Minister
CMSS	Chattisgarh Mines Shramik Sangh
CP	Chandra Pulla Reddy
CPI	Communist Party of India
CPI(M)	Communist Party of India (Marxist)
CPI–ML	Communist Party of India (Marxist–Leninist)
CrPC	Criminal Procedure Code
CRPF	Central Reserve Police Force
CSI	Church of South India
DRDA	District Rural Development Agency
DSP	Deputy Superintendent of Police
ECT	Electroconvulsive Therapy
EPW	Economic and Political Weekly
FIR	First Information Report
GRBT	George Reddy Book Trust
HBT	Hyderabad Book Trust
IAS	Indian Administrative Service
IIM	Indian Institute of Management
IIT	Indian Institute of Technology
IPC	Indian Penal Code
IPS	India Police Service
ITVCS	Ibrahimpatnam Taluka Vyavasaya Coolie Sangam
JNTU	Jawaharlal Nehru Technological University
KS	Kondapalli Seetharamaiah
KV	Kendriya Vidyalaya
KVIC	Khadi and Village Industries Commission

ML	Marxism–Leninism / Marxist–Leninist
MLA	Member of Legislative Assembly
MP	Member of Parliament
MPP	Mandal Praja Parishad
MPTC	Mandal Parishad Territorial Constituency
MRO	Mandal Revenue Office/ Officer
MVF	Mamidipudi Venkatarangaiya Foundation
NAPM	National Alliance of People's Movements
NCERT	National Council of Educational Research and Training
NCPCR	National Commission for Protection of Child Rights
NFE	Non-formal Education
NGO	Non-Governmental Organization
NH	National Highway
NIMH	National Institute of the Mentally Handicapped
NIRD	National Institute of Rural Development
NR	Neelam Ramachandraiah
NTR	N.T. Rama Rao
NTSE	National Talent Search Examination
OBC	Other Backward Classes
OU	Osmania University
PDS	Progressive Democratic Students
PDSU	Progressive Democratic Students Union
POW	Progressive Organisation of Women
PT	Protected Tenants
PUCL	People's Union for Civil Liberties
PWG	People's War Group
RDO	Revenue Development Officer
RPI	Republican Party of India
RSS	Rashtriya Swayamsevak Sangh
SC	Scheduled Caste
SI	Sub-Inspector
SP	Superintendent of Police
SSS	Stree Shakti Sanghatana
ST	Scheduled Tribe
TDP	Telugu Desam Party
TN	Tarimela Nagi Reddy
TRS	Telangana Rashtra Samiti
WDS	Water Development Society
YMCA	Young Men's Christian Association
YSR	Y.S. Rajasekhara Reddy
ZPP	Zilla Praja Parishad

Gita Ramaswamy is best known for her work with Hyderabad Book Trust that has published over four hundred titles since 1980. HBT pioneered low-cost books and translations from across the world—from Alex Haley to Mahasweta Devi. She was earlier associated with the Marxist–Leninist movement in Telangana. Going underground during the Emergency in 1975 with her husband Cyril Reddy, she taught English in a dalit basti in Ghaziabad, near Delhi. Starting in 1984, she worked for a decade with the dalits of Ibrahimpatnam and helped them in their fight against bonded labour and landlessness. Gita has authored several books in English (including *Jeena Hai To Marna Seekho: The Life and Times of George Reddy*, 2016, and *India Stinking: Manual Scavengers in Andhra Pradesh and Their Work*, 2005), translated extensively from Telugu into English (including Devulapalli Krishnamurthy's *Life in Anantharam*) and edited works like B. Anuradha's *Prison Notes of a Woman Activist*.